IMAGES
of America

CHIPLEY/ PINE MOUNTAIN

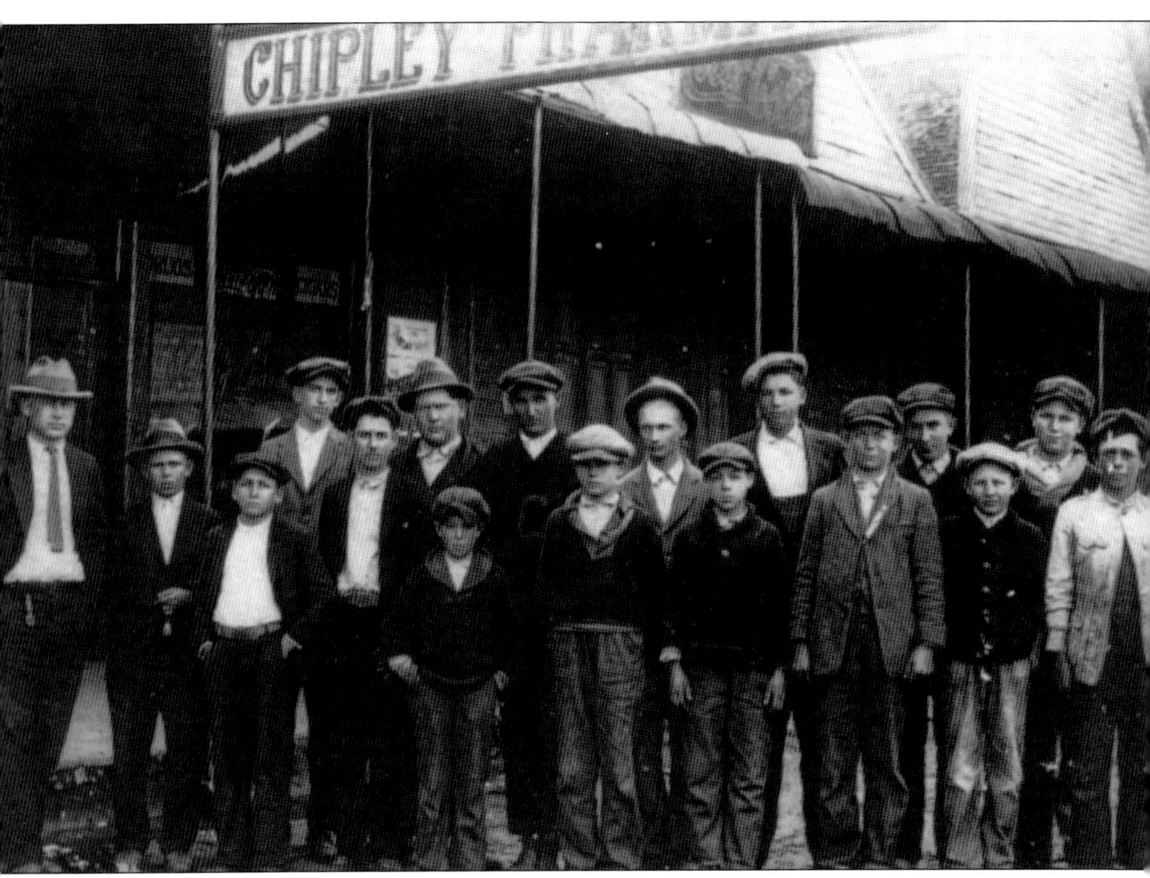

This group of boys and their teacher pose for a picture under the Chipley Pharmacy sign. They were out of school to visit the Tri-County Fair held in Chipley in 1925. Exhibitors included those from Harris, Meriwether, and Troup Counties. At that time, the Chipley Pharmacy was located on Broad Street. (Carolyn Bryant Hart.)

On the Cover: Chipley entered Georgia Power's Hometown Contest for several years in a row in the early 1950s. Here, young and old, Black and White, line up at city hall for a town cleanup day in 1952. Later, there was a picnic to celebrate their hard work. Chipley placed second in the 1949 and 1951 contests and earned honorable mention several other years. (Chipley Historical Center.)

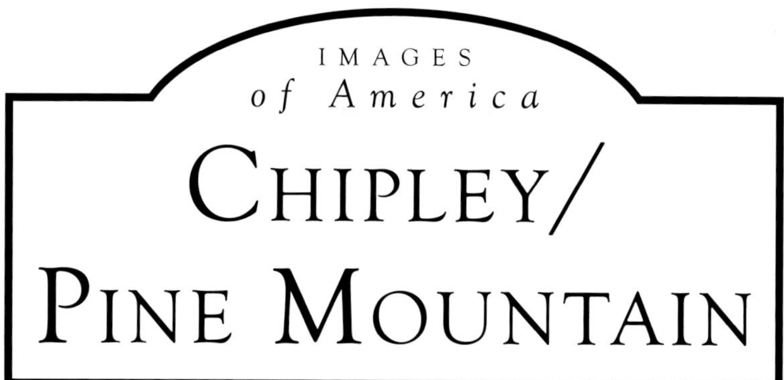

Helen L. Brackett and
Chipley Historical Center

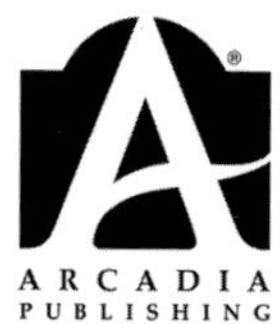

ISBN 978-1-4671-6270-8

Published by Arcadia Publishing
Charleston, South Carolina

Printed in the United States of America

Library of Congress Control Number: 2025937158

For all general information, please contact Arcadia Publishing:
Telephone 843-853-2070
Fax 843-853-0044
E-mail sales@arcadiapublishing.com

Visit us on the Internet at www.arcadiapublishing.com

Contents

ACKNOWLEDGMENTS

This book has been produced by the Chipley Historical Center. It is a compilation of Chipley and Pine Mountain images, the result of the collaborative efforts of many individuals associated with the center for over 40 years. Just over 100 years after Chipley was founded, as noted in the first recorded minutes of the center, two Chipley natives met with two newcomers who had married into Chipley families. Lillian Champion, a writer, and Alf Mullins, a merchant, both traced their Chipley roots back generations. Mayor Jim Edgar and town maintenance supervisor Franklin Davenport had for years considered themselves adopted sons of the town. The four met in July 1984 at city hall because they shared a common interest: the establishment of a center to preserve and showcase the town's past and its evolution into Pine Mountain.

In September 1985, the center opened in the old city hall after hours of work by countless volunteers. Since then, scores of volunteers, natives and newcomers alike, have continued the work of the center. One among many deserves special mention. Malinda Brooks, a lifelong Chipley/Pine Mountain resident, has served on the center board of directors for years. Before a book such as this was imagined, her research and interviews resulted in countless handwritten pages full of Chipley history and stories. Her meticulous work has contributed greatly to this volume.

From the center's beginning, Chipley natives and residents, past and present, have responded generously to make the original vision a reality. Contributions to the center, including family histories, books, documents, scrapbooks, letters, and artifacts, have been donated by Chipley folks for whom this small town holds a special place in their lives and hearts.

Chipley/Pine Mountain is the product of many minds and hands, all volunteers, to whom the town and all who visit and enjoy the Chipley Historical Center with its numerous collections and exhibits are most appreciative.

Unless otherwise noted, all images appear courtesy of the Chipley Historical Center.

INTRODUCTION

In 1958, the 76-year-old town of Chipley became Pine Mountain by an act of the Georgia State Legislature. It was not a result of any referendum and was not an especially popular change among the citizens. There is in the area a modest pine tree–covered mountainous ridge, a product, it is said, of an underlying amalgam of quartzite and other material that has withstood ages of erosion. Chipley's name had come from that of a Civil War survivor who was president of the railroad company that had laid the first rails to the spot that would become a town in 1882.

So, there was reason for both names, but neither is sufficient to define us or to describe our heritage. The land here is very old, but our climate is such that there are few surviving relics of prior inhabitants. There are no mastodon bones hereabouts. You could still find, however, bits and pieces of Aboriginal projectile points and potshards many years old. The Native Americans who were here when the first Europeans explored this area lived in towns generally confined to the bottomland near large streams. This area of the highlands was their hunting ground, with some well-worn trails leading to other regions.

The colony of Georgia was first settled in Savannah in 1733. It took nearly 100 years to encompass this part of Georgia, by then a state of the Union. Through treaties with the Creek Indian Nation, the land was acquired and opened to White settlers by land lotteries. Actual settlement was a slow, laborious process that required cutting and clearing of huge old-growth trees. There was virgin soil good for agriculture, but it was rocky. There are still ubiquitous piles of stones gathered during that era.

Counties and county seats were established, but other towns were scarce at first. Settlers congregated and established churches like Bethany Baptist at crossroads such as Goodman's, and hamlets and stores arose. One early settlement was Kings Gap at the foot of a trail on the north side of Pine Mountain ridge near a bold, pure spring, still the source of most of our town's water. Kings Gap had a tanning mill and was, for a time, a regular stagecoach stop. Now the area is the site of the Liberty Bell swimming pool in F.D. Roosevelt State Park.

After the Civil War and Reconstruction, thoughts finally turned to commercial development, and the idea of expanding the meager railroad service in the area gradually took hold. A rail line was built out of the city of Columbus, stage by stage, north into Harris County. Crossing Pine Mountain was no small feat, but the line eventually reached a level spot on the north side far enough from the foot of the mountain for the little locomotive to be able to gather enough momentum to cross back over the ridge.

That spot, about halfway between Kings Gap to the east and Goodman's Crossroad to the west, became the village of Hood, named for the president of the railroad at the time. It became a thriving community quickly, with a number of new businesses, but it lasted a very short time. For some possibly nefarious reason, the rail line was extended another mile north. The town of Hood died before it was fairly born, and a new settlement arose at the new terminus. The railroad president was now W.D. Chipley, and his name was given to the new town.

Chipley was a boom town right away, it seems. New businesses were started, and some just established in Hood were moved up the road, with a few buildings actually being rolled on logs. The railroad was naturally a boon to agriculture. The easy shipment of cotton and other crops resulted in an expansion of agriculture and an influx of new residents.

There was an edge to the boom, however, even a feel of a frontier town, with jealousies and resentments actually leading to family feuds and acts of violence. In 1908, there was violence of nature, too, as much of the town was destroyed by a tornado. More than a few citizens considered that to be divine intervention, if not retribution, and social interactions seemed to have become much calmer after that. It would still be many more years, however, before life improved significantly for Black residents.

Churches and schools, though still segregated by race, were all vital to the town's growth. Churches, especially, were and still are the town's core foundation. And until the era of countywide consolidation, local schools were also considered our society's guardians. The town was blessed with the best teachers and administrators, who were like stern but caring foster parents of all their wards.

Perhaps the most profound and lasting change to our town was the establishment of Callaway Gardens in the early 1950s. It began as gardens but evolved into a full-scale family resort at the foot of the Pine Mountain ridge. Cason Callaway proposed the name change for Chipley, apparently feeling that his resort would benefit from a more appealing and relevant address, especially since the name Pine Mountain was already well-known throughout this part of the state.

There was resentment on the part of some, especially those who had grown up and lived in the area for many years. The town leaders eventually accepted the idea. The name of Pine Mountain is now, of course, accepted by all, and all residents realize what Callaway Gardens has meant to our survival and subsequent growth.

Businesses have grown up all around the town proper and the surrounding area in response to the growth of tourism. The importance of agriculture was bound to diminish, and without tourism, there would have been relatively little to take its place in our commerce or serve as a reliable source of employment. We have also been blessed with a beautiful state park with unique hiking trails and a very popular campground, which has brought repeat visitors from across the country.

The importance of the railroad cannot be overstated, nor can the influx of early farmers and merchants. Tourism, businesses, and a variety of unique and flourishing restaurants are together the lifeblood now. Though the rails are gone, there is a permanent and splendid monument to Erastus Hood, Chipley, Callaway, later city fathers, and all the known or nameless former residents: the Man O' War walking and biking trail, aptly named for the daily passenger train that could carry you to downtown Atlanta in the morning and bring you back to your safe and peaceful home in the evening.

One

Kings Gap, Hood, and the Founding of Chipley

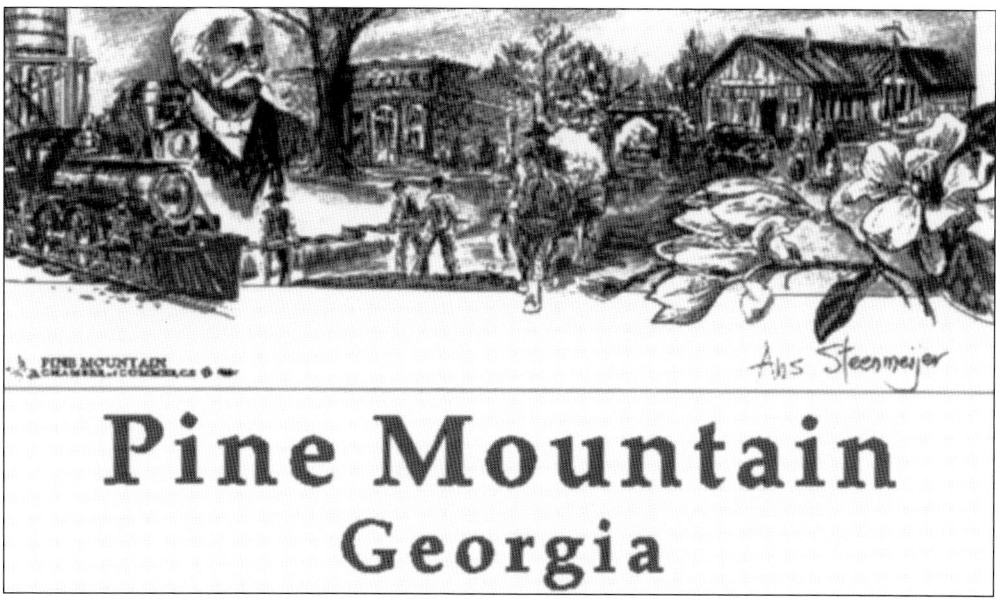

Welcome to Chipley/Pine Mountain! This is the original concept for one of the murals in Pine Mountain. It tells the story of Chipley and Pine Mountain from its beginnings as a rail and agriculture town. The concept drawing and original mural, located at the corner of North Commerce and Chipley Streets, was painted by Ans Steenmeijer in 1996 and repainted in 2013 by John Christian. (John Christian.)

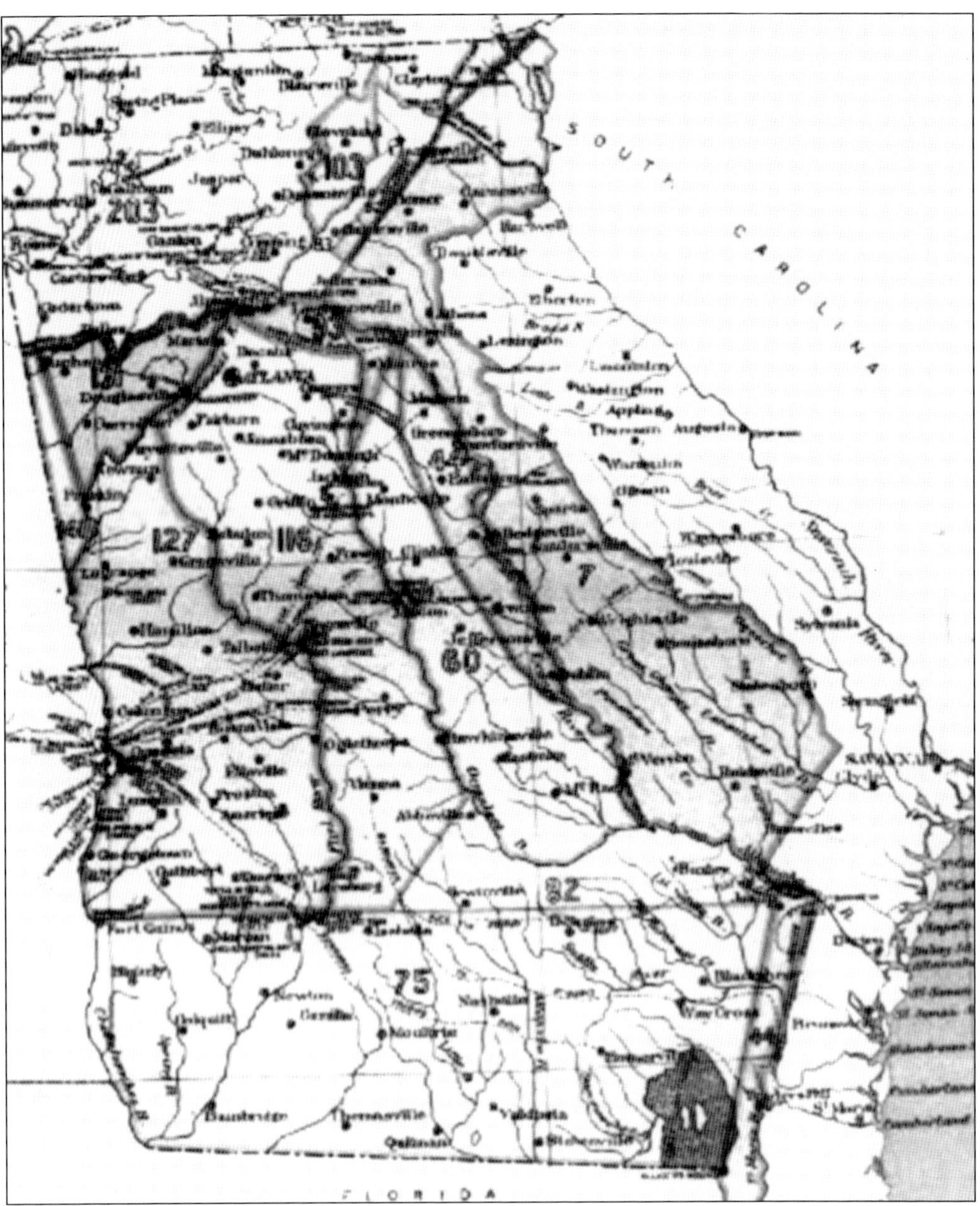

Beginning in the 1730s and continuing into the 1830s, the Cherokee and Creek Native American tribes ceded land to the state or to the federal government, often as payment for tribal debts or for being on the losing side in a war. This land, on the far left, numbered 127, the federal treaty number on this map, was ceded by the Creek Indians in the Treaty of Indian Springs in 1825. The treaty included all Creek land between the Flint and Chattahoochee Rivers. A land lottery was held to determine who could purchase acreage in the new territory. Participants in the lottery system were regulated by age, marital status, war service, and other factors. Lots were sold in parcels of about 200 acres for pennies an acre. This land cession was eventually divided into Carroll, Coweta, Lee, Muscogee, and Troup Counties. In 1827, Harris was, in turn, formed from parts of Muscogee and Troup Counties and named after Charles Harris, Savannah mayor and attorney. (Bureau of American Ethnology.)

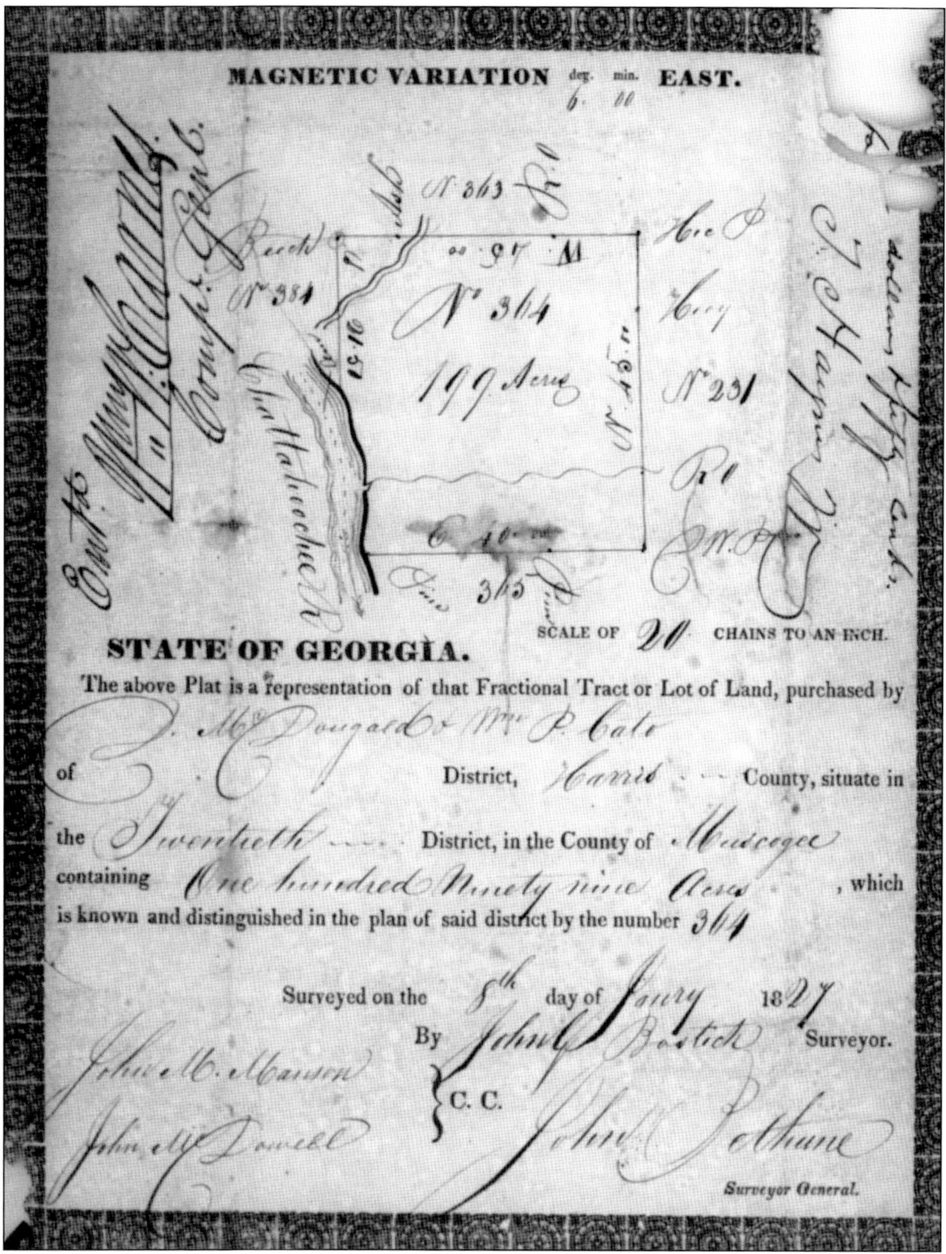

MAGNETIC VARIATION deg. 6 min. 00 **EAST.**

No 363

No 384

No 364

199 Acres

No 231

Chattahoochee R.

365

SCALE OF 20 CHAINS TO AN INCH.

STATE OF GEORGIA.

The above Plat is a representation of that Fractional Tract or Lot of Land, purchased by J. McDougald & Wm. P. Cato of District, Harris County, situate in the Twentieth District, in the County of Muscogee containing One hundred Ninety nine Acres, which is known and distinguished in the plan of said district by the number 364

Surveyed on the 5th day of Jany 1827

By John Bostick Surveyor.

John M. Manson
John McDowell } C. C.

John Bethune
Surveyor General.

This is an original land grant awarded to McDougald and Cato in the 1827 land lottery. Between 1805 and 1833, Georgia used a unique land lottery system to award land to settlers. Names were placed in a big barrel, and lot numbers were placed in another barrel. A drawing was held from both barrels, with the name drawn being matched to the land lot drawn. Although this particular grant was for land on the western side of Harris County bordering the Chattahoochee, one of the streets in Chipley/Pine Mountain was named McDougald, after one of the investors in the Columbus & Rome Railway, probably either this land grant recipient or one of his descendants. Very few of these original land grant documents still exist, and this one does not have the large official wax seal that was applied by the state. It was common for surveyors to draw landmarks on the map.

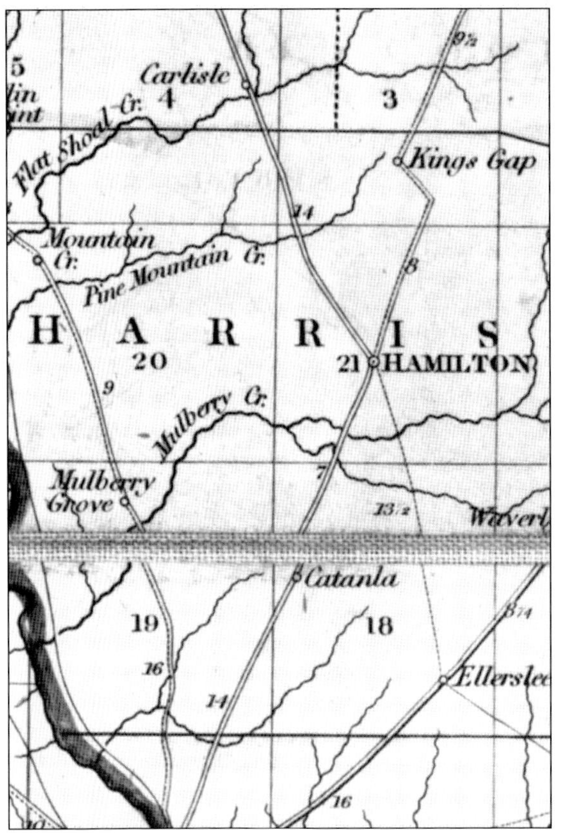

Kings Gap, where the Roosevelt Memorial Bridge spans Highway 354, is a natural gap in Pine Mountain. The site at the northern base of the gap became one of the earliest communities in the Chipley and Pine Mountain area. It was a stagecoach stop on the route from Columbus to the resort area of White Sulphur Springs in Meriwether County, and evidence indicates that a post office existed in Kings Gap as early as 1829. Beady McGee, pictured below with her children, grew up in Kings Gap in the 1870s. She often rode with her brothers to festivities at White Sulphur Springs, and she also went to school there, transported either by buggy or on horseback. According to her, she never missed a day of school. Her home was torn down when F.D. Roosevelt State Park was created. (Left, Library of Congress.)

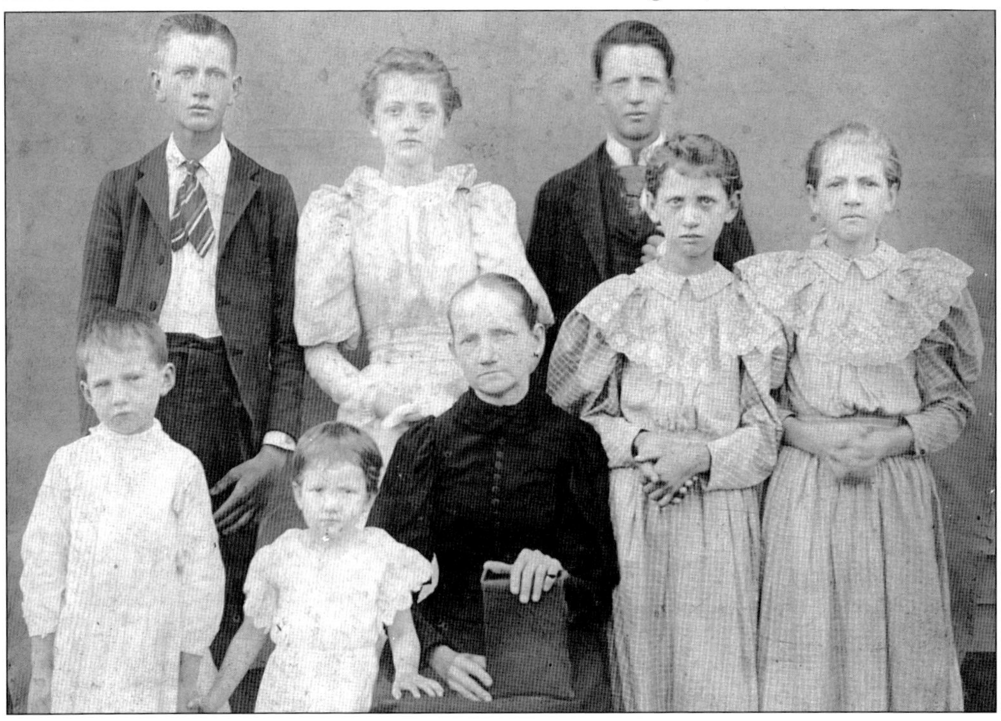

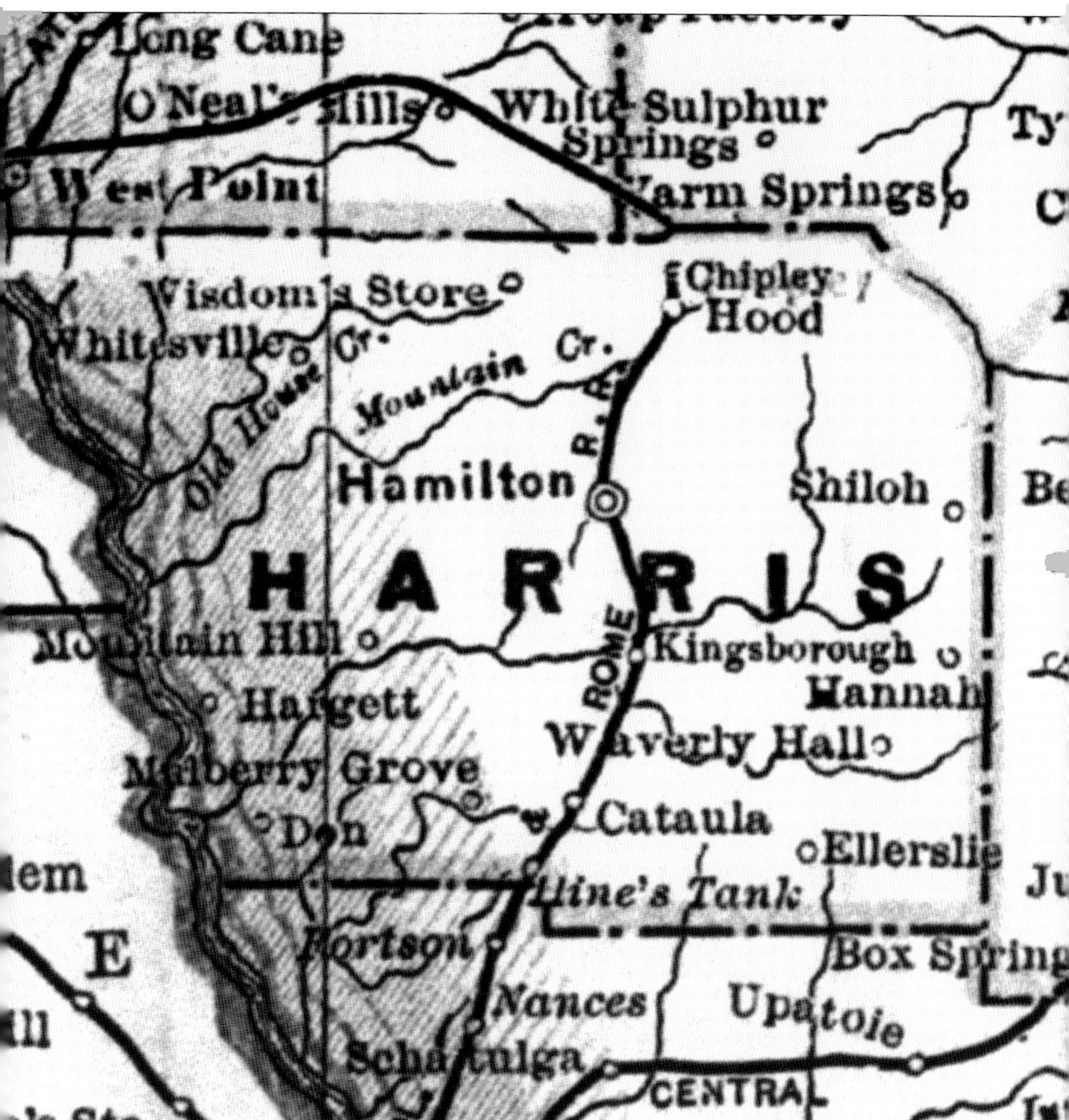

This map shows the route of the Columbus & Rome Railway through Harris County. It had started in 1870 as the North & South Railroad and was intended to connect the Georgia cities of Columbus and Rome. Progress had been slow, with only 20 miles of track laid by 1872. It would be another 10 years before it spanned the northern portion of the county. Note the names "Hood" and "Chipley" adjacent to each other at that point. Not indicated on the map is the Pine Mountain ridge just south of Hood. Crossing that modest ridge was a major undertaking at that time, but the rails had finally reached a suitable site for a terminus on the north side by 1880. At that point, the rails reached a wagon road connecting Kings Gap to Goodman's Crossroad, a small settlement to the west, and a new town arose.

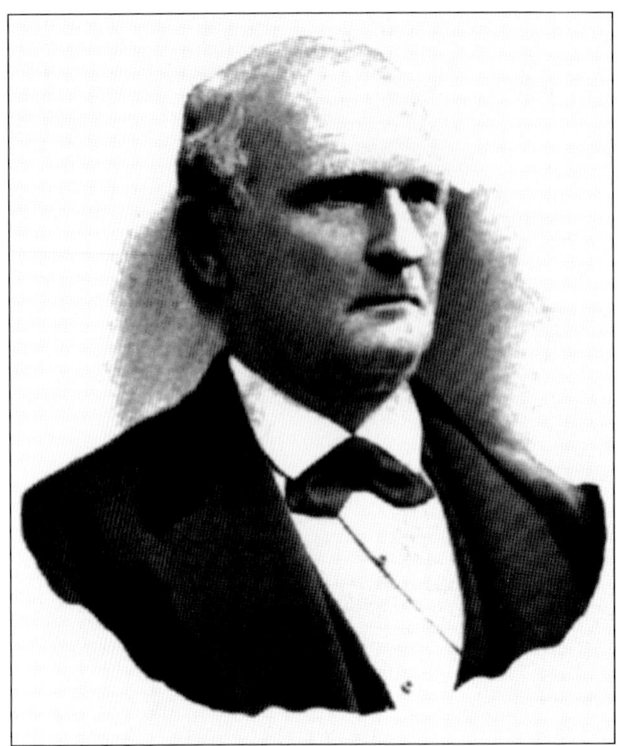

The new town was named for Erastus C. Hood, pictured here, a well-respected physician from Harris County and the president of the railroad. The town flourished immediately with new businesses arising, including stores and saloons as well as a lawyer's office and a photographer's shop. A number of people from Kings Gap, a mile to the east, moved to Hood. The photograph below shows Thomas L. Thomason; his wife, Samantha E. Sturdivant; and five of their seven children in front of their home at Hood in 1897. That house still stands on the campus of Impact 360, a gap year school. The town lasted barely three years, as history passed it by. The site today, where Highway 354 intersects US Highway 27, is a thriving business area and is still referred to by some locals as Hood or Old Hood.

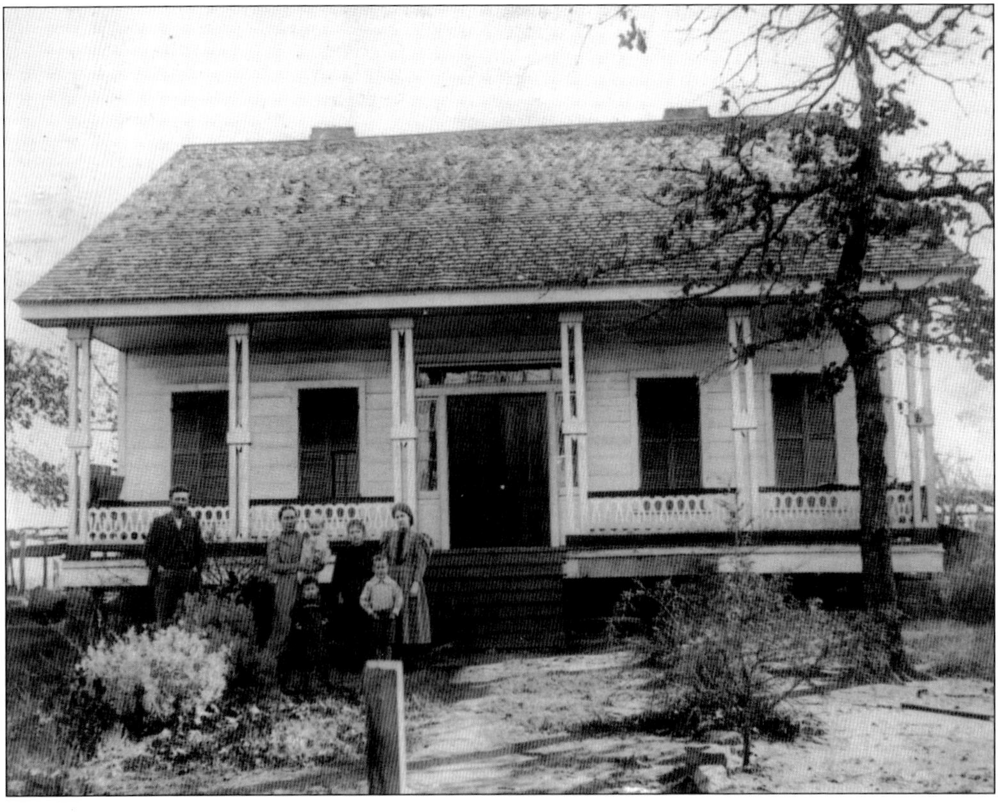

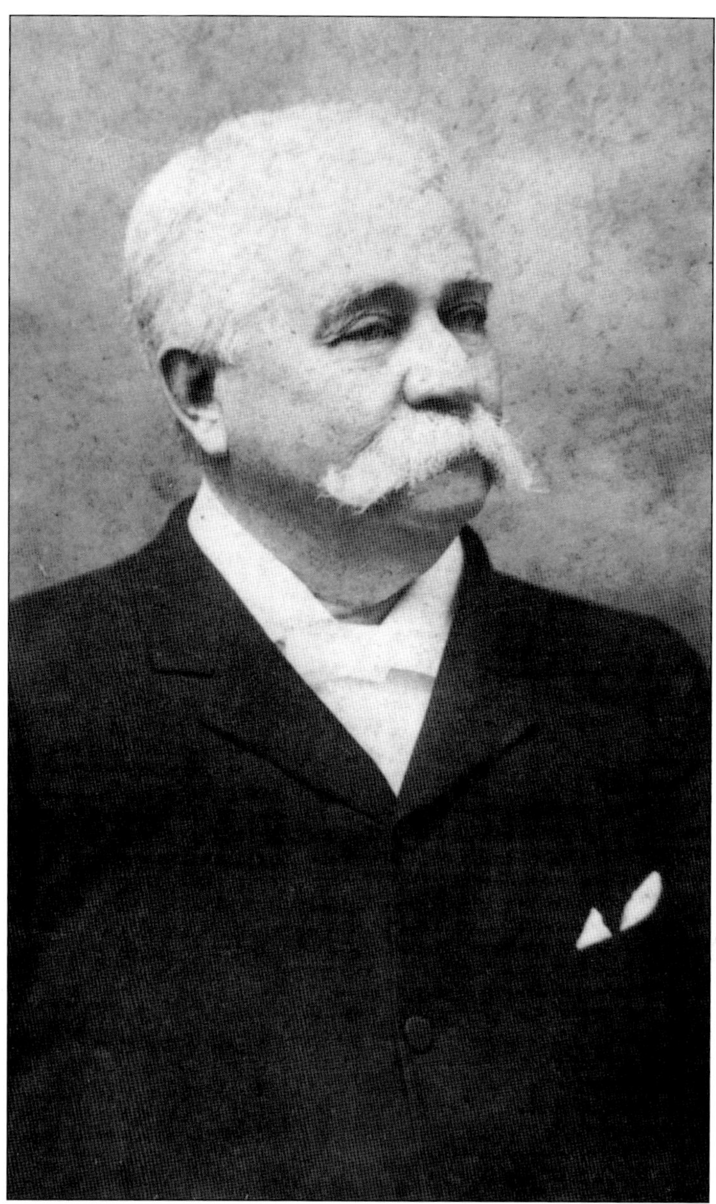

By 1882, the railroad had a new president, William Dudley Chipley, a Civil War veteran who had come to Columbus, Georgia, from Lexington, Kentucky. He had become an officer of the fledgling Columbus & Rome Railway in 1873. He relocated to Baltimore, Maryland, to work for a different railroad company for several years, but by 1881, he had come back to Columbus and assumed the presidency of the railroad, the northern terminus of which was at Hood. The tracks were then extended another mile north to a new terminus, where a new town was laid out and named Chipley in his honor. It prospered immediately and effectively doomed the town of Hood. As the *Hamilton Journal* reported, "Chipley is on a building boom. Hood is one of the things of the past." Several streets in Chipley, like McDougald and Blanchard, were named for railroad company investors. Chipley himself later moved to northwest Florida, worked on the Pensacola Railroad, and gave his name to another town: Chipley, Florida. (Collections of the University of West Florida Historic Trust.)

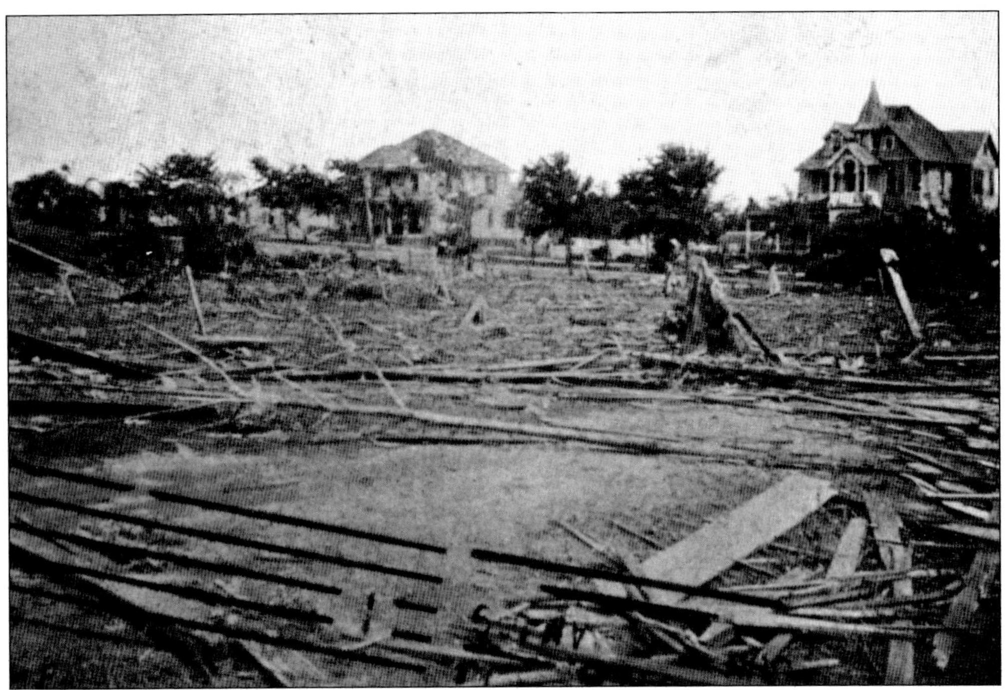

After only a few decades, Chipley was nearly wiped off the map. A devastating tornado struck Chipley in the early hours of April 25, 1908. It entered town from the west and made a path up Harris Street, damaging and destroying houses. Several people were killed, warehouses were destroyed, and businesses were damaged along West Railroad Avenue. The tornado crossed the railroad tracks and completely demolished the depot and the First Baptist Church. The loss was estimated at $101,000. Shown above is one of the few houses to escape damage, the Victorian home of R.E. O'Neal on West Harris Avenue. One of the warehouses in town had just received a shipment of wagon wheels, shown scattered in the photograph below.

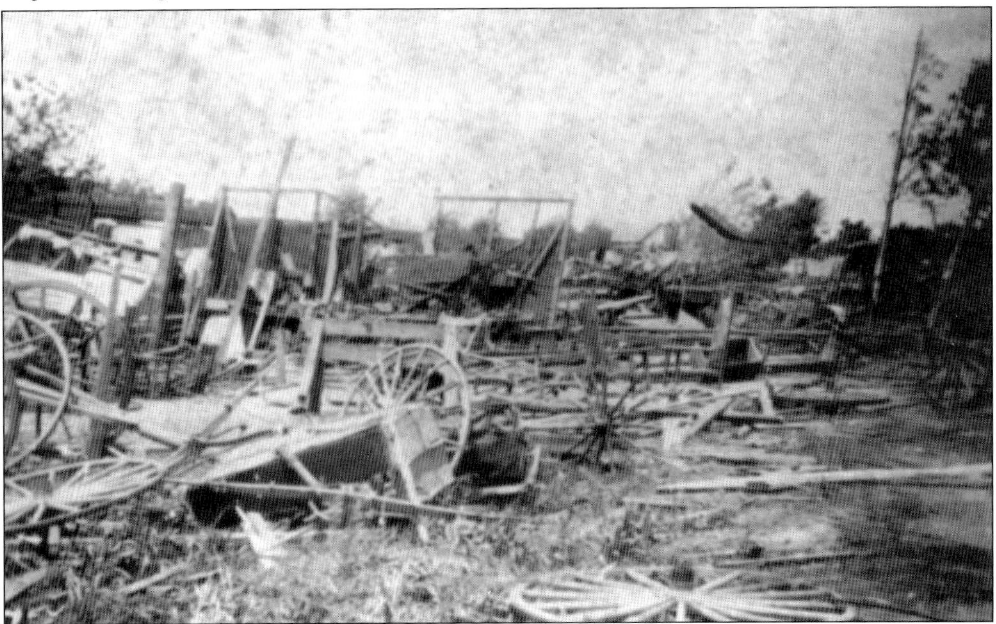

Two

Railroad Town

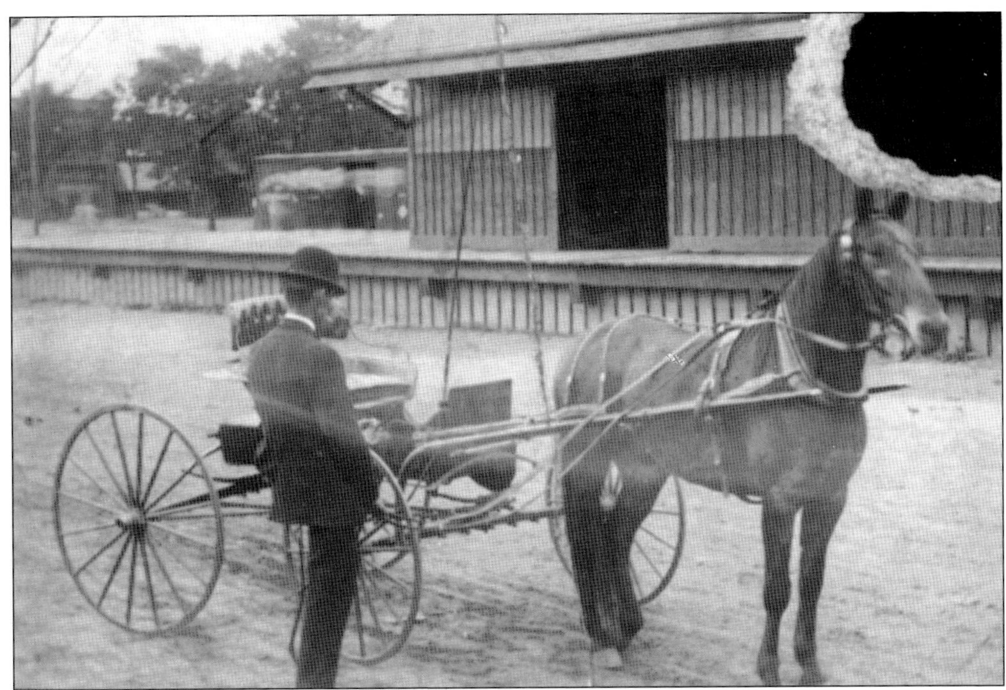

This dapper gentleman and his horse and carriage wait at the depot. Chipley's business district can be seen over the man's head on the other side of the depot. Although railroads started in the Chipley area after the Civil War, progress was slow. Crossing the ridge of Pine Mountain was difficult to accomplish and expensive.

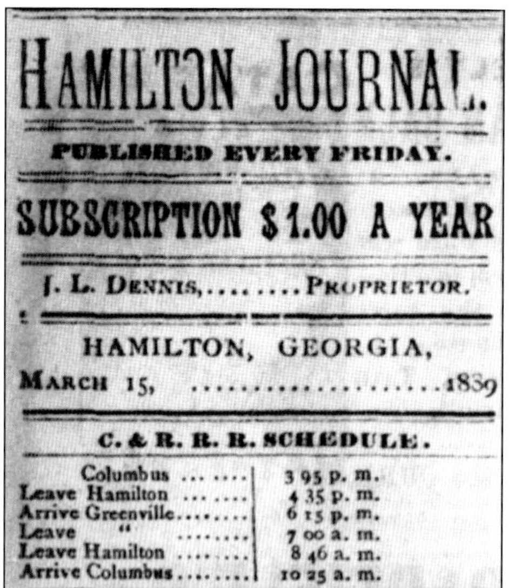

HAMILTON JOURNAL.

PUBLISHED EVERY FRIDAY.

SUBSCRIPTION $1.00 A YEAR

J. L. DENNIS, ... PROPRIETOR.

HAMILTON, GEORGIA,

MARCH 15, ... 1889

C. & R. R. R. SCHEDULE.

Columbus	3 95 p. m.
Leave Hamilton	4 35 p. m.
Arrive Greenville........	6 15 p. m.
Leave "	7 00 a. m.
Leave Hamilton	8 46 a. m.
Arrive Columbus	10 25 a. m.

The North & South Railroad, started by Dr. Erastus C. Hood, lasted only nine years (1870–1879). It was reorganized and renamed as the Columbus & Rome Railway (C&R) in 1882. The track was completed to Chipley in 1882 and to Greenville, Georgia, in 1885. The schedule shown at left is dated March 15, 1889, just a few years after the track was completed to Greenville. (The *Hamilton Journal.*)

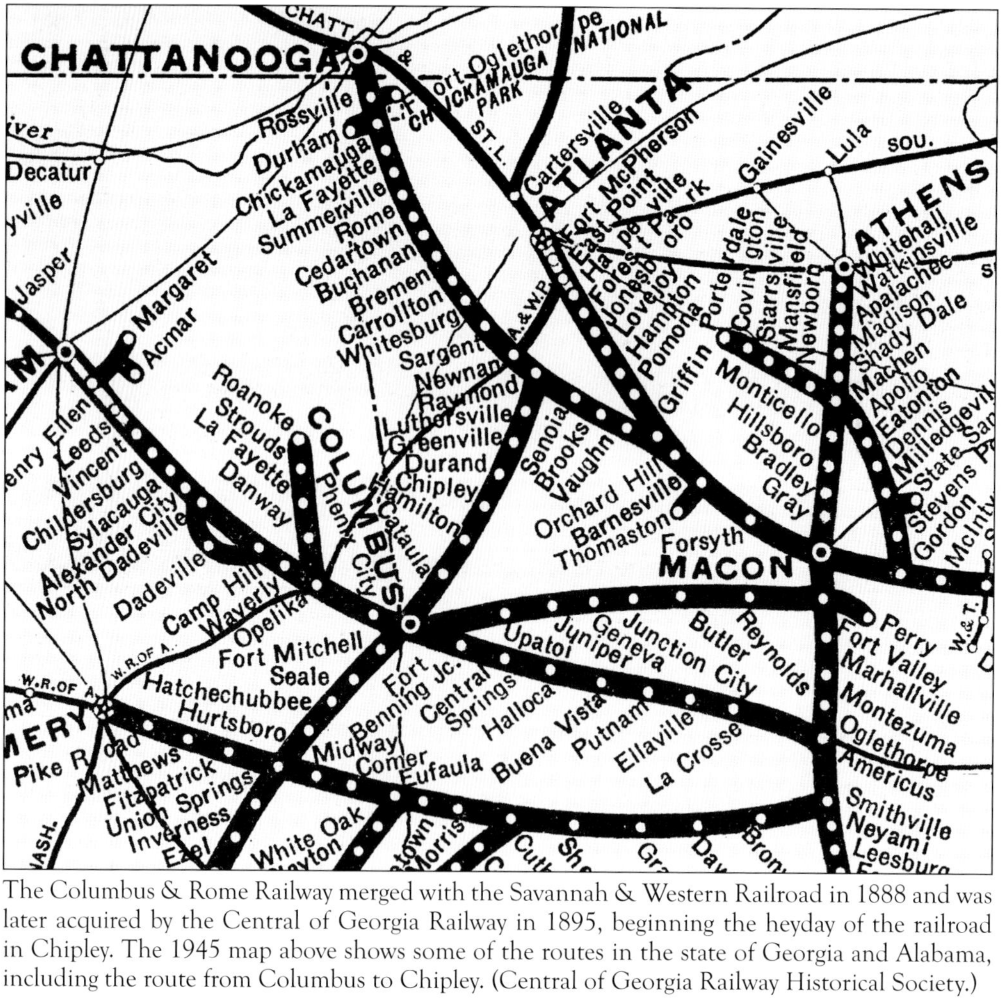

The Columbus & Rome Railway merged with the Savannah & Western Railroad in 1888 and was later acquired by the Central of Georgia Railway in 1895, beginning the heyday of the railroad in Chipley. The 1945 map above shows some of the routes in the state of Georgia and Alabama, including the route from Columbus to Chipley. (Central of Georgia Railway Historical Society.)

Central of Georgia R'y Co.

Inauguration of Daily Through Train Service between Columbus and Atlanta via Newnan, Central of Georgia Railway and Atlanta & West Point Railroad.

SCHEDULE EFFECTIVE JULY 7, 1907.

No. 17 Daily	No. 9 Daily	STATIONS	No. 10 Daily	No. 18 Daily
*6 30am	*5 30pm	Lv...COLUMBUS via C. of Ga...Ar	*11 00am	*8 50pm
6 35am	5 34pm	" C. & R. Junction via C. of Ga. Lv	10 53am	8 45pm
6 51am	6 00pm	" ......Nankipooh via C. of Ga...... "	10 35am	8 29pm
6 58am	6 11pm	" ...... Fortson via C. of Ga. ...... "	10 27am	8 20pm
7 07am	6 24pm	" ...... Mobley via C. of Ga. ...... "	10 17am	8 11pm
7 10am	6 27pm	" ....Cataula via C. of Ga....... "	10 14am	8 08pm
7 18am	6 39pm	" .....Kingsboro via C. of Ga...... "	10 00am	7 56pm
7 28am	6 52pm	" ......Hamilton via C. of Ga...... "	9 48am	7 45pm
7 35am	7 02pm	" ......Tip Top via C. of Ga....... "	9 38am	7 37pm
7 47am	7 22pm	" ...... Chipley via C. of Ga. ...... "	9 23am	7 22pm
7 59am	7 34pm	" Meriw'thr Wh. S'lph'r, C. of Ga. "	9 13am	7 14pm
8 11am	7 44pm	" ....Stinson via C. of Ga....... "	9 04am	7 03pm
8 24am	7 56pm	" ......HARRIS via C. of Ga...... "	8 49am	6 51pm
8 36am	8 10pm	" GREENVILLE via C. of Ga. "	8 30am	6 38pm
8 54am	8 25pm	" .... Allie via C. of Ga. .... "	8 14am	6 24pm
9 05am	8 34pm	" ......Primrose via C. of Ga....... "	8 03am	6 14pm
9 19am	8 47pm	" ... Luthersville via C. of Ga. ... "	7 49am	6 02pm
9 30am	8 59pm	" ...... Bexton via C. of Ga. ...... "	7 37am	5 51pm
9 45am	9 15pm	" ..... Raymond via C. of Ga. ..... "	7 20am	5 35pm
10 00am	9 30pm	Ar......Newnan via C. of Ga. ...... "	6 49am	5 20pm
10 05am	....	Lv....Newnan via A. & W. P.....Ar	....	5 15pm
....	....	Ar... Palmetto via A. & W. P. ...Lv	....	....
....	....	" ... Fairburn via A. & W. P. ... "	....	....
11 15am	....	" .....Atlanta via A. & W. P...... "	....	4 10pm

This timetable for the Central of Georgia Railway Company from 1907 lists several towns and communities that no longer exist, including Nankipooh, Mobley, Kingsboro, Tip Top, Stinson, Harris, Allie, Primrose, and Raymond. Nankipooh, just north of Columbus, was named after a character in the Gilbert and Sullivan opera *The Mikado.* Mobley and Kingsboro are north of Nankipooh. The Callaway Gardens Country Store is located near Tip Top, which was the high point of the track over Pine Mountain. Stinson, in Meriwether County, was renamed Durand when the Central of Georgia Railway came through the town. Harris (now known as Harris City) was south of Greenville in Meriwether County on Highway 18; Allie and Primrose were north of Greenville, and Raymond was five miles south of Newnan in Coweta County. At Newnan, the train switched to Atlanta & West Point Railroad tracks to complete the trip into Atlanta. (The *Hamilton Journal.*)

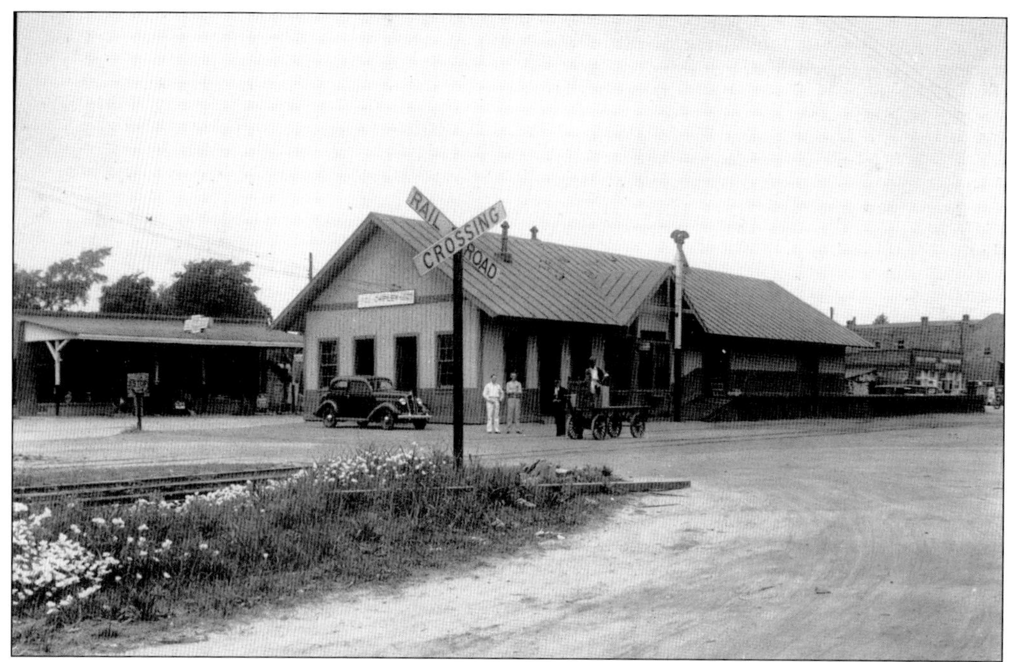

The first Central of Georgia depot, built in Chipley in 1881 before the track was completed, was destroyed by the spring 1908 tornado. It was quickly replaced by this depot, completed in the fall of 1908. It handled freight and passengers until it was torn down in 1961. D.C. Royal, Depot Agent, is on the left, and E.L. Howard, Section Foreman, is on the right in this c. 1938 photograph.

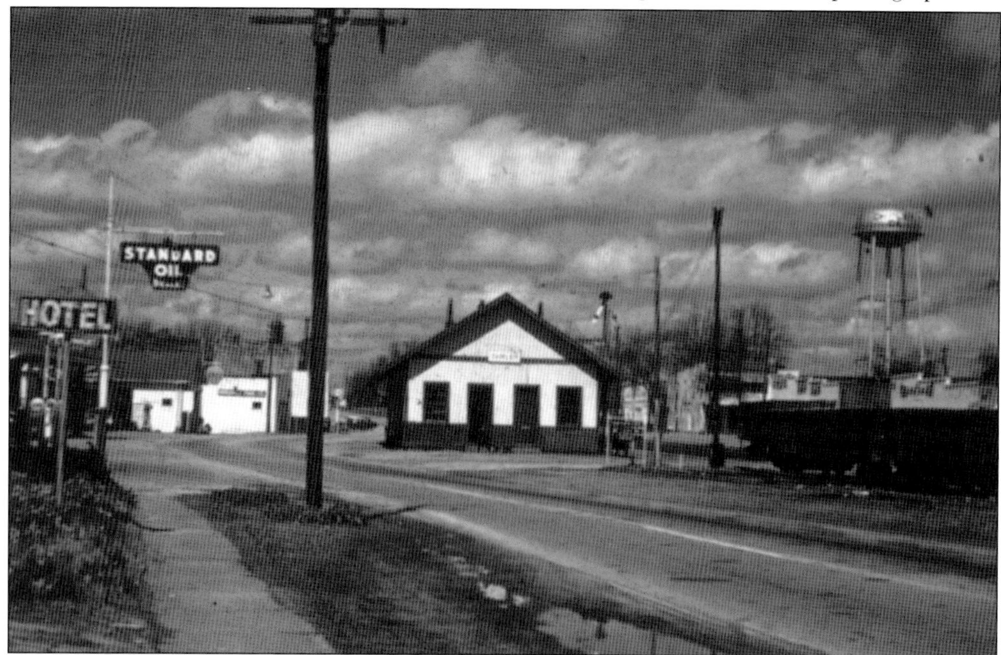

This photograph shows the "jog" that US Highway 27 took around the depot. As automobile traffic increased, and in an effort to make the town look better, the town of Chipley requested the removal of the depot in the late 1950s. It was demolished in 1961, and US Highway 27 was straightened out at that time. The Strickland Hotel can be seen on the left side of the picture.

Time Table No. 56, February 15, 1900, advertised "1554 miles of perfectly equipped railway, traversing the greatest agricultural, fruit and timber sections of the south," emphasizing the reliability of the Central of Georgia Railway in getting the farmers' goods to market in a timely and efficient manner, in addition to providing passenger service. (Central of Georgia Railway Historical Society.)

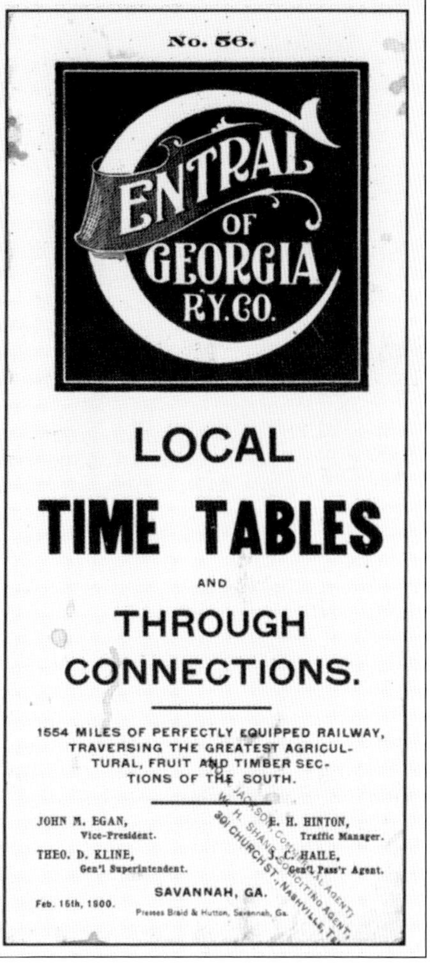

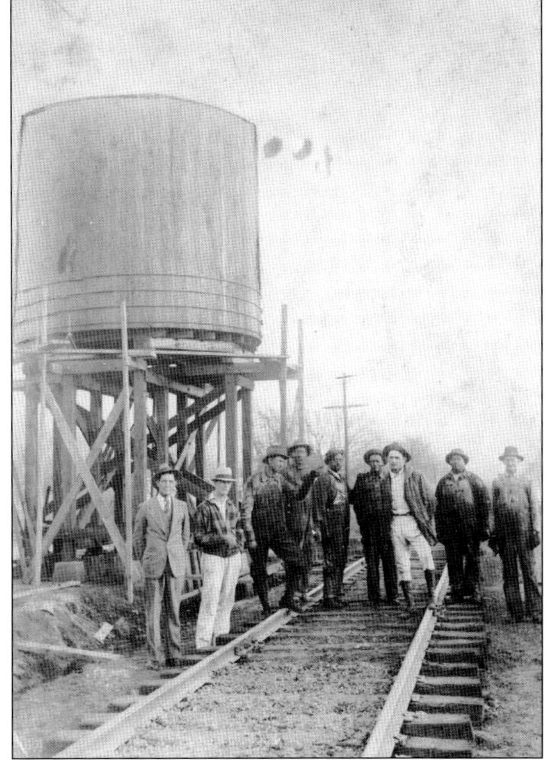

Prior to World War II, trains were primarily pulled by steam engines, which had to have a good supply of water along the track. This 1911 photograph is a picture of the section crew, led by E.L. Howard, section foreman, on the far left, gathered at the water tank just south of the depot.

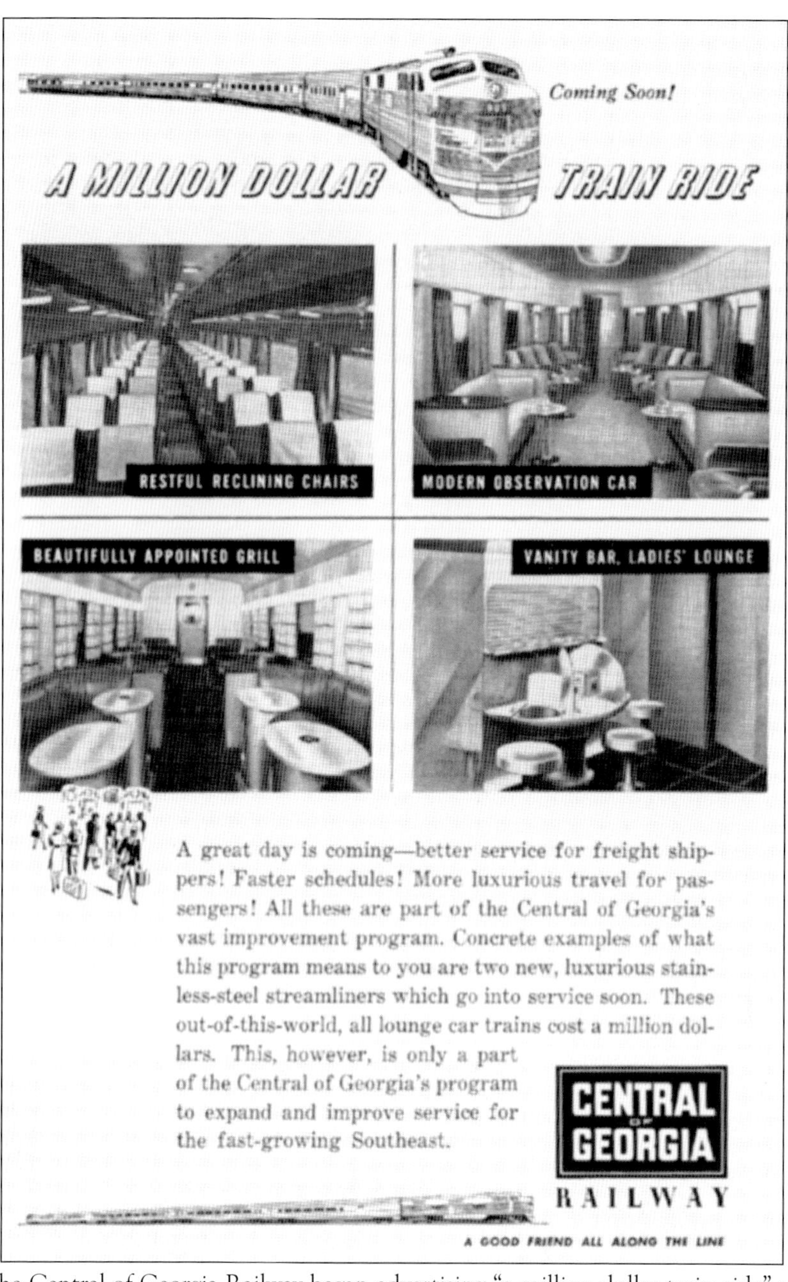

In 1947, the Central of Georgia Railway began advertising "a million dollar train ride" and "more luxurious travel for passengers" on the *Man O' War* and the *Nancy Hanks II*. The *Man O' War* made two daily round-trip trips from Columbus to Atlanta, while the *Nancy Hanks II* ran between Atlanta and Savannah. Chipley ladies wore hats and gloves to travel to Atlanta for a day trip to shop at Rich's and other department stores downtown. There were two round trips daily. The ladies could shop and have a leisurely lunch, then catch the afternoon train back to Chipley. Passengers were often treated to fashion shows on the trips, and many children held their birthday parties on the train. In the 1950s and the 1960s, end-of-school-year excursions to either Cataula or Columbus and back were also a treat for schoolchildren, and those trips often included a factory tour. These trains represented the golden age of rail travel. (Central of Georgia Railway Historical Society.)

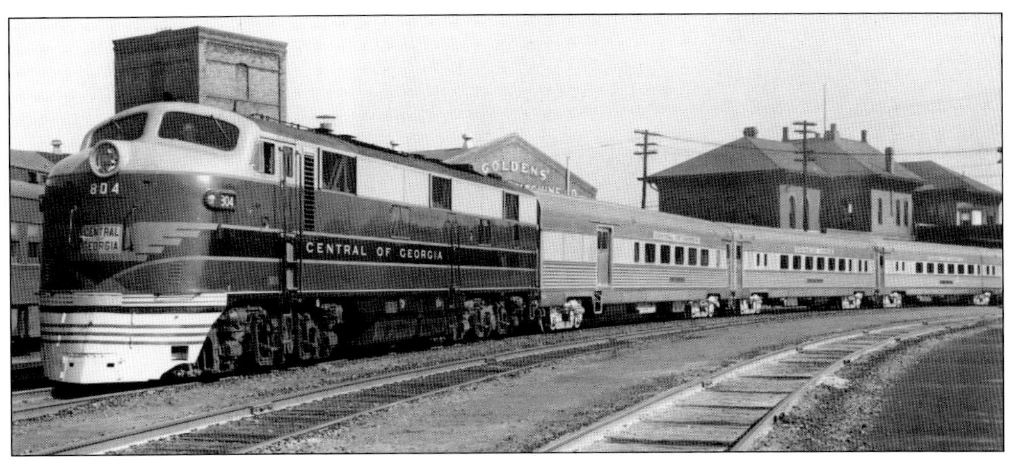

All shiny and new, the *Man O' War* is shown above on display in Columbus before going into service on June 24, 1947. The *Man O' War* and the *Nancy Hanks II* represented considerable investment, and Central of Georgia management was optimistic that train travel revenue would make that investment worthwhile. However, by the mid-1950s, passenger rail travel began declining as automobiles gained in popularity. Below, *Man O' War* waits at the Chipley depot before continuing its Columbus to Atlanta run. The *Man O' War* made its last run on May 16, 1970. (Above, Central of Georgia Railway Historical Society; below, Chipley Historical Center.)

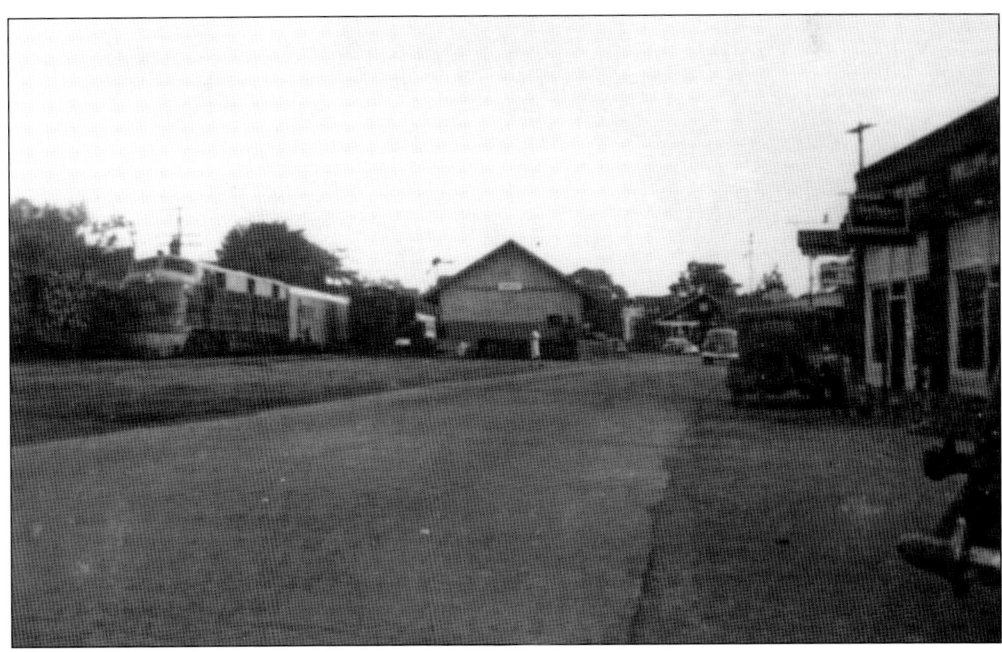

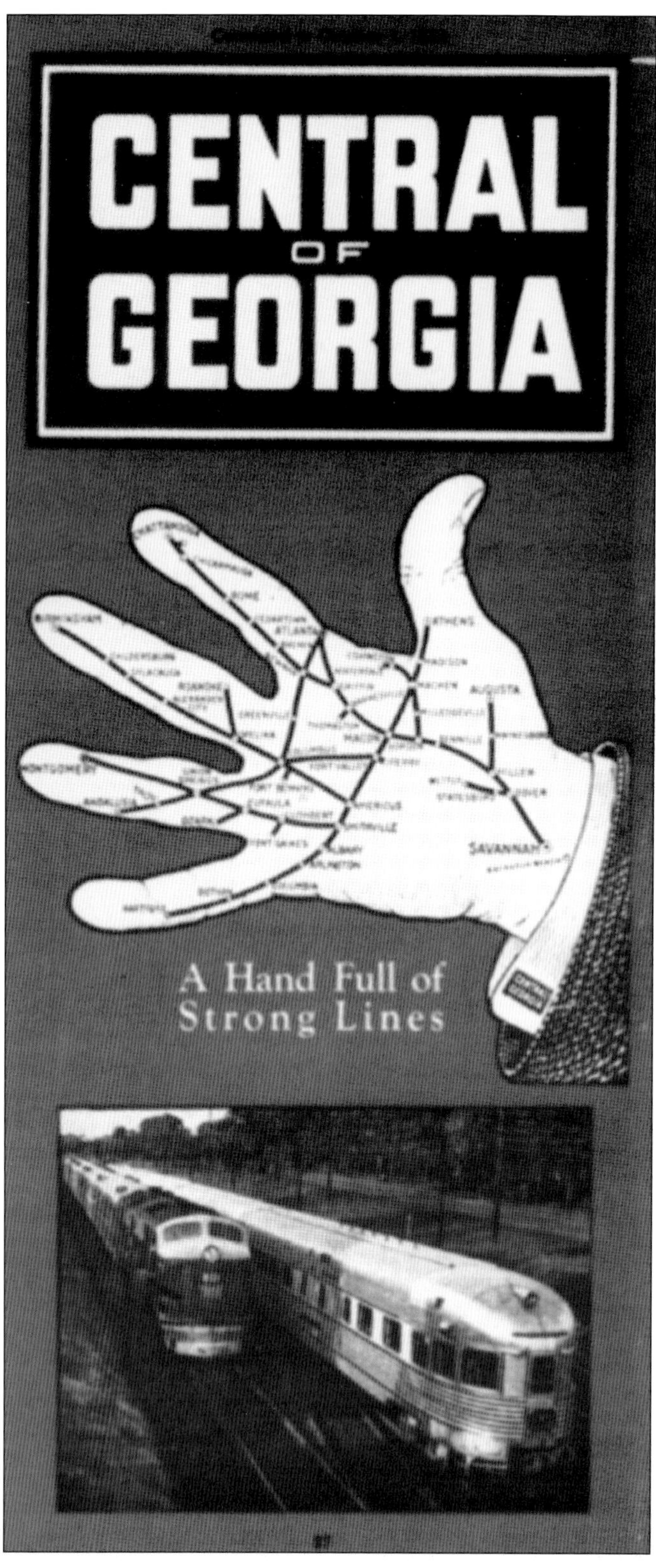

This Central of Georgia timetable from October 1952 features a staged photograph meet between *The Man O' War* and the *Nancy Hanks II* at Fort McPherson just south of Atlanta. Named after sleek, fast racehorses, both trains were built for speed, comfort, and style. The streamlined cars were meant to impress passengers with modernity and glamour, reflecting the post–World War II period of optimism. The timetable also featured Central of Georgia's hand and map logo, representing "a handful of strong lines." This logo appeared on most of its timetables between 1914 and the 1950s. While the prime routes connected Atlanta with Columbus and Savannah, there were a number of spurs with connecting service to Athens, Augusta, Chattanooga, Birmingham, Montgomery, and points beyond. Later, Central of Georgia also began using the slogan "The Right Way." (Central of Georgia Railway Historical Society.)

This 1953 advertisement encourages travelers to avoid traffic and enjoy the ride over the Thanksgiving holiday. At this point, automobiles were becoming more popular and easier to purchase, but interstate highways were still not readily available. According to the advertisement, the *Man O' War* was the "safe, smooth, and luxurious" way to get to Grandma's for the holiday.

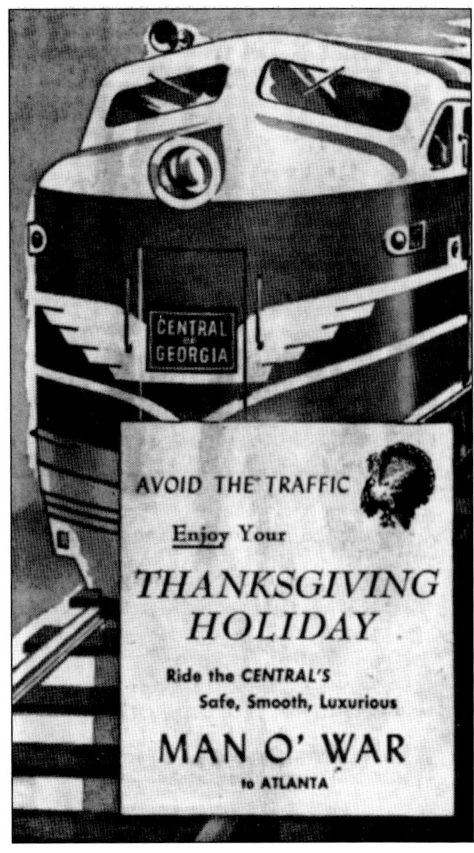

Just a month after its inaugural run, this July 1947 timetable promotes air-conditioned comfort on the *Man O' War* runs from Columbus to Atlanta. In 1947, air-conditioning was a new and very attractive way to beat the southern summer heat. The advertisement also notes reclining seats and a tavern/lounge/observation car. (Central of Georgia Railway Historical Society.)

TABLE 10—COLUMBUS, ATLANTA

19	17	Miles	EASTERN TIME	20	18
PM	AM		**Air-Conditioned**	PM	PM
* 3 15	* 7 30	.0	Lv.......**Columbus**....... Ar	2 10	10 10
3 19	7 34	0.7	...**Columbus,** Second Ave....	1 58	9 58
3 42	7 55	16.0	...........Cataula...........	f 1 37	f 9 37
3 56	8 06	23.9	..........Hamilton..........	1 25	9 25
4 11	8 20	32.6	...........Chipley...........	1 10	9 10
f 4 21	f 8 30	39.6	...........Durand...........	f 1 00	f 9 00
4 34	8 43	49.1	..........Greenville..........	12 47	8 47
			(Warm Spgs. 10 miles by highway)		
4 55	9 02	62.8	.........Luthersville.........	12 28	8 28
5 09	9 15	72.5	...........**Raymond**..........	12 15	8 15
5 25	9 25	78.4	Ar.........**Newnan**........ Lv	12 05	8 05
a	a	113.5	........Ft. McPherson........	b	b
6 15	10 20	117.0	Ar..........**Atlanta**......... Lv	*11 10	* 7 10
PM	AM			AM	PM

MAN O' WAR

Trains Nos. **17, 18, 19** and **20** Diesel Powered Streamliner. Reclining seats, Tavern, Lounge, Observation. Seats reserved.
a–Stops to let off passengers from Columbus.
b–Stops to take passengers for Columbus.

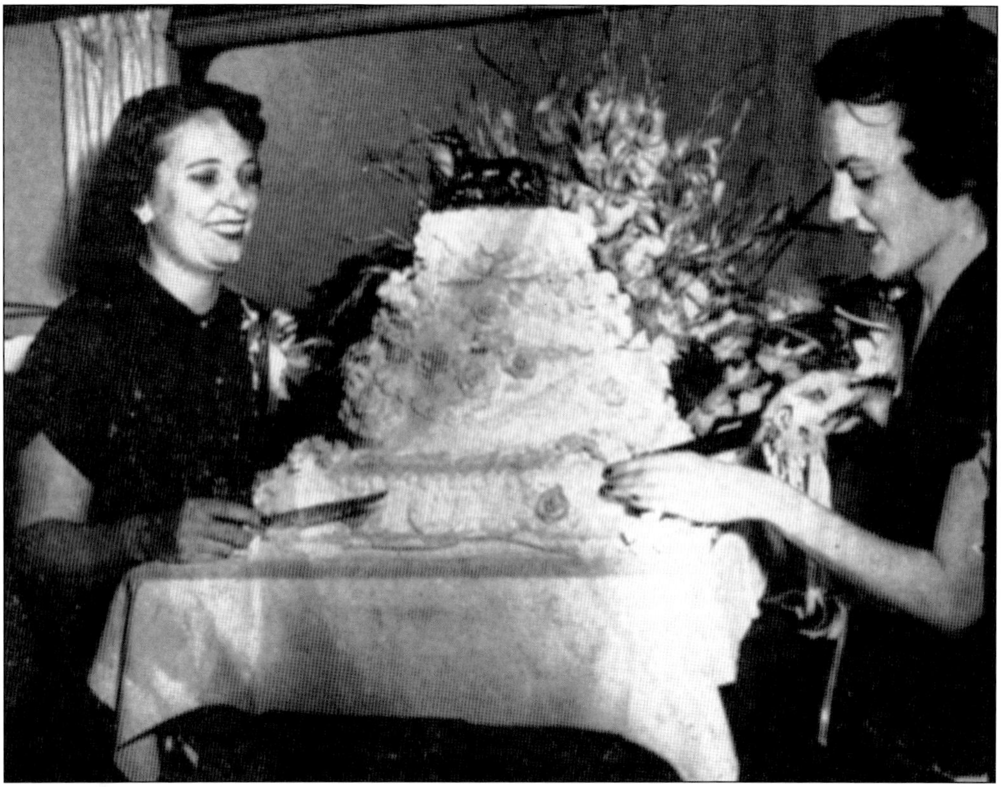

In 1951, *Man O' War* celebrated its fourth birthday in style. An invitation from Ben J. Tarbutton, president of the Central of Georgia, was sent to all "first day" riders to join in the festivities, touting over a half-million passengers served. A birthday cake was featured on both runs that day. Above, Mrs. Tom Starling (left) and Nancy Benton (right) cut the cake on the second trip of the day; below, from left to right, Chipley mayor J.W. Caldwell; Capt. J.H. Williams, assistant transportation officer at Fort Benning; and Robert W. Brown, editor of the *Columbus Ledger*, admire the cake on their run. In addition to being mayor, Caldwell was also a retired Central of Georgia agent. (Below, Central of Georgia Railway Historical Society.)

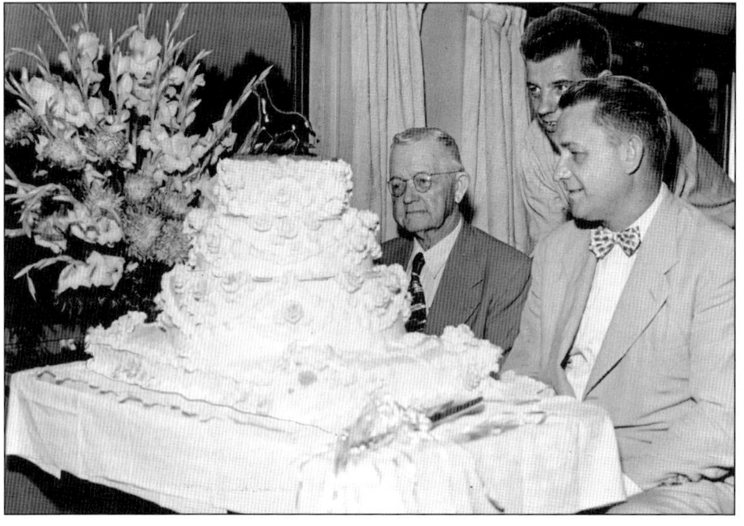

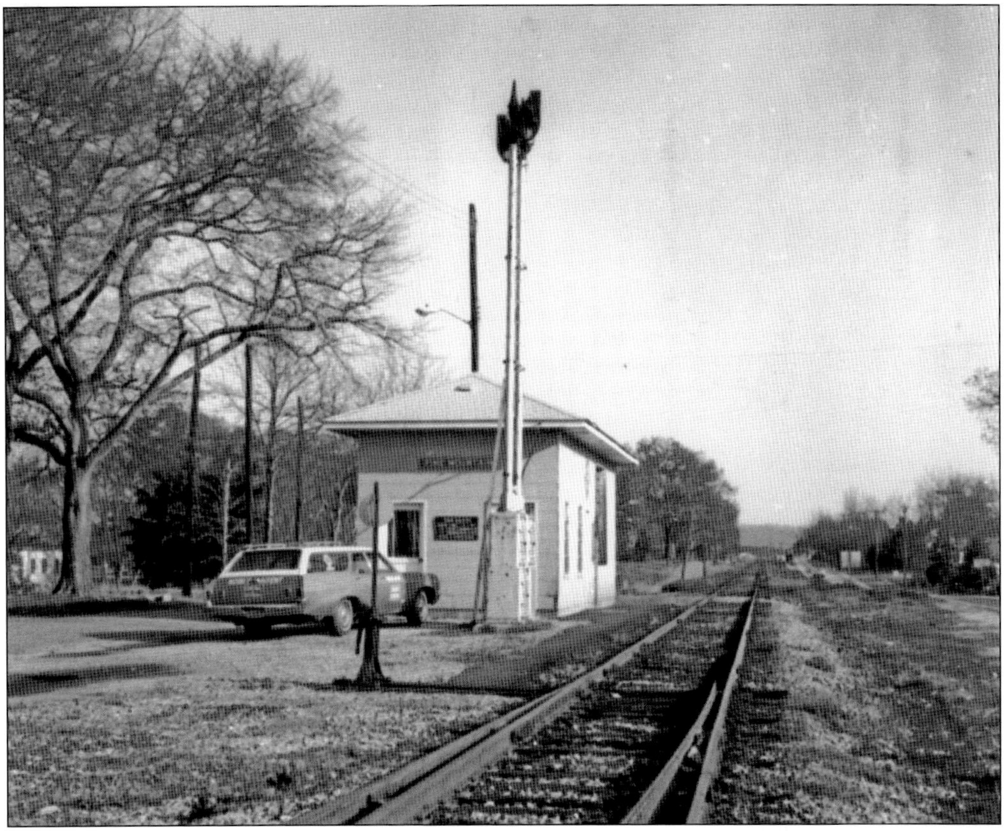

After the depot at the center of town was demolished in 1961, the railroad business moved to this small concrete block building south and east of the former depot location. Since rail traffic was decreasing in favor of the automobile, this small building had no trouble handling the job. Note that, since this was post-1958, the location on the building now reads Pine Mountain.

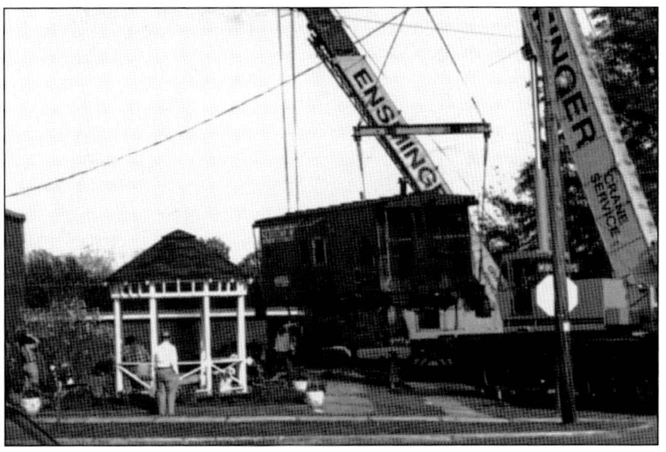

Southern Railway absorbed Central of Georgia in 1963, and in 1982, Norfolk & Western Railroad merged with Southern, becoming Norfolk Southern. In recognition of Chipley/Pine Mountain's long railroad history, in 1989, Norfolk Southern donated a retired Southern caboose to the Chipley Historical Center. In this picture, the caboose is being lifted to its new home behind the Chipley Historical Center.

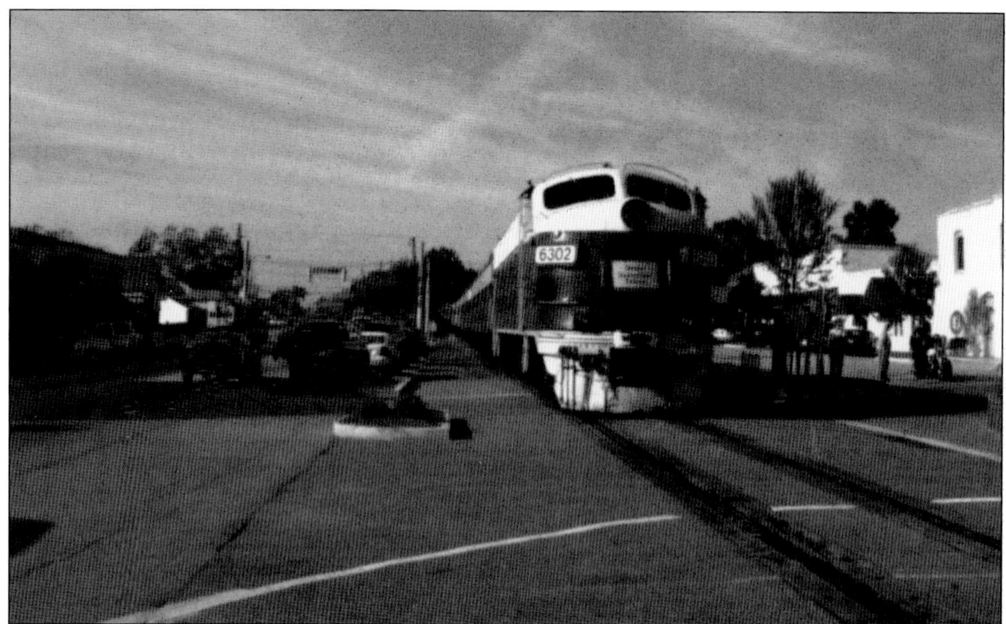

The final train ran in Pine Mountain on November 17, 2007. Passenger trains had long been absent from this track, but the Georgia Southwestern Railroad made one last excursion run. Tracks were removed shortly after that, and after more than a century, the railroad era officially ended in Chipley/Pine Mountain. (Helen Brackett.)

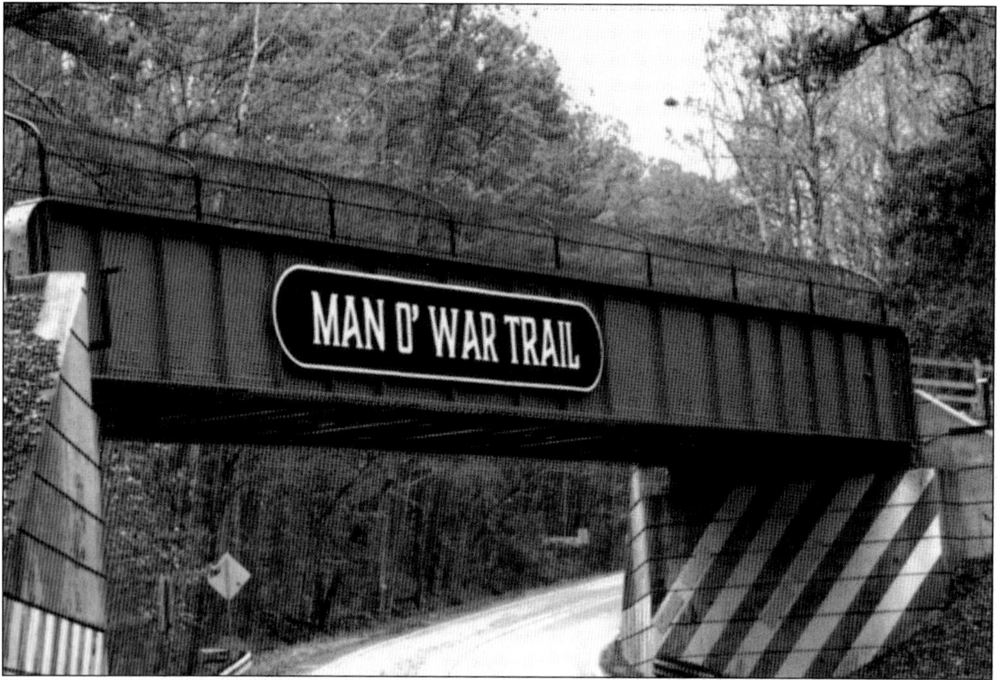

Once the rails were removed, the track bed sat empty for several years. However, Harris County has begun converting the old railbed to a walking and biking trail. Beginning in Pine Mountain, the trail winds its way over the mountain and currently ends in Cataula. Fittingly, the trail has been named the Man O' War Trail after Central of Georgia's famous passenger train. (Robert Brackett.)

Three

Agriculture

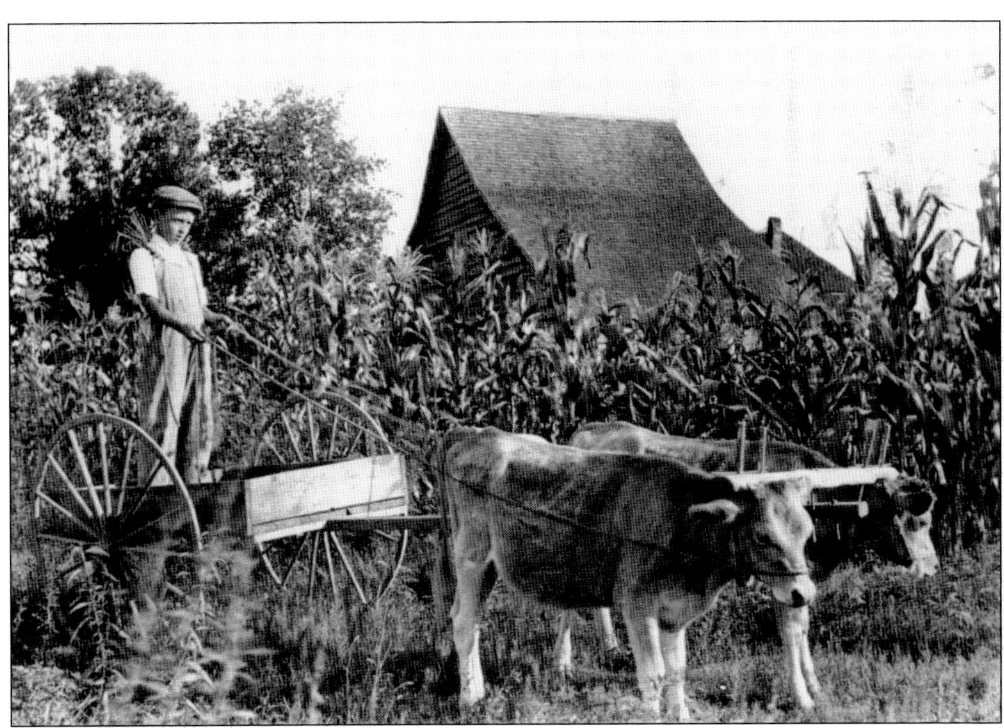

On early family farms, child labor was a necessity and was restricted by common sense rather than regulation. Pictured here around 1914 is Henry Kimbrough Jr., later in life always referred to as "Judge Kimbrough," managing a team of oxen, used generally for heavy loads but ultimately replaced by the mule. He earned his nickname as a shrewd horse and mule trader and merchant.

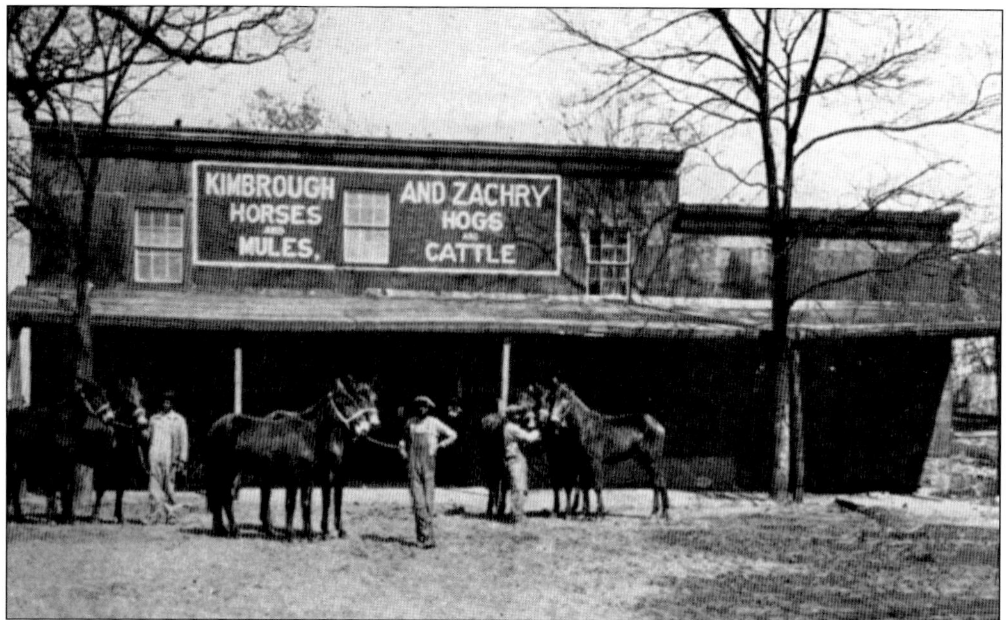

By 1925, Judge Kimbrough and Henry Zachry were business partners in the Kimbrough and Zachry Sale and Feed barns. It was a growing business and could feed, exchange, buy, sell, and ship horses, mules, hogs, and cattle. The photograph below shows S.A. Surles in the background shoeing in 1901. The Vardeman and Surles blacksmith business started in the early 1880s. In 1908, he and his son Ernest were operating the Surles and Son Blacksmith shop, and later Ernest's wife, "Miss Pinky," had a hat shop upstairs in their building. Both the livery and blacksmith businesses declined, however, as farming became more mechanized. The structures of both had been razed by the early 1960s. Old South Antiques is now located at the Kimbrough and Zachry site, and the Pine Mountain Post Office is located on the Surles site.

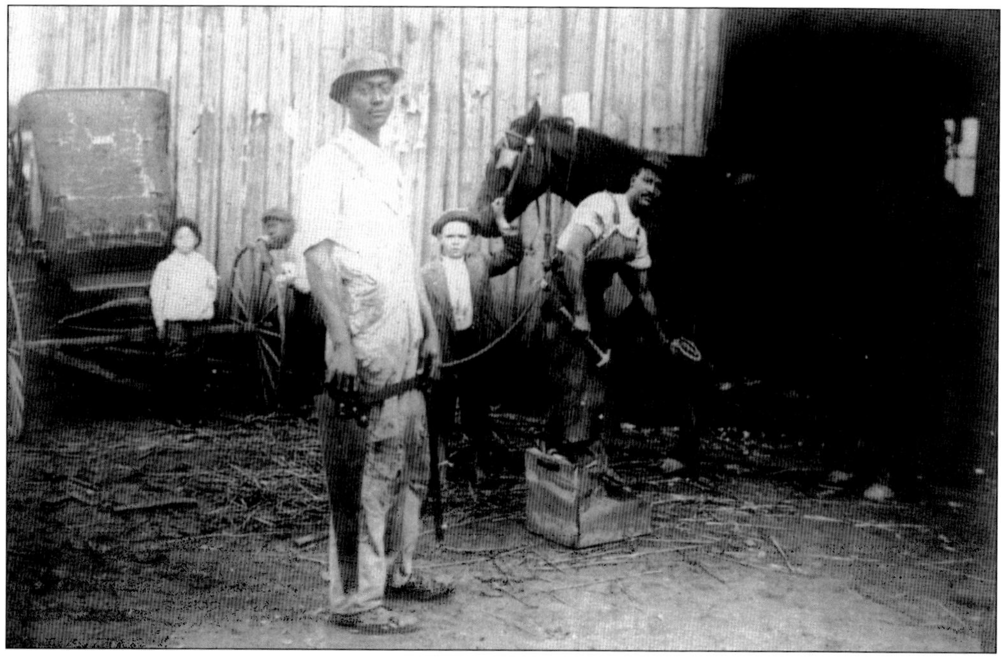

ALLIANCE WAREHOUSE.

TUCKER & HUNT, Proprietors.

Chipley, Ga. Dec 5 189 3

MARKS	Nos.	WEIGHTS	P. MARKS	RE-WEIGHED	REMARKS
W	11	558		7¢	

Received from Alvin Phillips

One Bales of Cotton.

Marks, Nos., &c., as per margin, deliverable to this Receipt only, by paying customary charges and all Advances. (Acts of Providence and fire excepted.)

D J Tucker

Weigher.

Wagoner:

Cotton was one of the few money crops for early yeoman farmers with limited acreage and few, if any, hired hands. Imagine the time required to prepare, plant, and manage the crop and the backbreaking effort in picking enough cotton by hand to make 558 pounds of ginned and baled lint at 7¢ per pound, for a total of $39.06 on the above receipt. After purchasing the bales, the broker would store them in warehouses to capacity and line up the overflow along an alley to await shipment by rail or later by trucks. In the early days, local transport of raw cotton and bales was made by mule and wagon.

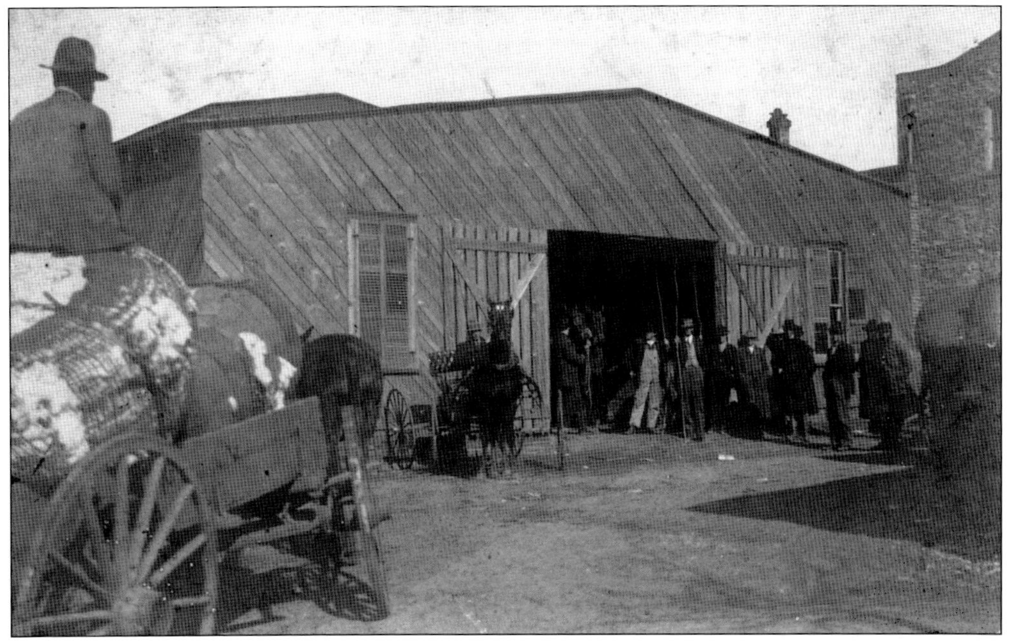

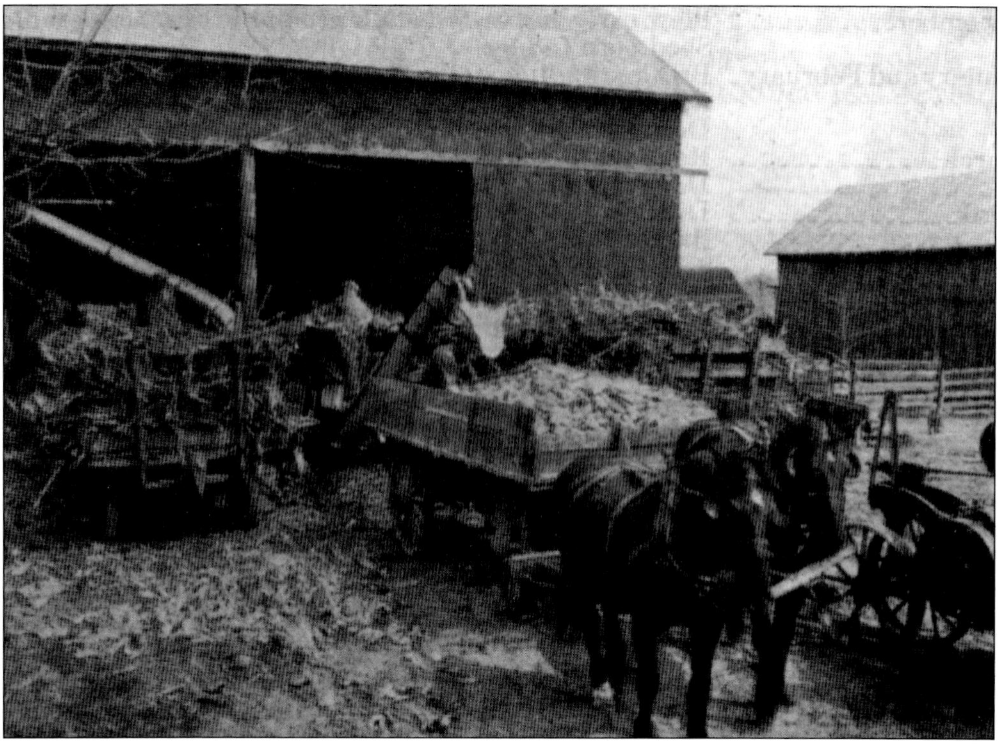

A successful farm was in many ways a village unto itself. Outbuildings, particularly barns, were constructed as the need arose. Generally of rough, unpainted pine boards, they were meant above all to be functional. They had stalls for horses and mules and cribs for storage of feed corn. Some farms had separate buildings that served as dairy barns. There were central fenced lots for livestock with water tanks and troughs. Elsewhere about the farm were sties for swine and houses or coops for fowl. Particularly before general rural electrification, there would be a smokehouse for the preservation and storage of meat. Near the farmhouse would be a well house or open well with rope, bucket, and pulley. And, of course, there would be a privy or outhouse at an adequate distance from the house and well.

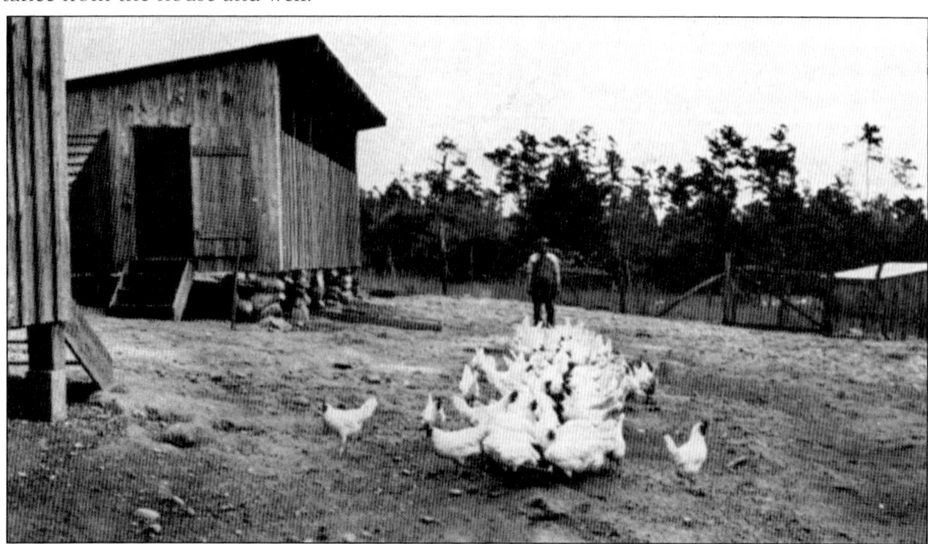

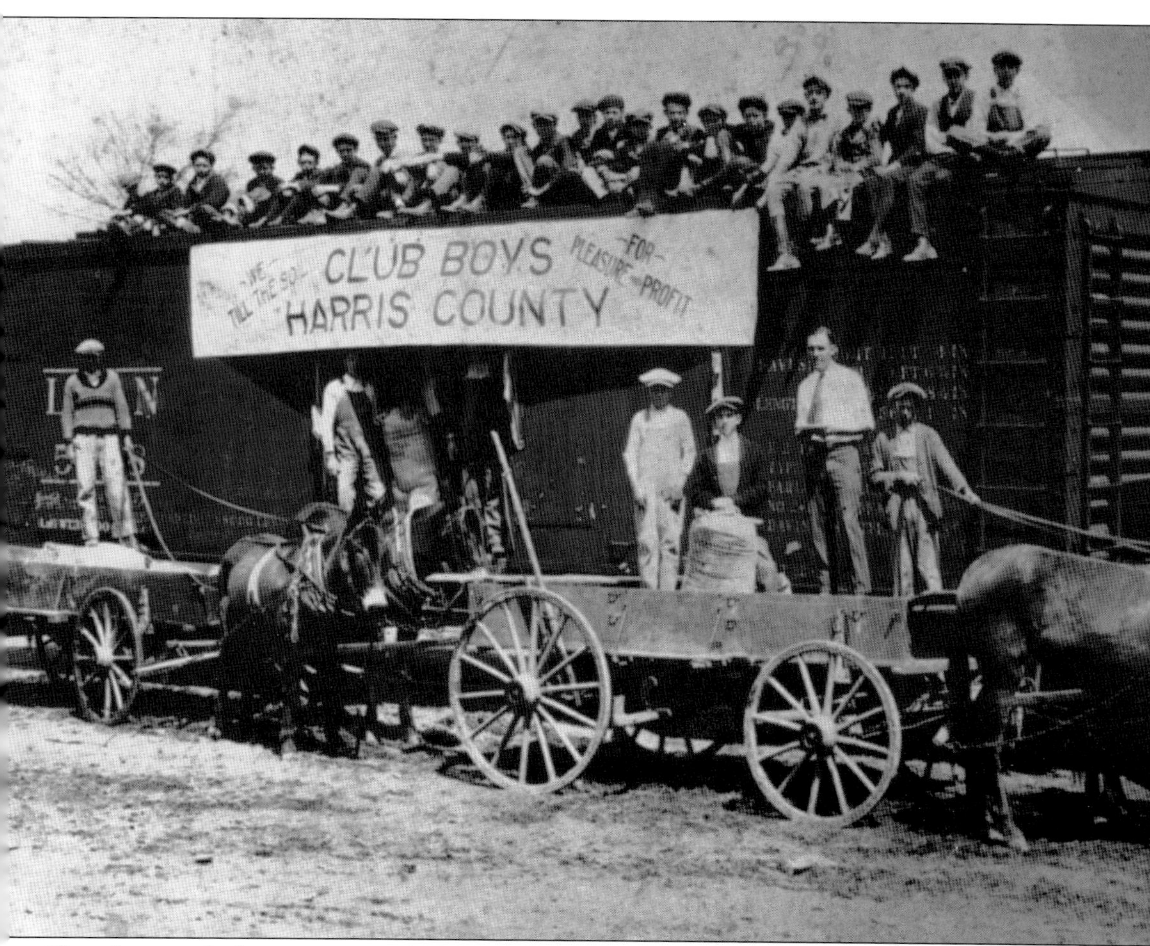

This photograph shows many members of the Corn Club of northwest Harris County, including Chipley, Whitesville, and the communities of Hopewell and Sunnyside. It was taken in the 1920s with the boys sitting on the roof of a railroad car in Chipley. The club, which was a forerunner of the 4-H Club in Harris County, was started by J.T. Cox Jr., wearing a dress shirt and tie and standing in a wagon. He was from Macon, a graduate of the University of Georgia, and worked for the US Department of Agriculture as an assistant to the extension agent in Columbus. He started the club to teach Harris County youth modern, more productive methods of agriculture. Cox met and eventually married Mary Hopkins, a first-grade teacher at Sunnyside School, located between Chipley and Whitesville. Their children included Betty Cox Beegle, a longtime resident of Whiteville, and Franklin Cox, later a resident of Pine Mountain.

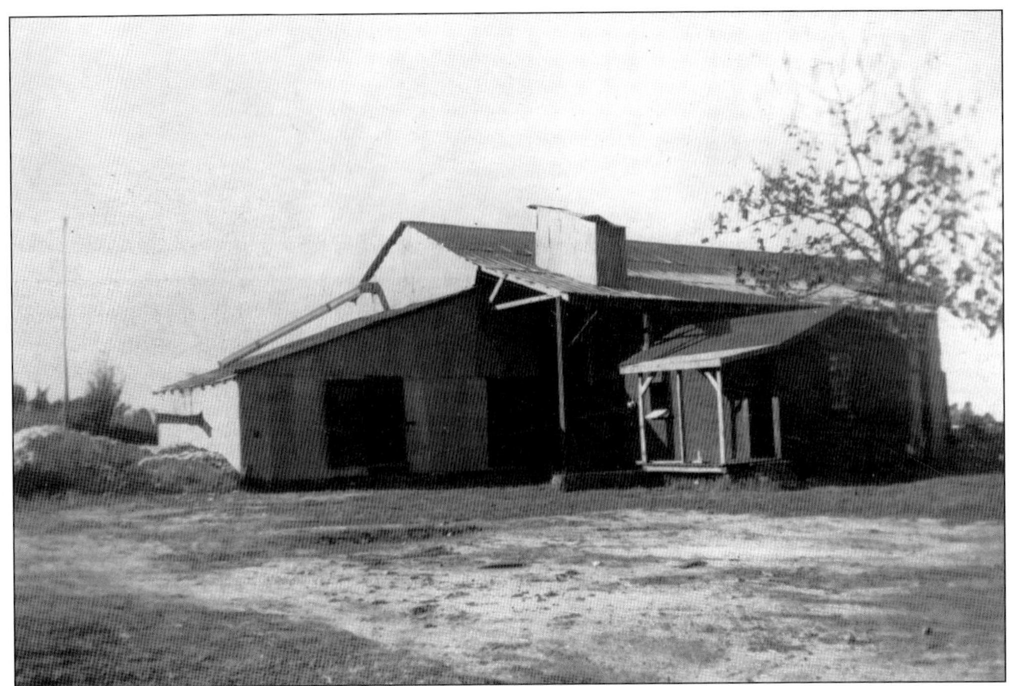

In 1951, there was a "sensational cotton crop," up to one and a half bales per acre reported. J.M. Dunn's gin (above) noted 1,850 bales ginned and 700 tons of seed bought and sold, with an approximate value of $426,000. Another 280 bales were ginned by the Hastey Ginning Company (below). Kimbrough Brothers Warehouse handled 1,316 bales. By the mid-1970s, however, the white fields of cotton were no longer found near Pine Mountain, and the gins were closed for good. There are cotton conglomerates now in southern Georgia and Alabama, Texas, and elsewhere, but the yeoman and small family growers near Pine Mountain are no more.

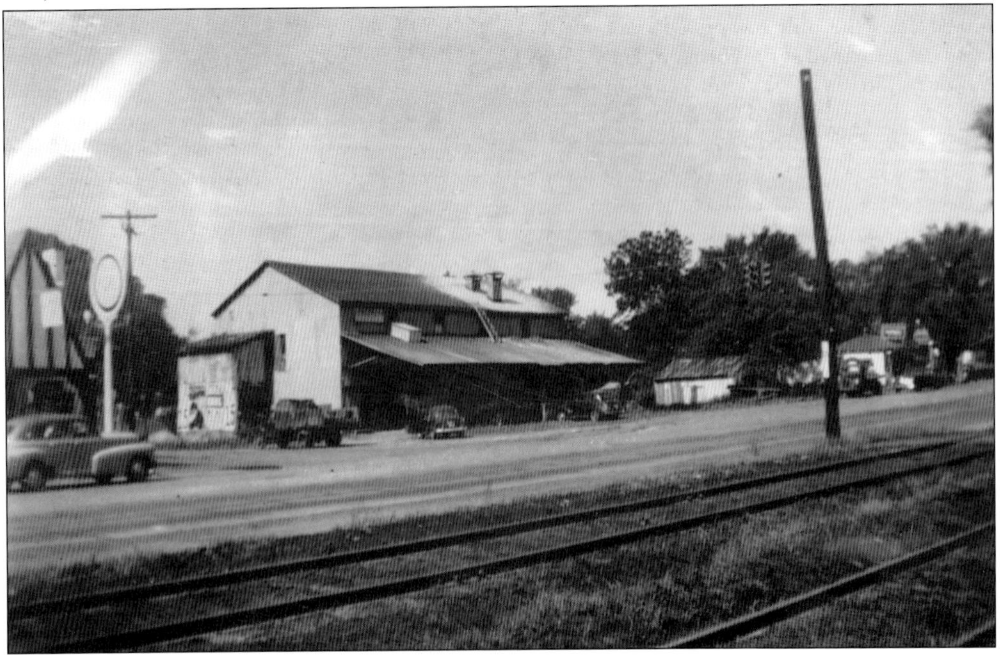

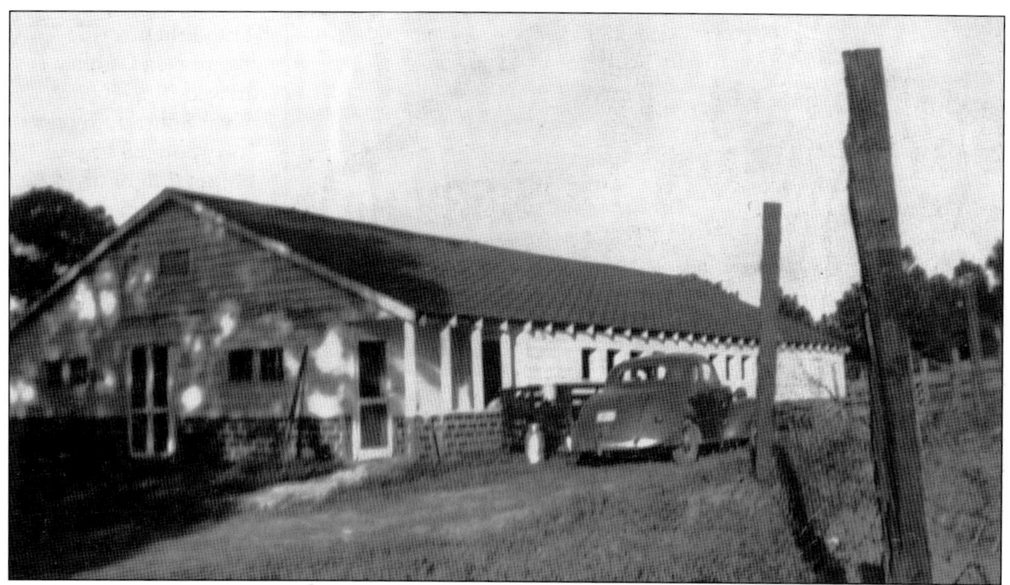

Dairy cattle were part of every farmer's herd. Many farmers entered the commercial dairy business, which reached its peak in the early 1950s. Within a 10-mile radius of Chipley, there were as many as 15 active dairies providing milk to processing and distribution facilities in the nearby cities of Columbus and LaGrange. In one year, a total of over eight million pounds of milk was produced by local family-operated dairies with a value of $502,600. The dairy business waned, however, in later years for smaller operations, and there are no dairies now in the Pine Mountain vicinity. Raising beef cattle and hogs is a better alternative. Even farmers with small herds can supply the commercial meat processors with a few head of cattle and hogs over and above those raised for their own consumption.

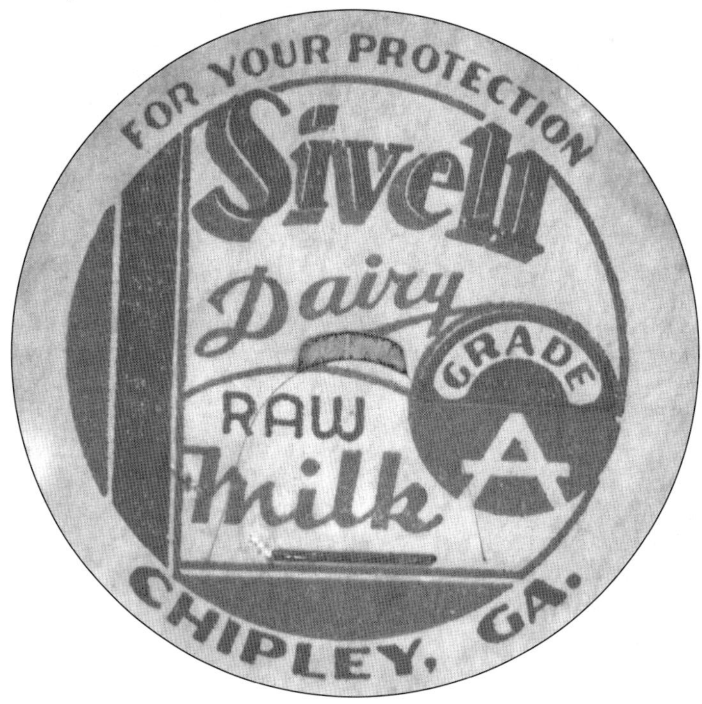

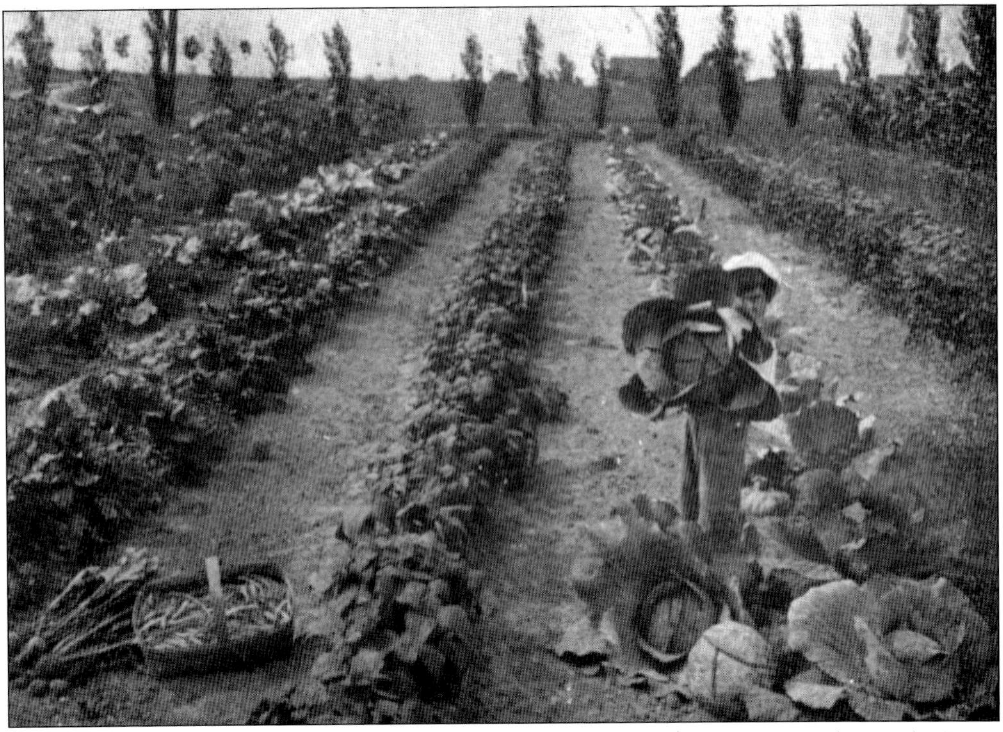

Chipley was established at the northern edge of Harris County. The counties to the north, Troup and Meriwether, came together at Chipley. So, when Chipley held a country fair in October 1925, it had to be the "Tri-County Fair." There was then extensive and diverse agriculture and horticulture in the area. Awards were offered for the best apples, pears, pecans, potatoes, beets, tomatoes, cabbage, onions, carrots, and pumpkins as well as for field crops like corn, millet, alfalfa, wheat, rye, oats, peanuts, sugar cane, sorghum, and soy beans. All areas of cooking and preserving food, sewing, weaving, and quilting were judged. Of course, all categories of cattle, swine, horses, and fowl were considered, but not turkeys. By 1950, though, the Bruce Champion family had entered that market and had 1,300 turkeys, processing equipment, and freezer units.

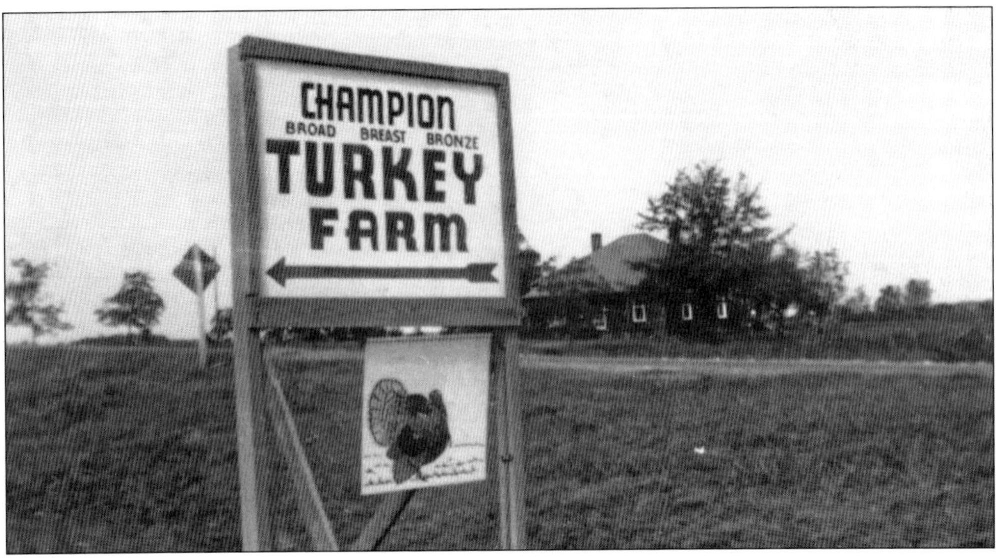

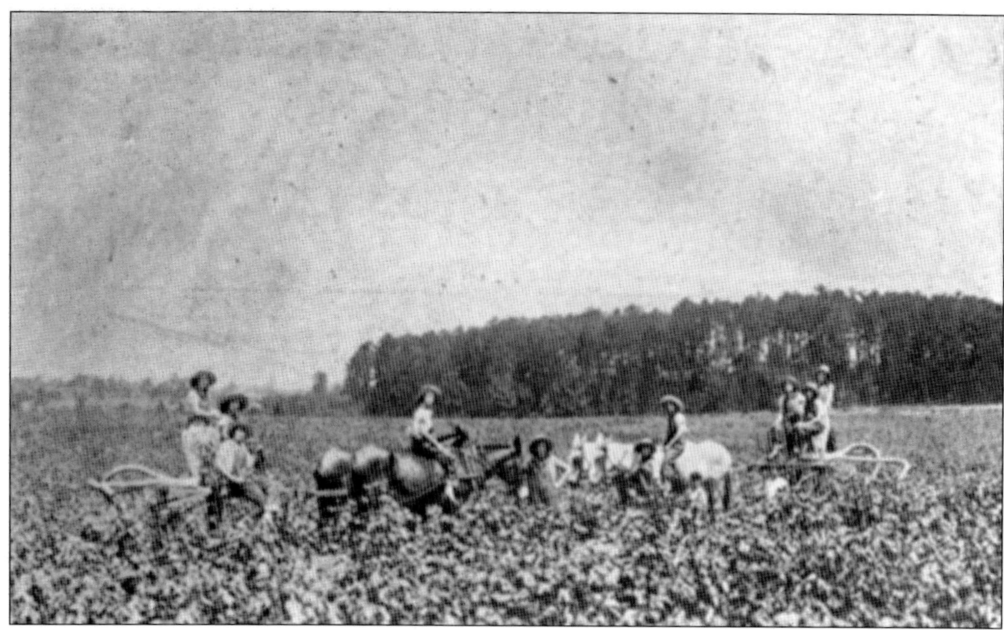

At the time of Chipley's Tri-County Fair in October 1925, there were white fields of cotton all around. Even young belles could be persuaded to pose while pretending to be working for King Cotton. By then, however, the boll weevil had arrived, and fields planted only in cotton year after year were being exhausted of their natural minerals. Application of commercial fertilizers could help for a while, and farmers began to practice rotation of their crops. There was, however, usually a much lower immediate cash value in other crops. Before the end of the century, the local cotton fields had gone fallow, had been converted to hay fields or pasture, or had been planted in pine trees. The beef cattle industry was the new monarch, and hay and pulpwood had taken over as the long-term renewable resources.

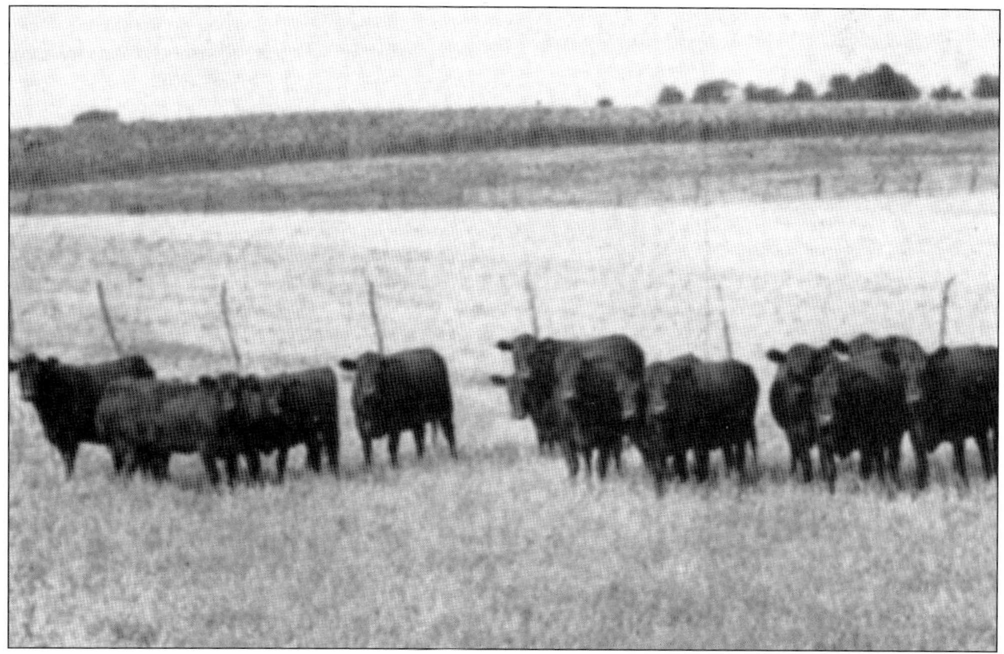

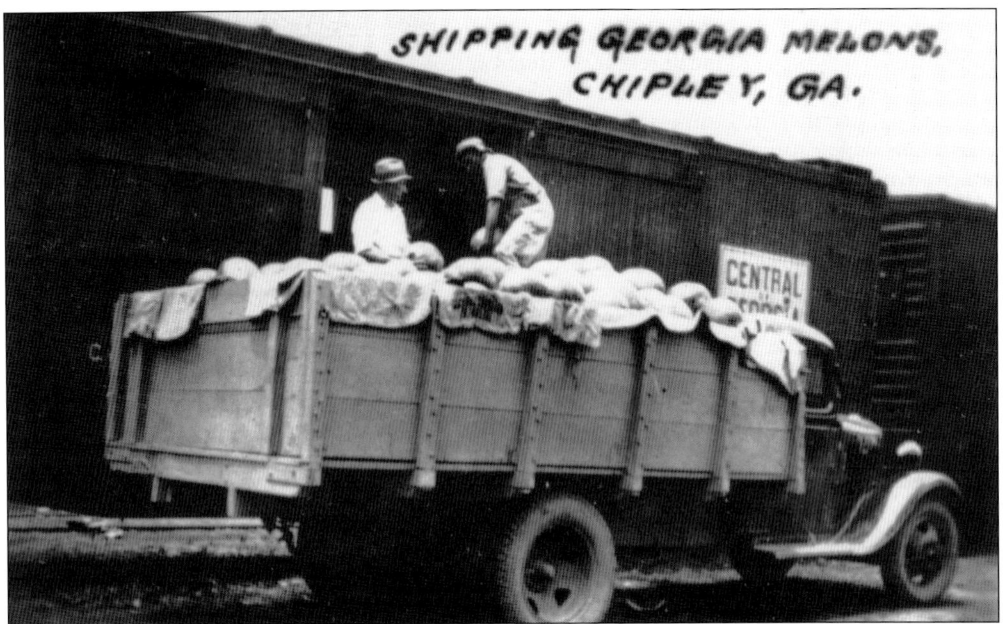

Produce grown by farmers at a modest level for immediate consumption or preservation for later use became, for some, commercial commodities because of the proximity to the railroad. Larger crops of melons, sweet corn, potatoes, peaches, and other fruits were made possible by the easy shipment of large amounts to markets and distribution points. Even before refrigerated railcars were available, fresh items could reach distant markets in good condition.

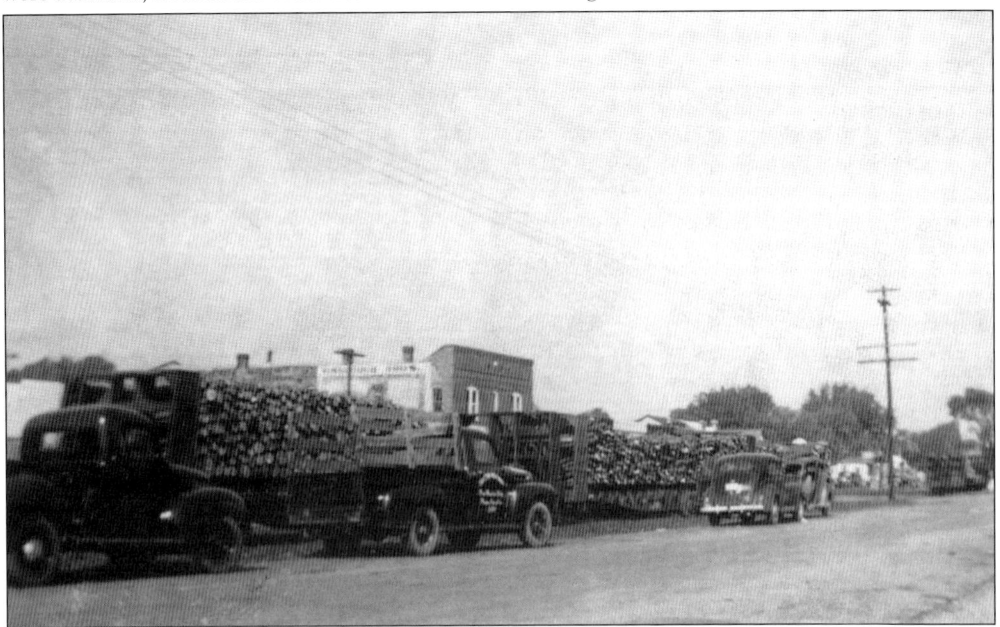

The sidetracks in Chipley were often full of flat cars designed particularly for shipping standard lengths of pulpwood. The cars were divided longitudinally, with each side sloping slightly inward so logs could be loaded from both sides and be stable in transit. This sight was more common as cotton planting declined and more fields either grew up in volunteer pine trees or were intentionally planted in seedlings.

Four

PLACES OF WORSHIP

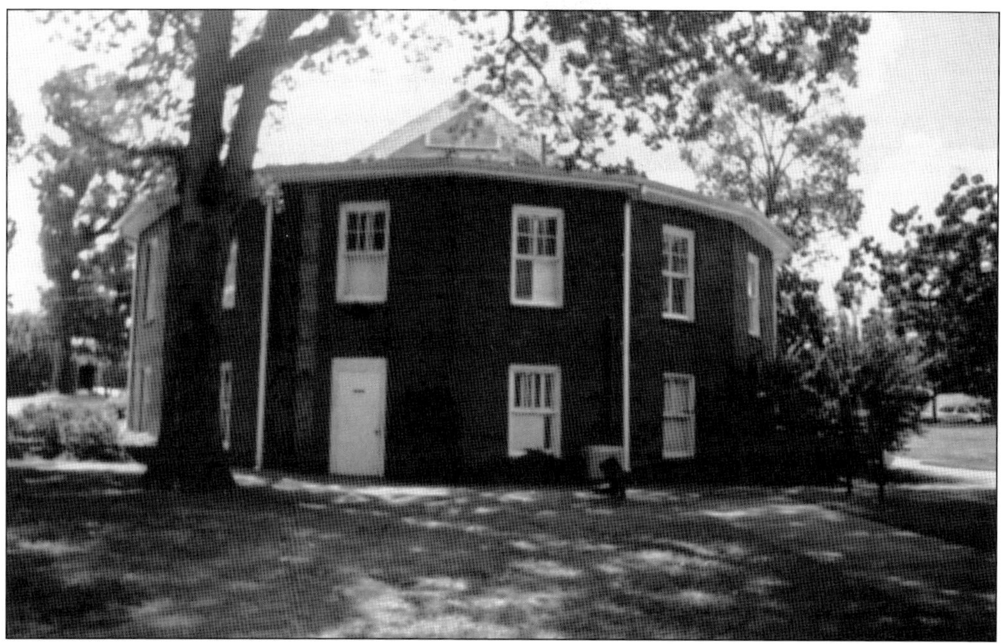

One of the most unusual structures in Chipley was the First Methodist Church, built in 1920. The rear portion of the church was an octagon. It had classrooms on the upper floor and a common room and kitchen on the lower floor. This portion was demolished in 2003 and replaced with the current two-story educational annex. (First United Methodist Church of Pine Mountain.)

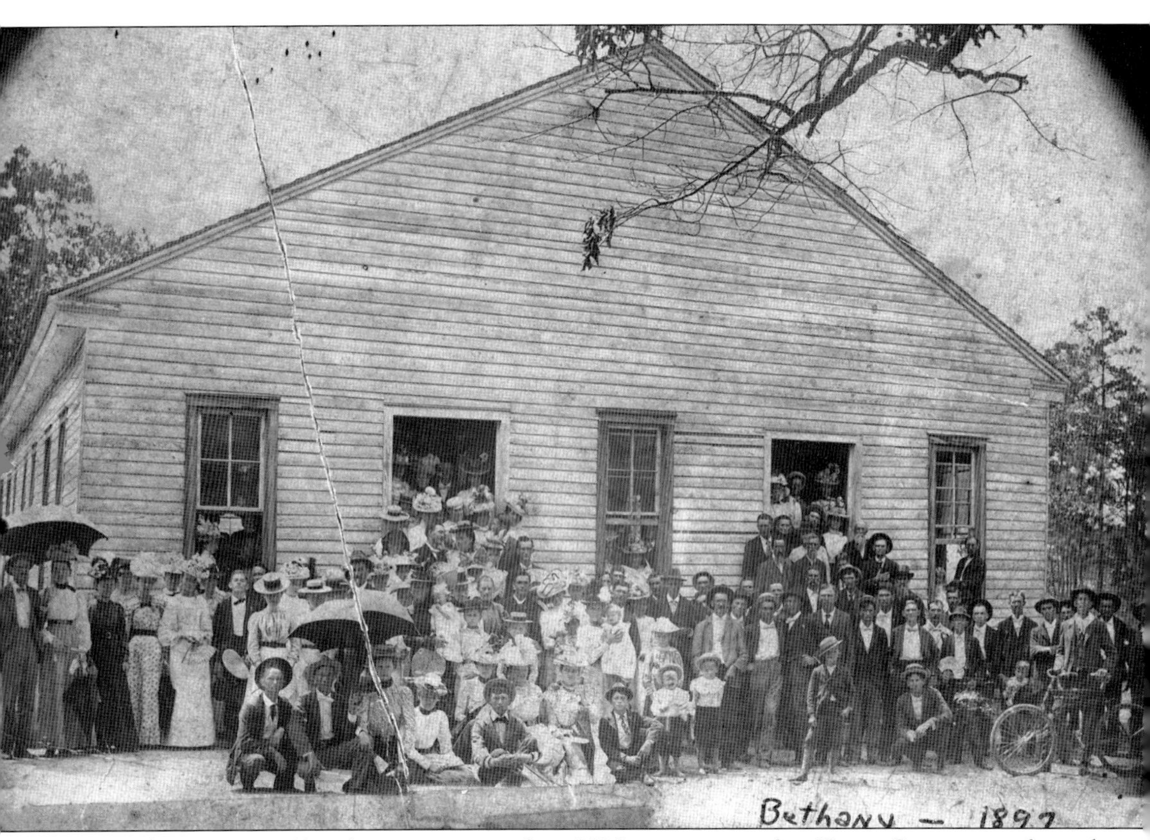

Bethany Baptist Church was constituted in 1828, just a year after Harris County was formed, in an area known as "Goodman's Crossroad" near what would eventually become Chipley. The first pastor was John W. Cooper, who served from 1828 to 1847. By 1836, the church had a total membership of 73 people. There have been several church buildings, but all have been located within just a few miles of the current structure on Bethany Church Road, which was constructed in 1847. In the years prior to the Civil War, enslaved African Americans worshipped with their owners at Bethany until they eventually formed their own church in 1877. Some are buried in the old part of the cemetery at Bethany. In 1886, several more members left Bethany to form a new Baptist Church in the town of Chipley, now the First Baptist Church of Pine Mountain. The original Bethany Baptist was the "mother" church to two other congregations.

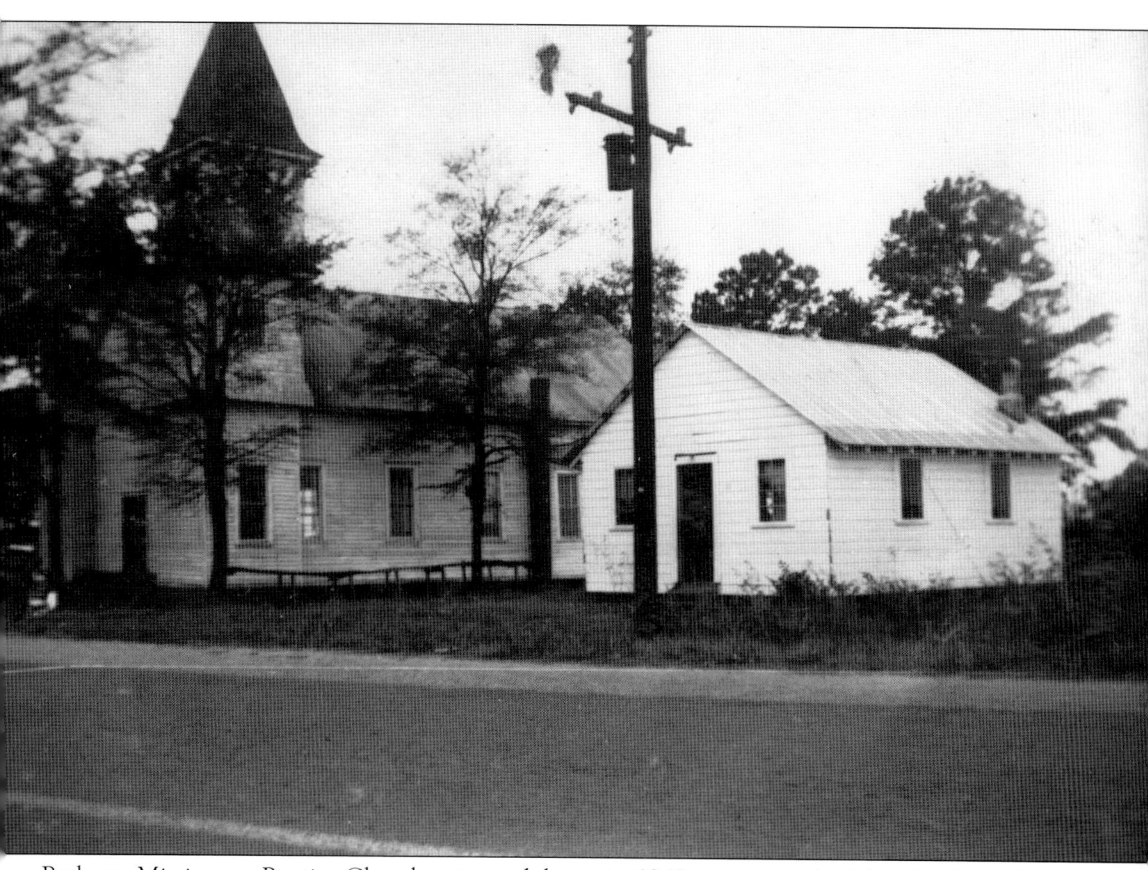

Bethany Missionary Baptist Church, pictured here in 1949, was organized by the formerly enslaved Black members of the original Bethany Baptist Church in 1877. The first pastor was Rev. J.D. Walker, who served until his death in 1880. They held services there until 1885, when they purchased an old freight house for $125 that they moved from the town of Hood to their property on Highway 18 West. That building was destroyed by the 1908 tornado that swept through Chipley, leaving only the floor. Other community churches, along with church members, contributed toward a new building. The new church was erected across the road and still stands today. Brick veneer was added to the building in 1952 along with a fellowship hall. The cemetery that extends behind and to the side of the current building has been the site of an identification and restoration project from 2022 to 2025.

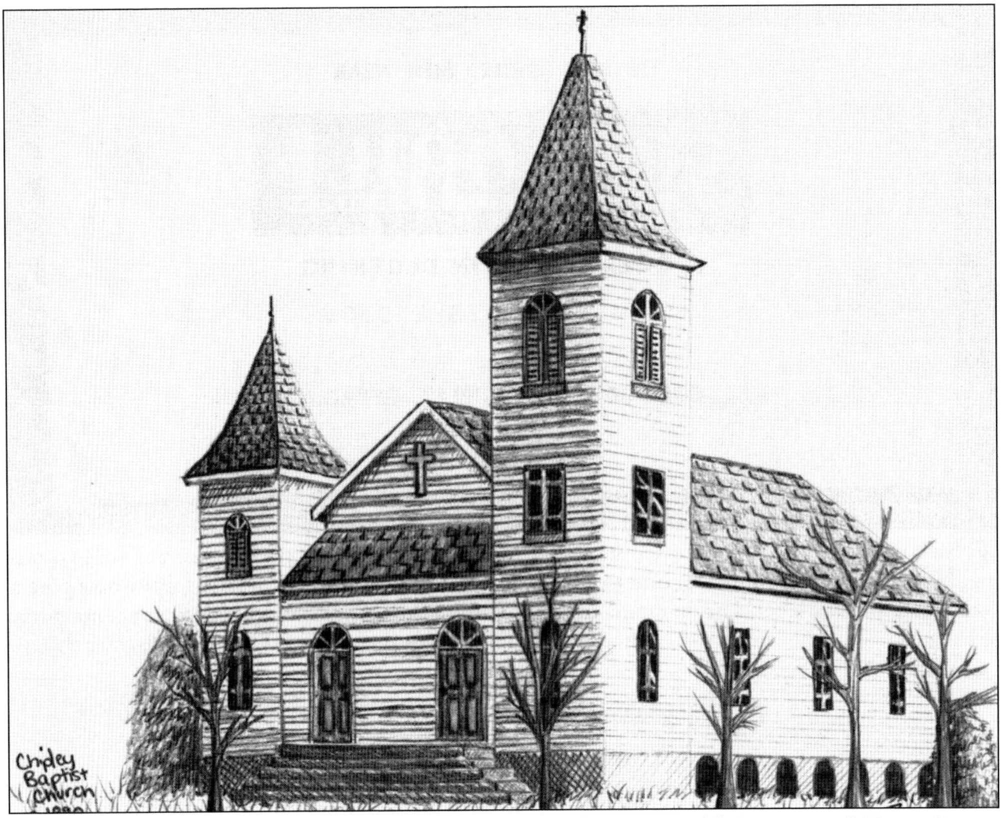

The First Baptist Church, located at the corner of South McDougald Avenue and Harris Street, was organized in 1886 by 37 members of Bethany Baptist Church. Families from that church west of town who transferred their memberships to the new "in-town" church, shown above, included Hastey, Huguley, Jenkins, Stripling, Bowles, and Surles. Chipley Baptist Church first met in "a good, neat house, finished off nicely and all paid for in 1887." Unfortunately, the wood-frame church building was destroyed by the 1908 tornado. The current brick building, pictured below in 1951, was completed at the same location and was dedicated in 1910, which, with some additions, remains today. Following her mother church's lead, Pine Mountain First Baptist Church was instrumental in founding New Life Church, located northeast of Pine Mountain, a congregation primarily of Black members. (Above, Katie Wright.)

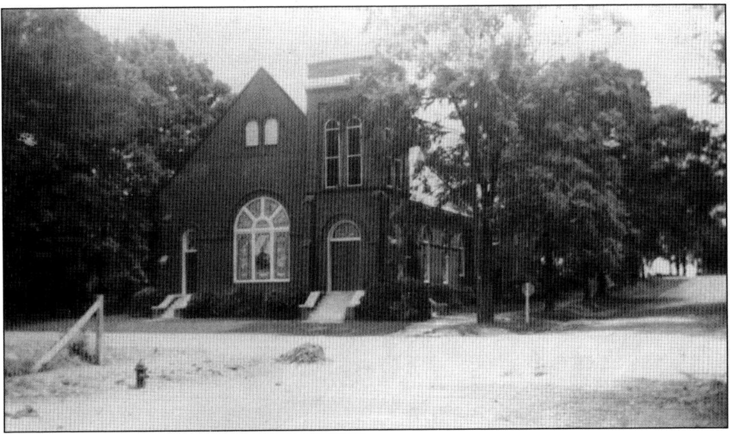

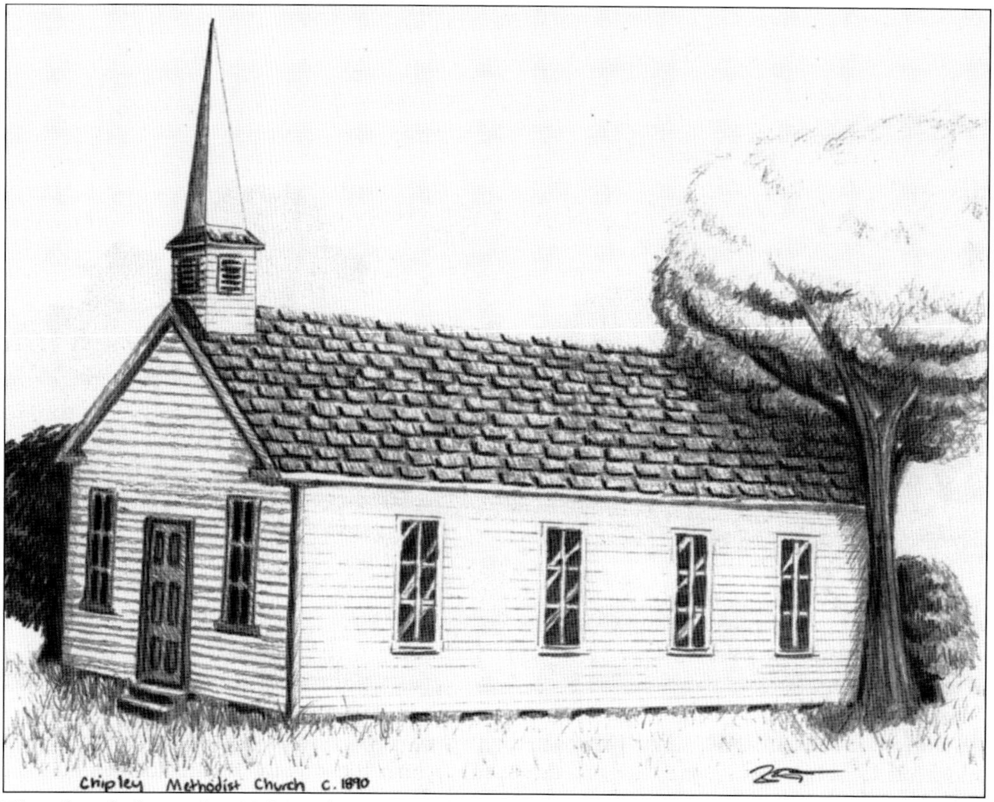

Chipley Methodist Church c. 1890

This church, located at 206 North McDougald Avenue, was chartered on October 20, 1882, by the North Georgia Conference as the First Methodist Episcopal Church South. Rev. S.D. Clements was the first minister. The frame building pictured above was completed in 1883 and survived the 1908 tornado. After the storm, since the Baptist church just a few blocks down the street had been destroyed, both the Methodist and Baptist congregations shared the building until the Baptist church was rebuilt. In 1920, this frame structure was dismantled, and the present building, shown below in 1951, was constructed at the same location at a cost of $10,000. In 1939, the name was changed to the First Methodist Church of Chipley, and it became the Pine Mountain United Methodist Church in 1968. (Above, Katie Wright.)

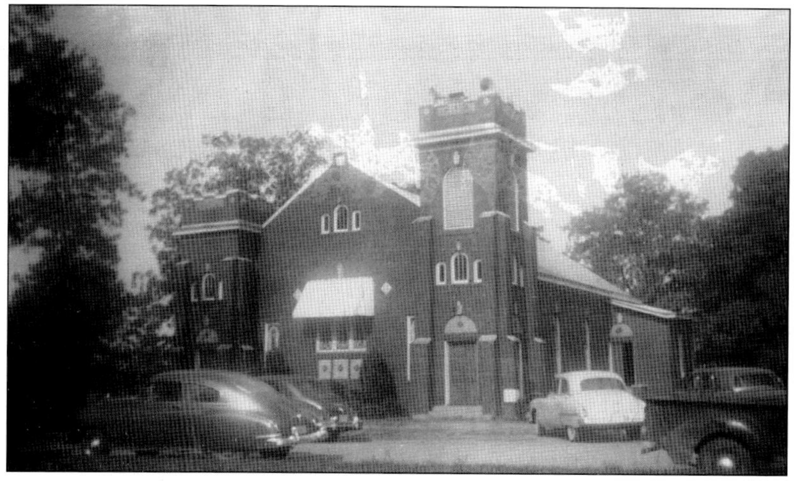

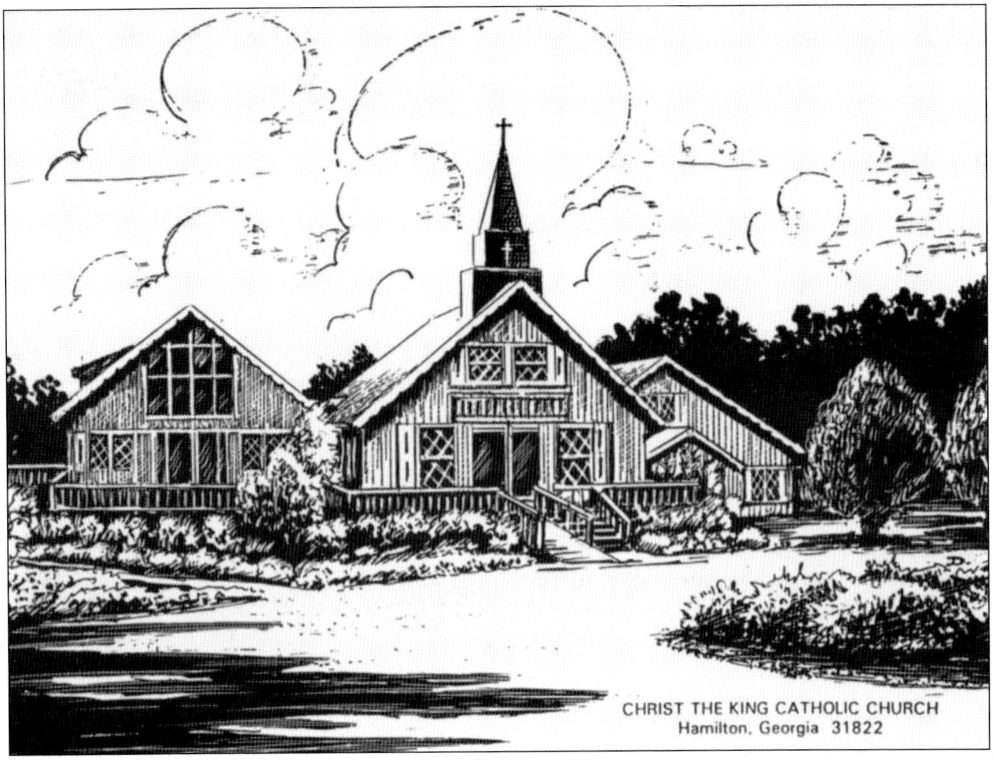

CHRIST THE KING CATHOLIC CHURCH
Hamilton, Georgia 31822

In the early 1960s, Fr. Lawrence A. Lucree began celebrating Mass in people's homes and at Callaway Gardens. A chalet-style church, shown above, was built on US Highway 27 between Hamilton and Pine Mountain. In 2002, Fr. Ronnie Madden and his parishioners purchased a site on Highway 354 near Pine Mountain on which to build a new church and parish hall. Christ the King Catholic Church, shown below, was completed in 2003. In August 2017, lightning struck the church steeple during a terrible storm, causing a massive fire that nearly destroyed the steeple and roof. Only an alert neighbor and the fortunate passing by of the local fire department kept the entire structure from going up in flames. It took three years to rebuild. The church started with 12 families and now has 150. (Above, Christ the King Catholic Church; below, Robert Brackett.)

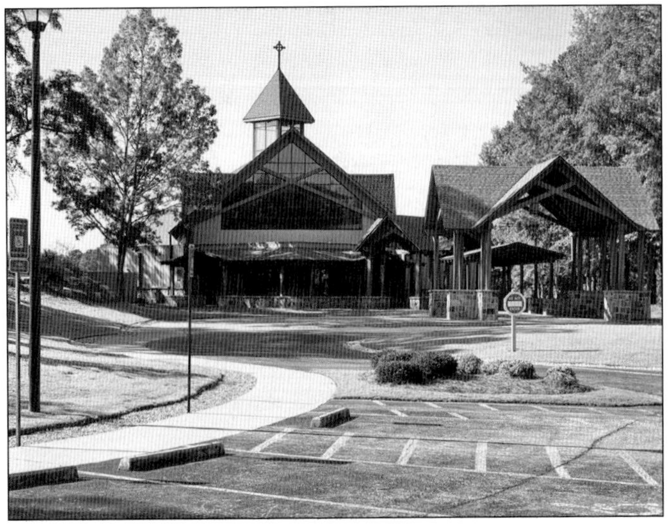

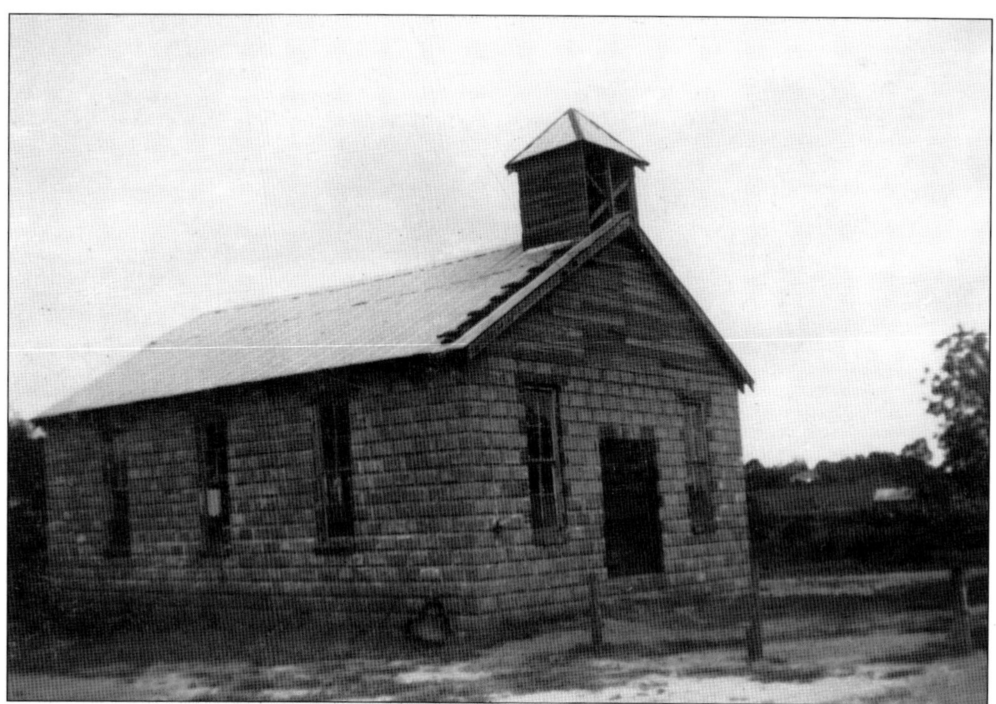

The establishment of St. John CME Church, an early Black church, pictured above in 1949, occurred on or about May 18, 1891, in Troup County. The trustees were Elbert Carter, Howard Turner, and Lee Jones. The church prospered through the years until the 1940s. Serving as trustees and stewards in the 1940s were Byron Copeland, Tom Dunlap, Lovie Roberts, and Hudson McGruder. These men continued serving until the 1960s. In November 2001, construction of a new building of 3,550 square feet in Pine Mountain began. The church voted that its members and community volunteers would be asked to complete work on the interior of the building to save as much as possible on construction costs. Work was finished in just 18 months, and the new facility was dedicated in September 2003. The church is located on Davis Lake Road. (Below, Robert Brackett.)

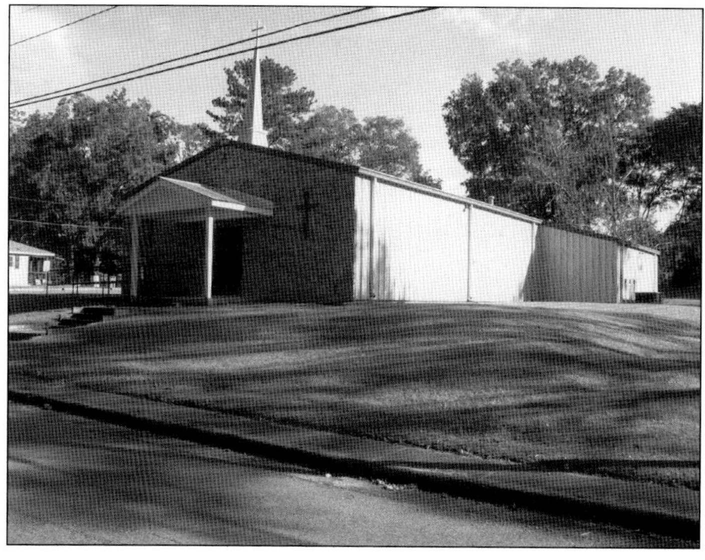

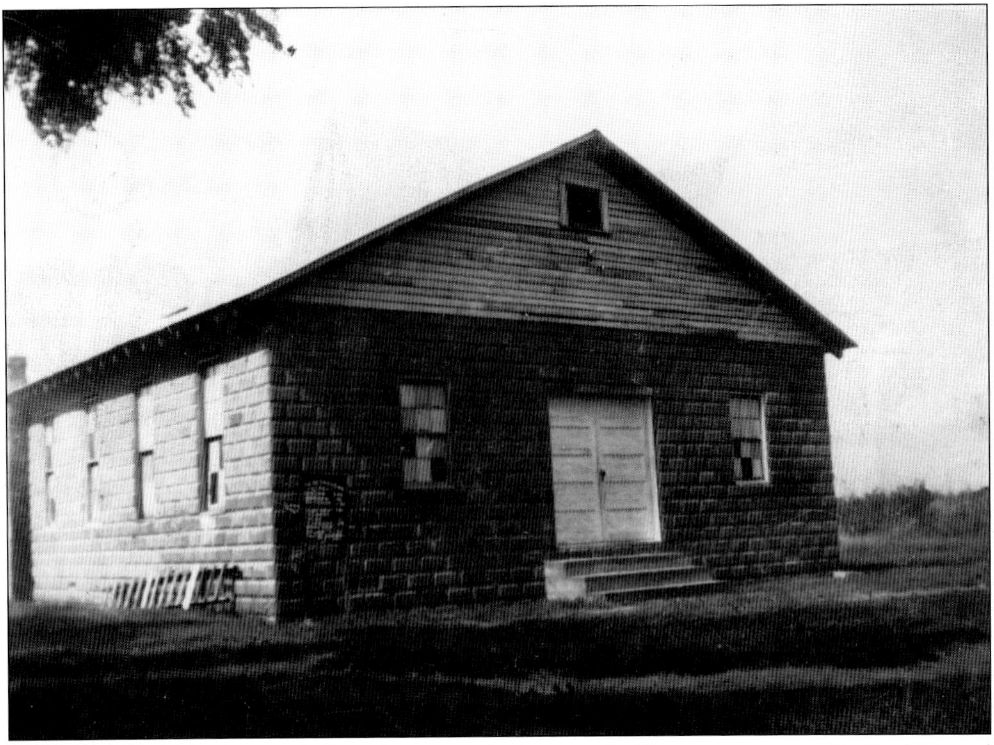

St. Paul Methodist Episcopal Church, pictured above in 1949, now known as St. Paul United Methodist Church, stands as one of Chipley's earliest Black churches. While the original founding date remains unknown, the church was reestablished in 1908 under the guidance of Rev. J.S. Stripling, who served as the district superintendent. The church cornerstone commemorating this event also mentions P.B. Gibson, likely as a parish associate, along with trustees A.L. Cameron, J. Brooks, Jno. (Jonathan) Tramell, and James Scott. The 1908 tornado caused extensive damage to the church and necessitated its rebuilding. In 1980, the church's parking lot was paved, and in 2002, a fellowship hall was added. Today, the church sits on a one-acre lot between Hardy and Wood Avenues. (Below, Robert Brackett.)

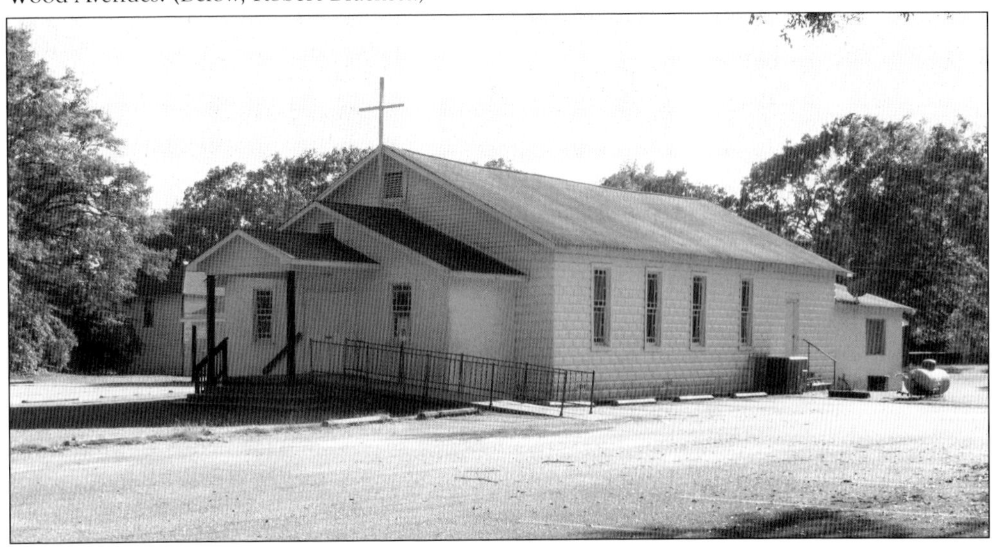

Five

Early Schools

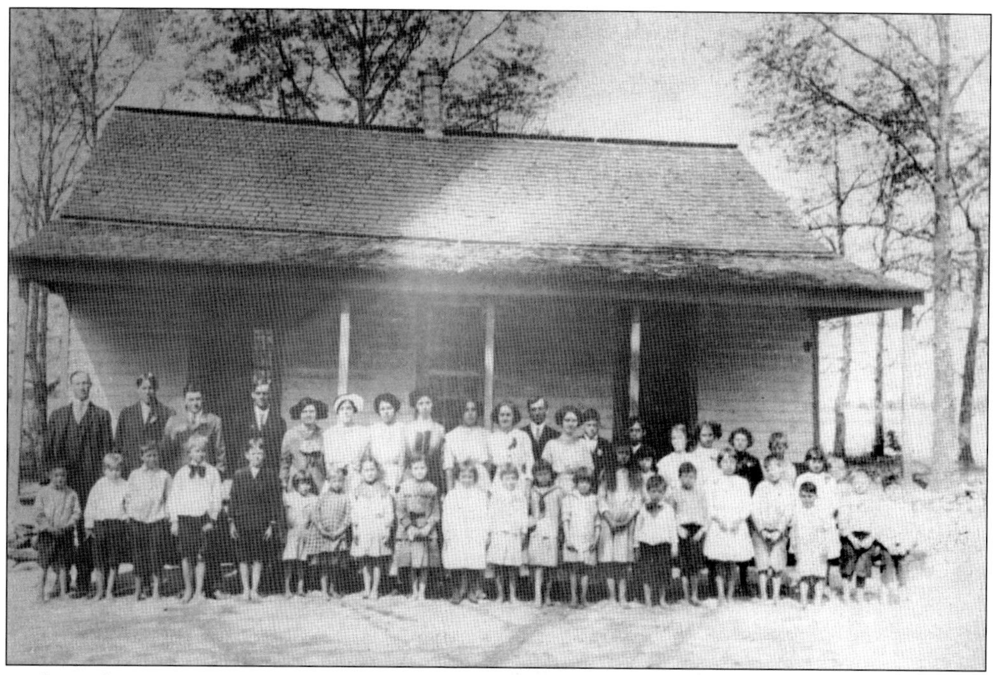

In the early 1900s, education in the Chipley area consisted of many local, one-room schoolhouses, often funded by the families of the children who attended them. Hopewell School was located on the southwest corner of Wright Road and Hopewell Church Road. One of Hopewell's teachers was Belle Holland (second row, eighth from left). Her great-grandfather, Thomas Holland, drew two tracts of land in the 1827 land lottery.

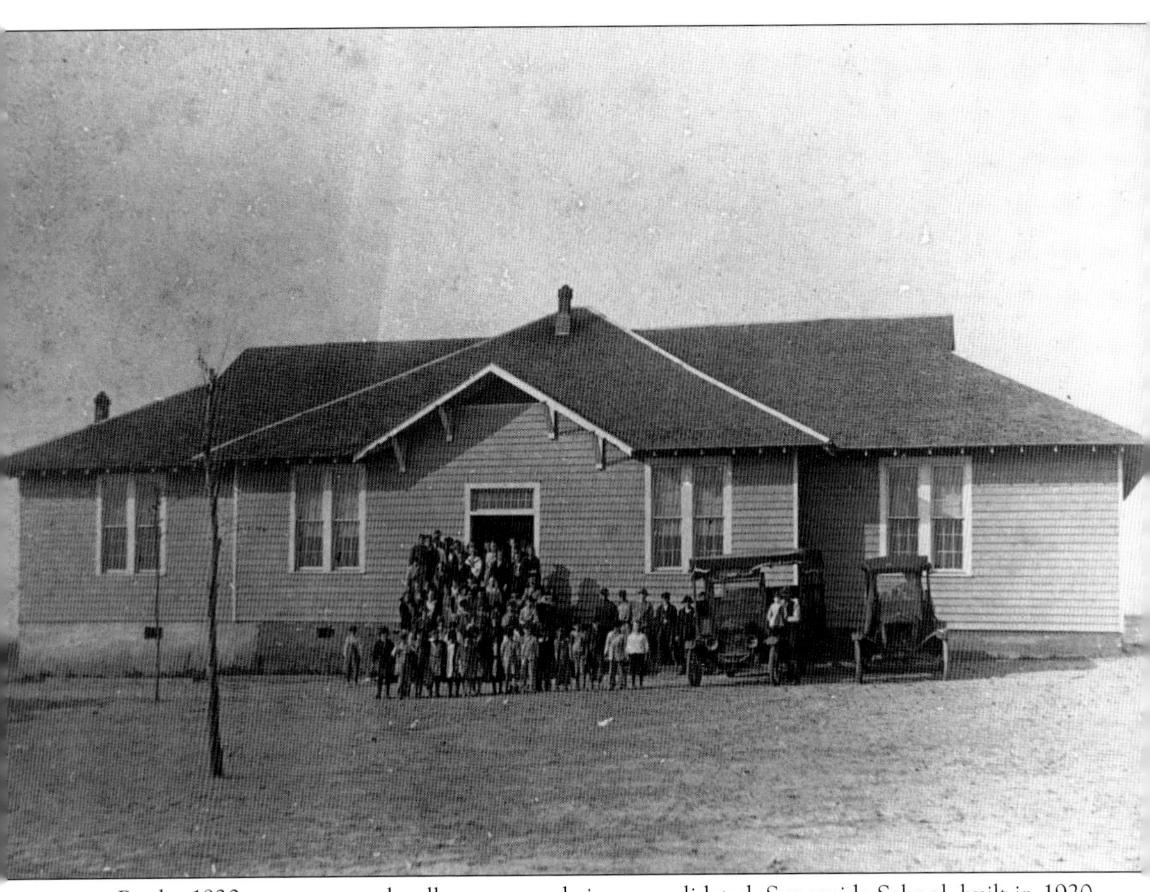

By the 1920s, one-room schoolhouses were being consolidated. Sunnyside School, built in 1920, took the place of five smaller schools in the area, including Hopewell. Belle Holland, a former teacher at Hopewell, became a teacher and the principal at Sunnyside. The four-room school housed grades one to eleven (Georgia had no twelfth grade at that time) with four or five teachers. In the 1930s, high school students began attending Chipley High School, and Sunnyside finally closed in the 1940s. Former student Lillian Moncrief Murphy reminisced about Sunnyside, remembering that "after five years at Old Hopewell, Sunnyside looked like fairyland. . . . We had lights, we had several windows to each room . . . we had a place to put our coats and hats. In the winter, we had to keep them on at Hopewell to try to stay warm." Today, Sunnyside is cared for by a community group that meets for covered dish suppers each month.

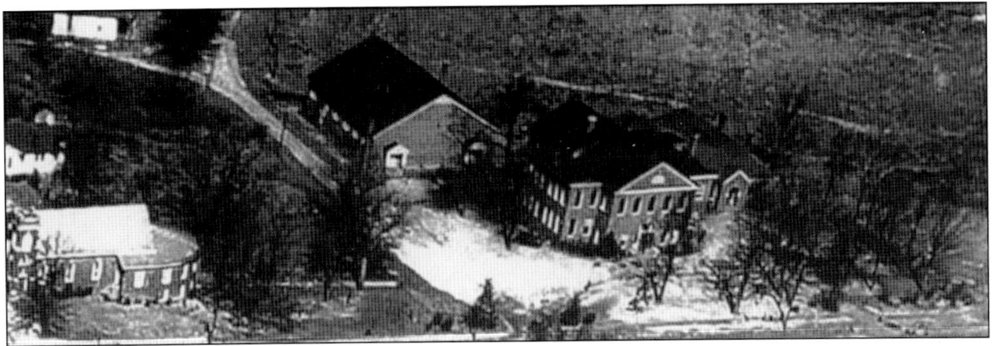

Shown here are the 1908 brick Chipley school; the annex built in the 1930s; and the gymnasium, also constructed in the 1930s. A large auditorium on the second story of the school was used for various activities, such as plays, music recitals, and PTA meetings, as well as for magic shows and movies for students' entertainment. Occasionally, it was available for use by the town for meetings.

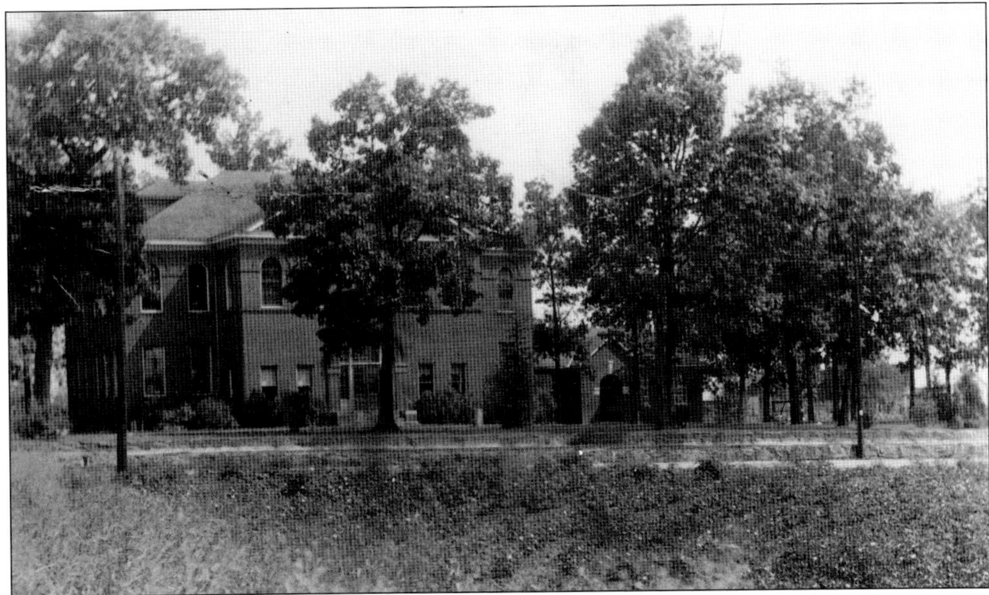

The first two Chipley schools were wooden. In 1909, classes began in a new brick building, shown above, located in a hickory and oak grove. It was far more modern but still lacked electricity and indoor plumbing. An outhouse was available just to the east of the building. Elementary children were taught by three teachers, with one instructor for high school. There were 223 students in 10 grades.

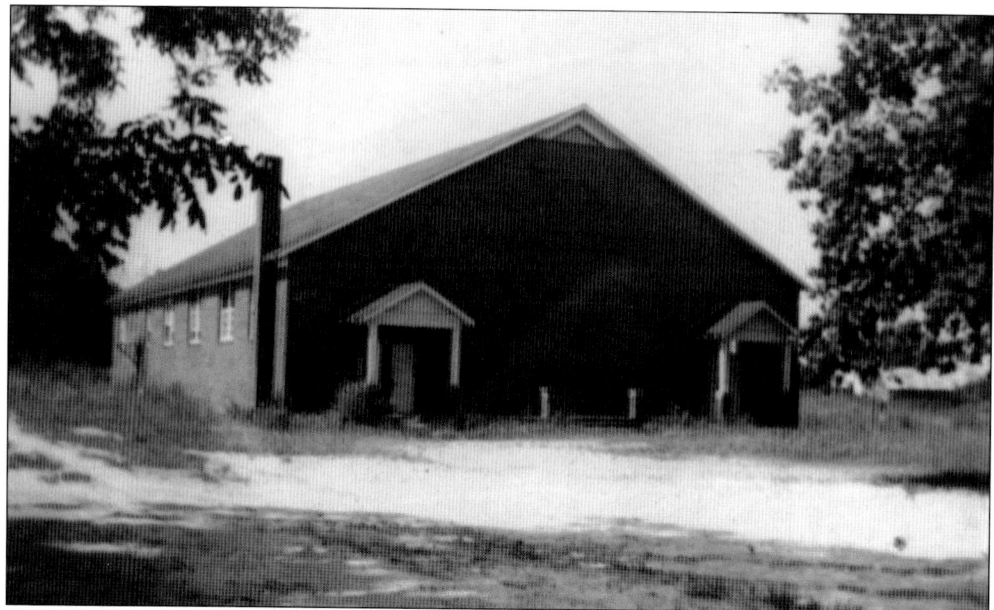

The gymnasium was home to the Chipley Panthers basketball teams and the site of Halloween carnivals, school parties, and dance classes. Today, the gym is the property of the Town of Pine Mountain. It is named in memory of A.D. Davis, former principal of Chipley Elementary School, and is available for community events.

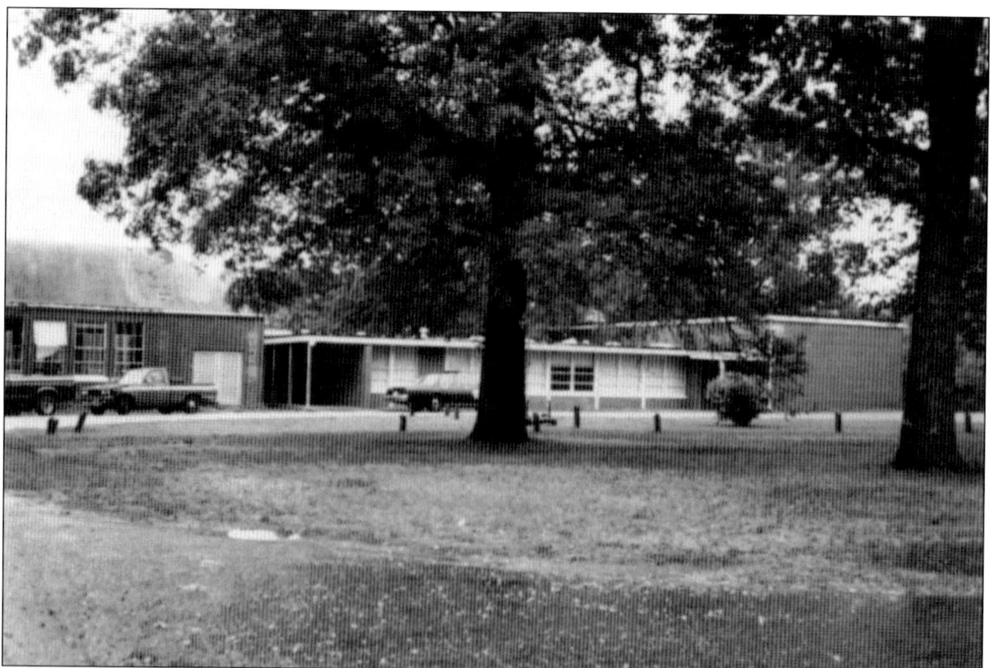

In 1962, the old two-story school was torn down, and this addition to Chipley Elementary School was built. There were two additional classrooms, a cafetorium, and the principal's office. The PTA led a fundraising drive for the purchase of new playground equipment. When elementary schools were consolidated, part of the building housed the Pine Mountain Police Department.

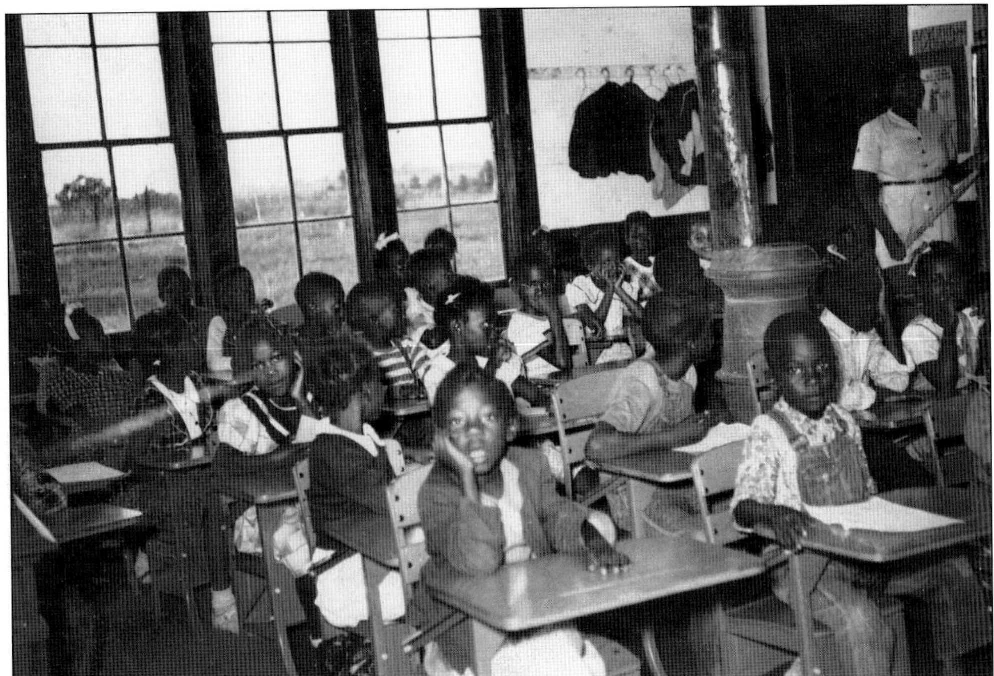

An early 1950s report from a Harris County citizens' committee stated, "Our negro [*sic*] schools are entirely too small. Most of them are of the one room type, in which seven grades of 20 to 40 pupils are taught by one teacher. . . . All of these schools are in bad physical condition...They would all be considered 'fire traps.'" This photograph shows one of those overcrowded classrooms, heated by a potbellied stove.

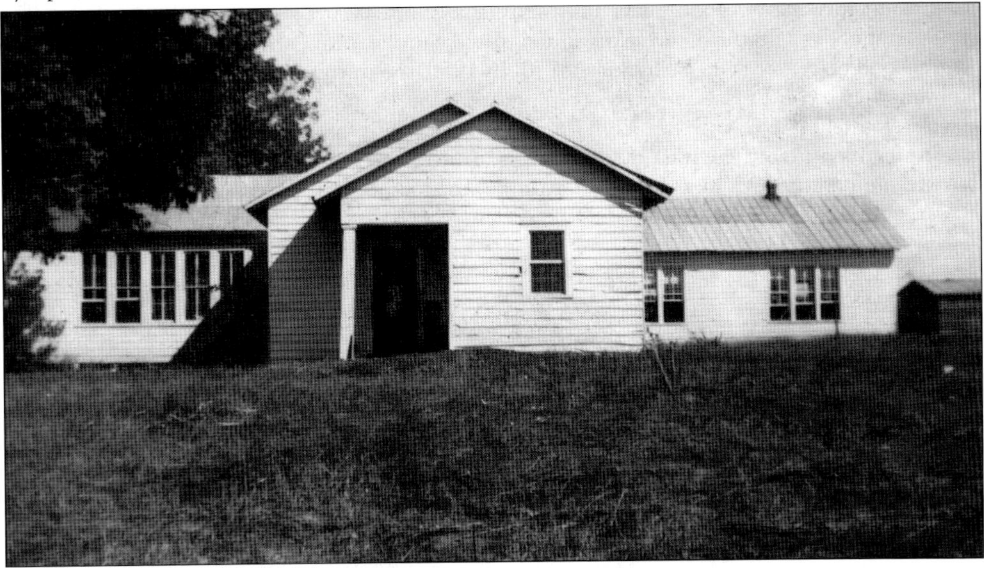

Black children attended the Chipley Colored School, a rambling frame structure just off Highway 18. Bonds were issued by the Harris County School Board in 1951 for a new school on the same site. The old building was purchased by the Town of Chipley and leased to the school trustees. The building was then converted into a teacherage to provide housing for teachers, many of whom were from Alabama.

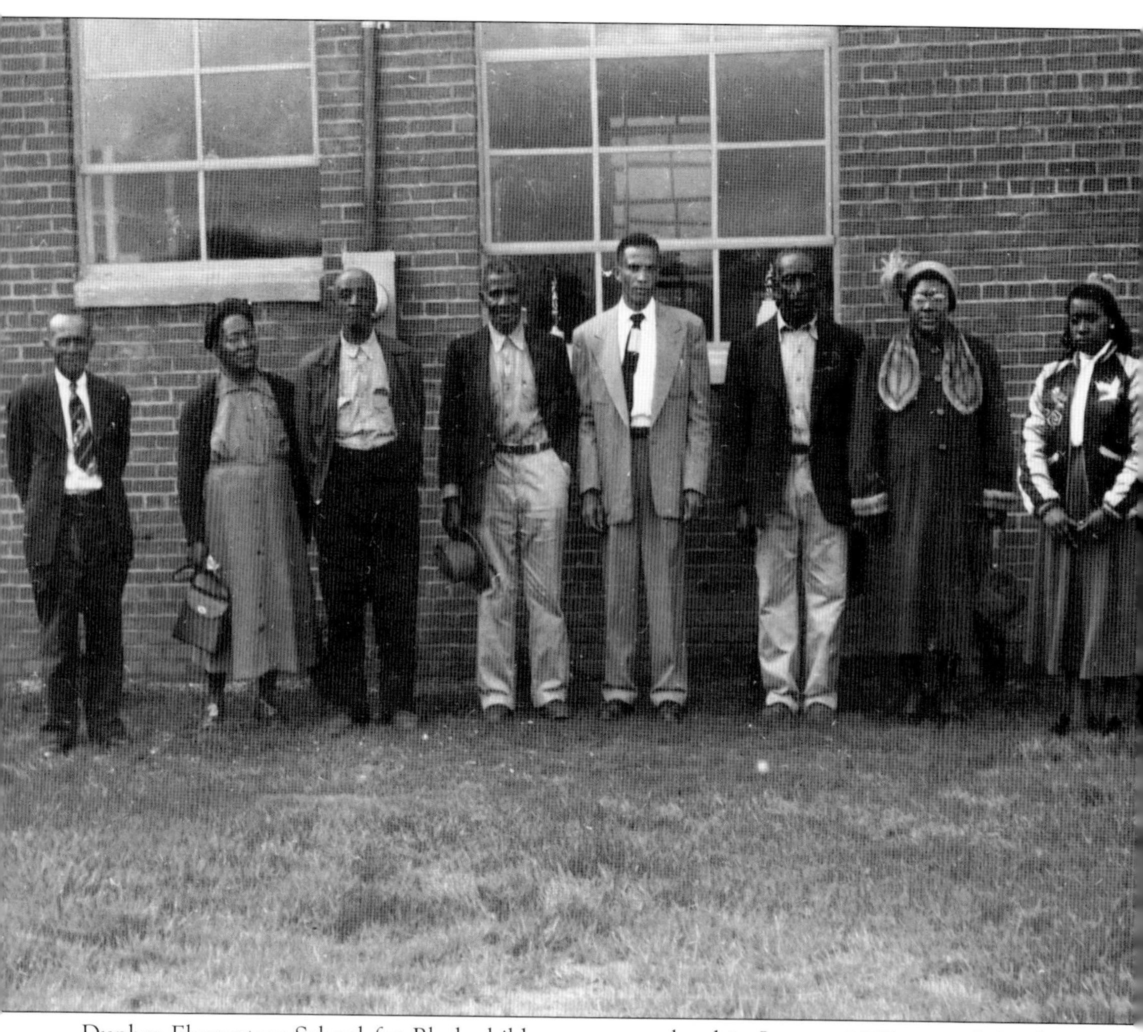

Dunbar Elementary School for Black children was completed in January 1953, named for the Black poet Paul Laurence Dunbar. According to a 1953 Chipley scrapbook, "This school building is as modern and comfortable as any in the country. . . . Many fund-raising activities were carried out for the purpose of providing funds for the equipping of the school lunchroom and kitchen. Donations, box suppers and other community functions helped in raising the necessary funds . . . further, the local school board, through the cooperation of the PTA, had purchased a new $475.00 piano to be used at musical programs at the school." School board members posed in front of the new school are, from left to right, Early Spratling, chairman of the school board; unidentified, possibly Lonnie Williams's wife; Lonnie Williams; Fairchild "Bud" McGee; Principal Robert Sease; Zeke Fitzpatrick; Pearlie Spratling, wife of Early Spratling; and Wylene Spratling, daughter of Early and Pearlie Spratling.

Six

Business and Economy

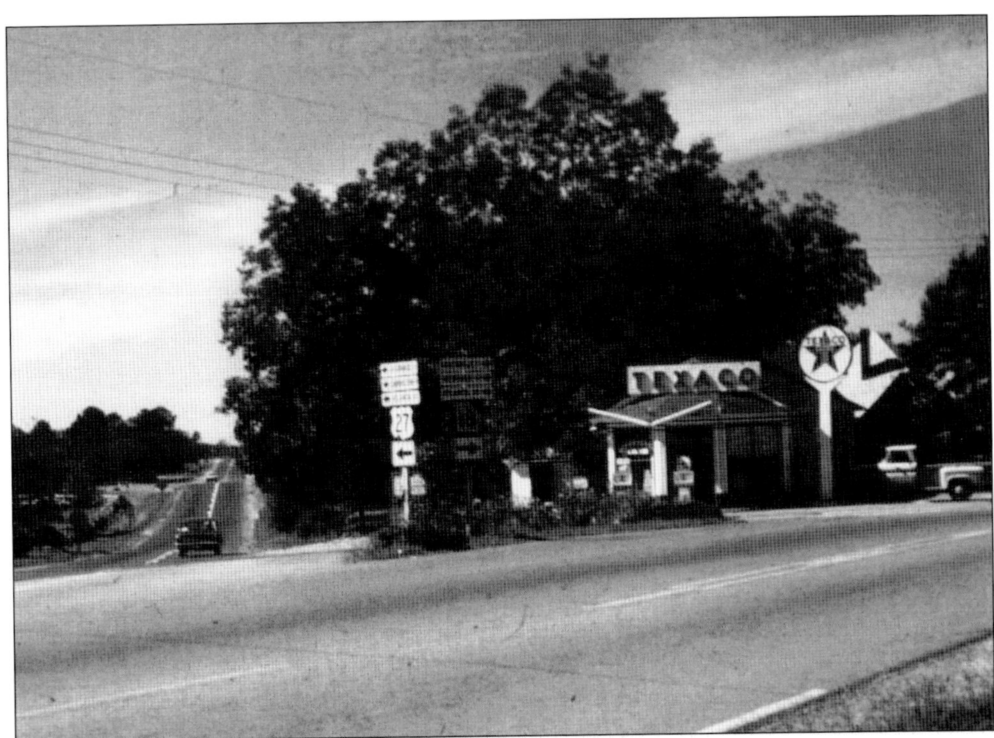

At the "V" where US Highway 27 and Highway 18 part ways sits a building that has undergone several transformations. In the 1930s, Alvah Swint ran a gas station/market here. Later, Broughton Myhand took it over. Still later, A.G. Akin managed it, followed by J.D. Dunn. In more recent times, three restaurants have occupied the space, and now it is a bakery.

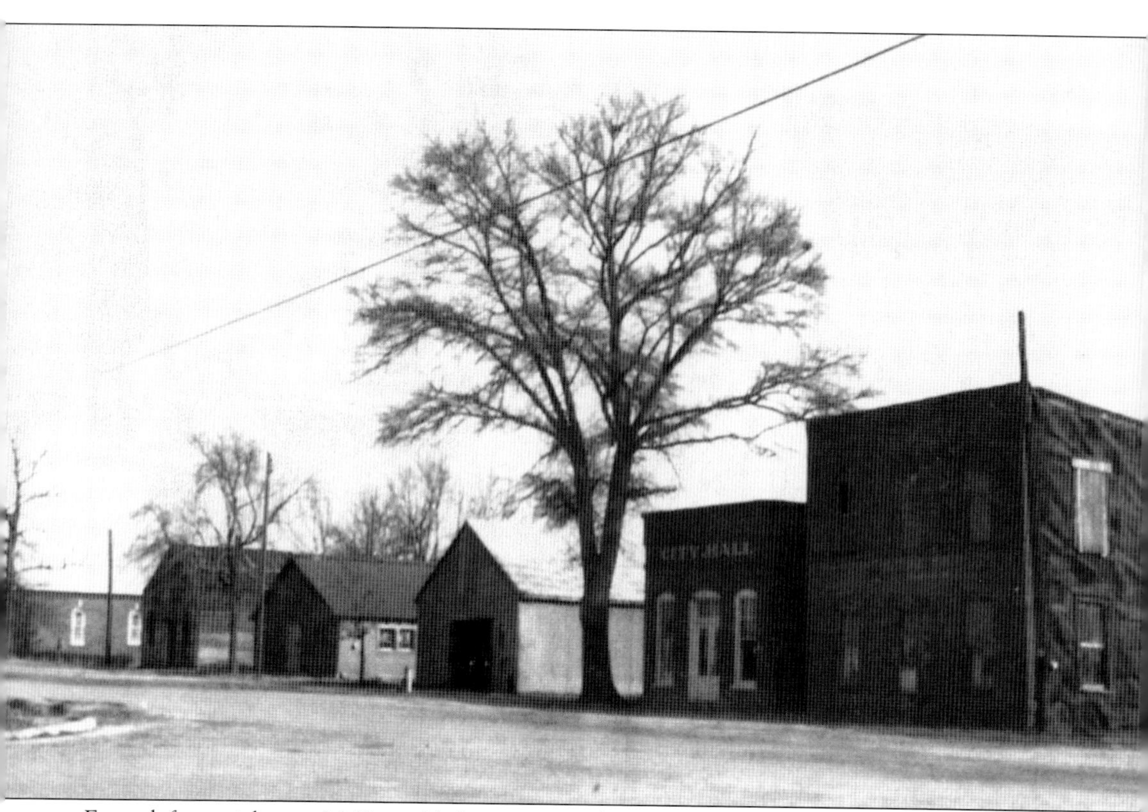

From left to right on McDougald Avenue are Chipley Methodist Church, Surles Blacksmith Shop, Old Chipley Canning Company, fire truck storage building, city hall, and two-story former drugstore and Coca-Cola building. The city hall structure is in the National Register of Historic Places and serves as one of the Chipley Historical Center buildings. Beginning in 1883, the Glass Brothers Apothecary was located in the two-story building on the right. That building was also a Coca-Cola bottling plant from 1909 to 1917. Chipley Motors briefly used the building after the Coca-Cola plant moved to Manchester, Georgia, followed by a variety of other businesses. The building was demolished in the 1960s, and the Chipley Historical Center constructed a new structure there in 2021. An archaeological dig from 2024 to 2025 behind the building has turned up apothecary bottles, construction materials such as square nails, and Coca-Cola and other soda bottles.

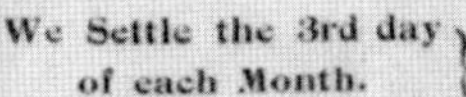

We Settle the 3rd day of each Month.

Chipley, Ga. July 15 18

CHIPLEY CREAMERY,

Bought of Emiline Cox

For Month of June

1137 lbs. Milk, at 83 per 100 lbs. 943 Test 4.6		943
Less Account,		
Cash Herewith,		

Please Pay J H P

contributed by (great) grand daughter Mary B. Dixon

An early business in Chipley was the Chipley Creamery, established in 1895. Milk was purchased by the pound for the production of ice cream. The creamery was located near downtown on Cherry Street. Another boon to farmers in the area was a cheese factory, opened in 1925, located in a residence with a spring in the basement, ideal for a supply of fresh water necessary for making cheese. The house was near the present-day site of Chipley Village. Equipment was brought to Chipley from Zebulon, Georgia, in sawmill trucks driven by Rob Bryant and Cecil Champion, a trip which took a whole day. Three hundred gallons of milk daily was guaranteed by local farmers who were paid 10¢ per gallon. A buyer in Atlanta purchased cheese wheels wrapped in cloth and greased with lard or paraffin for approximately $2,500 monthly.

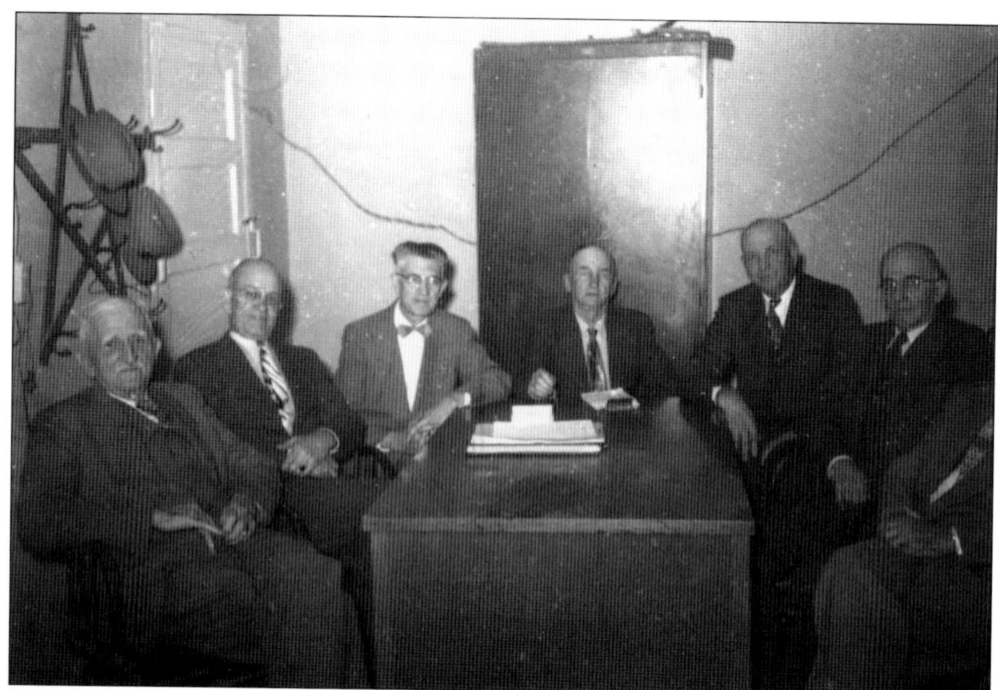

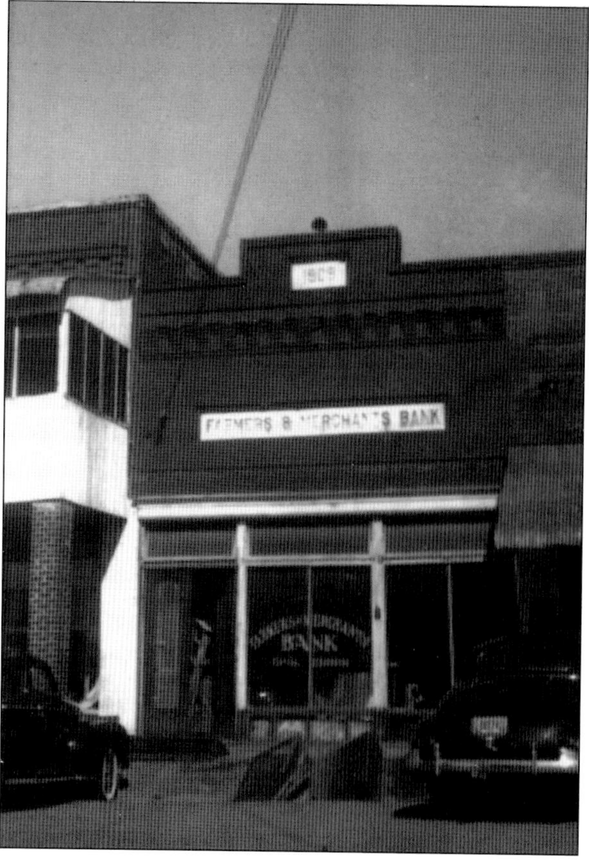

In 1950, from left to right, Henry Kimbrough, J.O. Kimbrough, Roy Askew, Henry Zachry, Hiram Jenkins, Wiley Wisdom, and P.H. Layfield (not shown) served as directors of Farmers & Merchants (F&M) Bank, founded in 1909. The first bank in town was the Bank of Chipley, chartered in 1901. The two banks merged in 1921, keeping the name of Farmers & Merchants and remaining in its original location, next door to the present Pine Mountain Tourism Center. In 1962, the bank moved across Broad Street to a much larger building where Wells Fargo is today. Over the next several years, what had been the local F&M bank was purchased by several banking companies and became a branch of the large banks. In 1987, most of those on the local advisory board to the parent bank, Wachovia, felt that the small-town flavor was missing in the Pine Mountain branch. In December 1987, First Peoples Bank was founded by local folks who had deep Chipley roots.

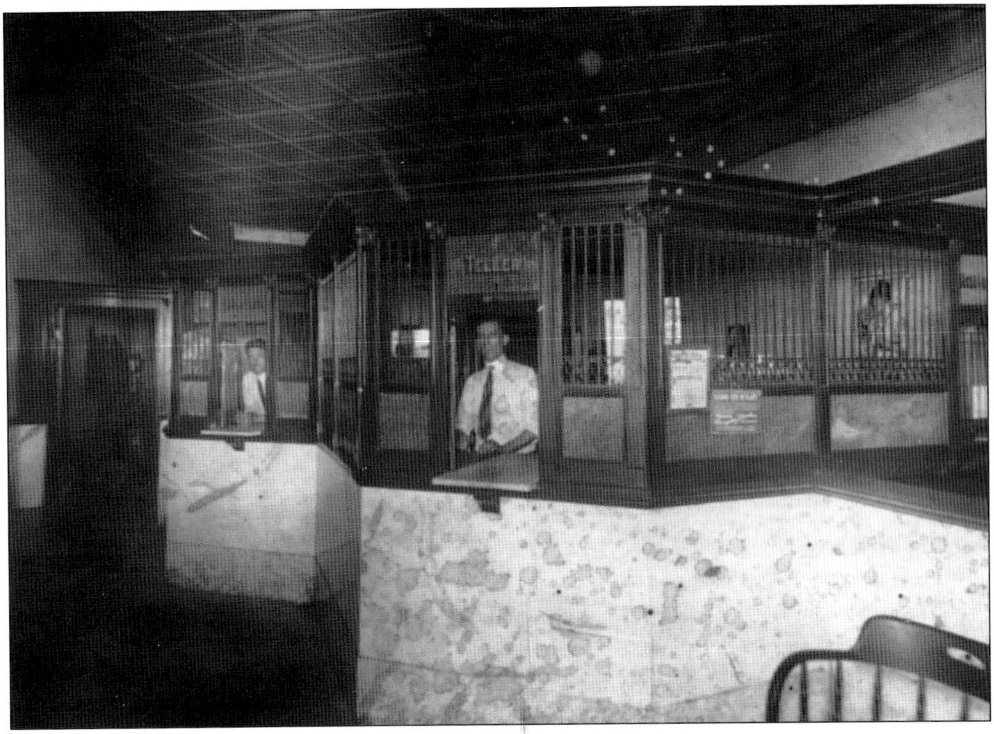

After the two banks merged, Farmers & Merchants Bank advertised in the 1926 *Harris County Journal* that the Bank of Chipley property was for sale at its original location on Main Street. Listed was a "bank outfit" comprising a "manganese lug door safe, vault, door equipped with burglar trap, and one nine column Burroughs adding machine." The Chipley safe must have been superior to the lug door safe, for it became a fixture in the newly merged bank. Apparently, no other changes were needed. Fixtures remained for cashiers Roy Askew and Arthur Priddy to take their places behind the tellers' cages. The bank safe from the original Bank of Chipley was donated to the Chipley Historical Center, where it is now displayed.

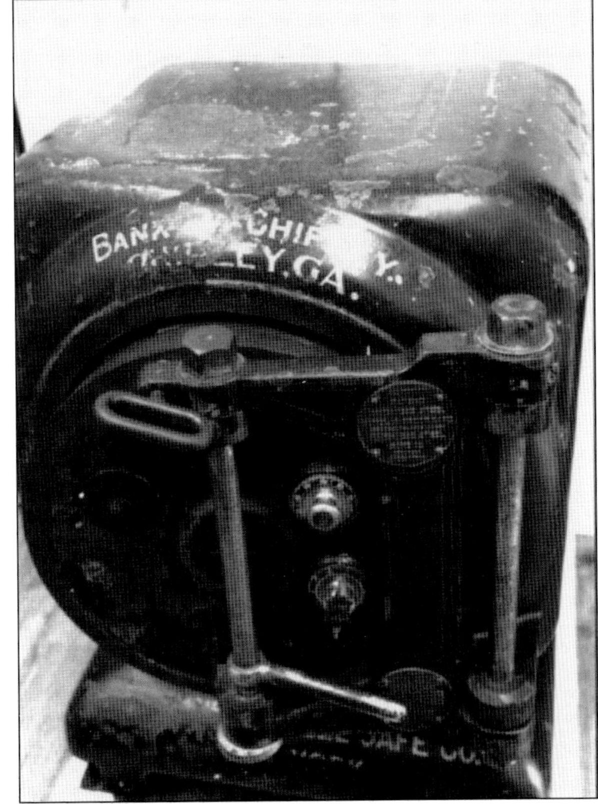

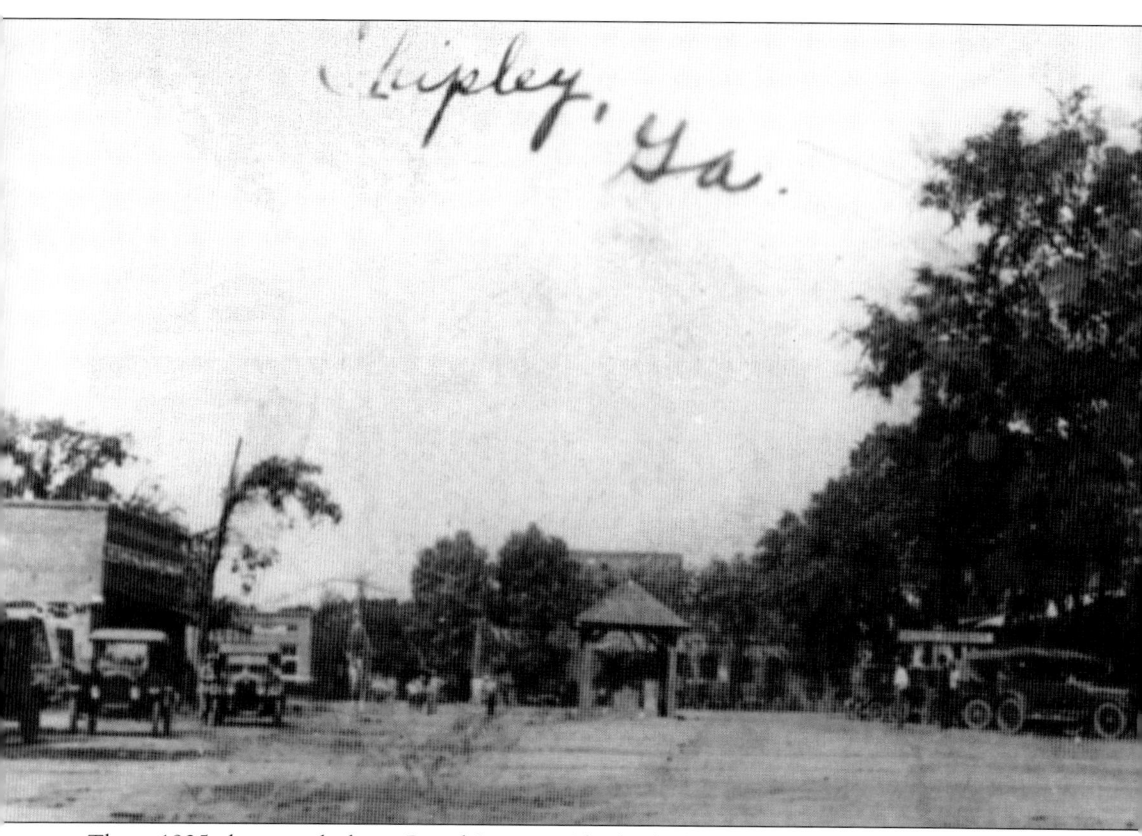

The c. 1925 photograph shows Broad Street in Chipley looking west toward US Highway 27 from McDougald Avenue. The well house is in the foreground, and the two-story Kimbrough Brothers building is in the background. The building on the left with the name written on it was Floyd and Hill General Merchandise. Floyd and Hill sold almost everything, including caskets. C.S. Swanson, Henry A. Mullins, and then Farmers & Merchants Bank eventually occupied this location. Wells Fargo Bank is now at that corner. Although obscured by trees in the photograph, the two-story Chambers building on the right, now the Pine Mountain Tourism Association, is directly across from Floyd and Hill on the north side of Broad Street. The well house was eventually removed after this photograph was taken, and Broad Street now features a median filled with seasonal flowers and holiday decorations.

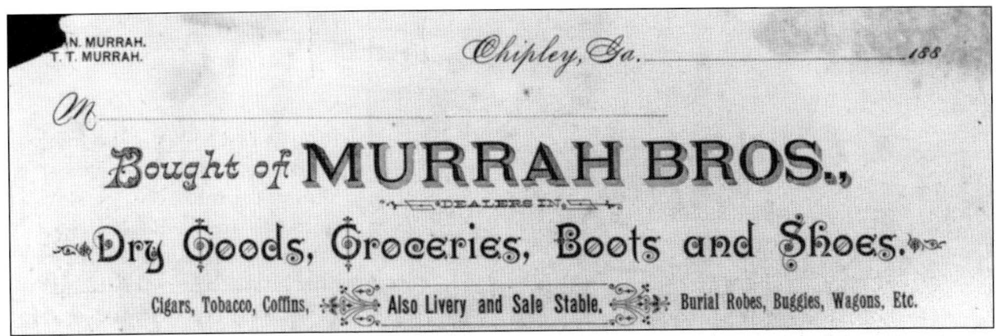
N. MURRAH.
T. T. MURRAH.

Chipley, Ga. 188

M ....

Bought of MURRAH BROS.,

DEALERS IN

Dry Goods, Groceries, Boots and Shoes.

Cigars, Tobacco, Coffins, Also Livery and Sale Stable. Burial Robes, Buggies, Wagons, Etc.

This two-story rock structure on US Highway 27 directly across from Broad Street is one of the oldest buildings in Chipley/Pine Mountain. Originally located where the Masonic Building is today on Broad Street, the business was moved across the railroad tracks to a new two-story structure, creating another area of commerce. The store carried just about everything, including shoes, cigars, dry goods, and even coffins, as advertised in the letterhead above. It was the only store in town with a hand-cranked elevator, necessary to move caskets between floors. Most of the construction is believed to have been done by George King, son of former slave and master bridge builder Horace King. In 1908, the Murrah business was acquired by Chipley Mercantile Company, with Henry Kimbrough as manager. The photograph below is a picture taken on the opening day in 1892. (Below, Chad Kimbrough.)

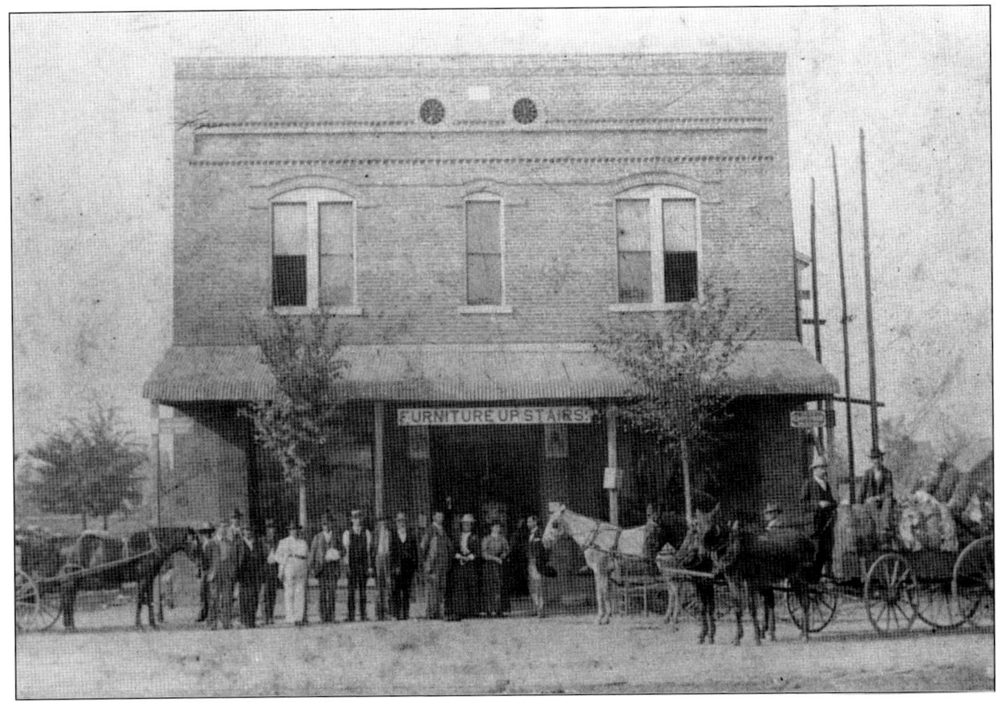

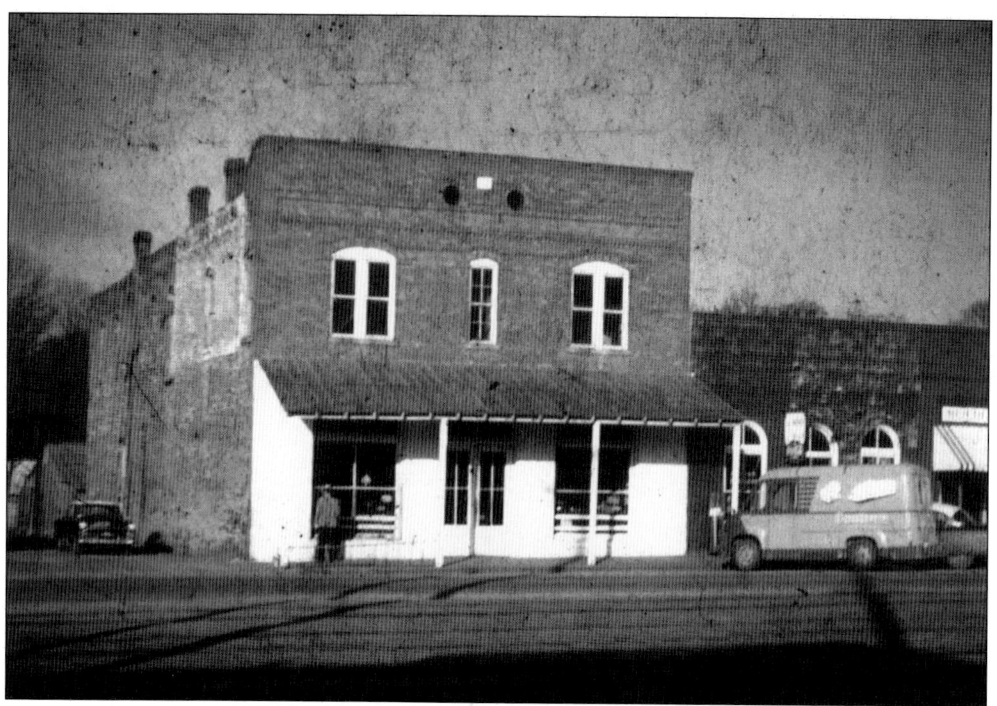

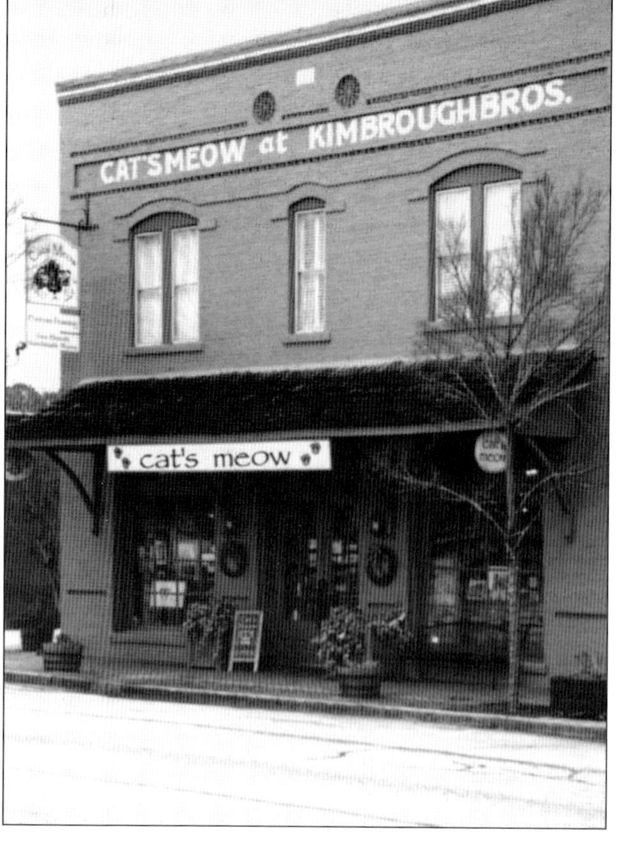

After the Murrah business was acquired in 1908, Henry Kimbrough was joined in 1910 by his brother Heywood. For over 100 years, the business flourished as Kimbrough Brothers, later run by Henry's grandson Billy and then by Henry's great-grandson Chad. Besides clothing, hats, and shoes, they handled most agricultural products, including seeds, fertilizer, feed, and farm tools. For years, they were agents for the collection and shipping of locally grown cotton, their warehouses and alley crowded with bales in season. By the 21st century, though, the town had become a tourist mecca, and businesses were being patronized by a different clientele. The old building now houses a gift and picture framing business, the Cat's Meow. Kara Cable assumed ownership of the building in 2020. (Left, Robert Brackett.)

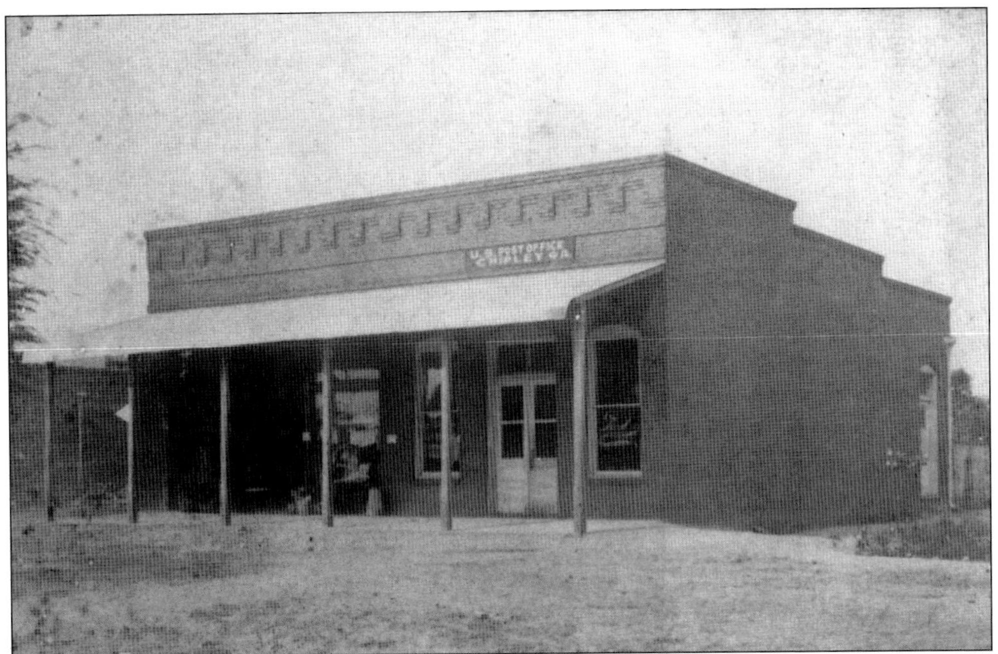

In 1913, the post office was located on the corner of Harris and North Commerce Streets, where Eatz on the Corner is now. W.J. Key's Fancy Grocery store adjoined the post office. Olivia Floyd Anderson was appointed postmistress in 1922. Mailbags were placed on a cart and pushed across East Railroad Avenue to the train. A new post office opened on North McDougald Avenue in 1961.

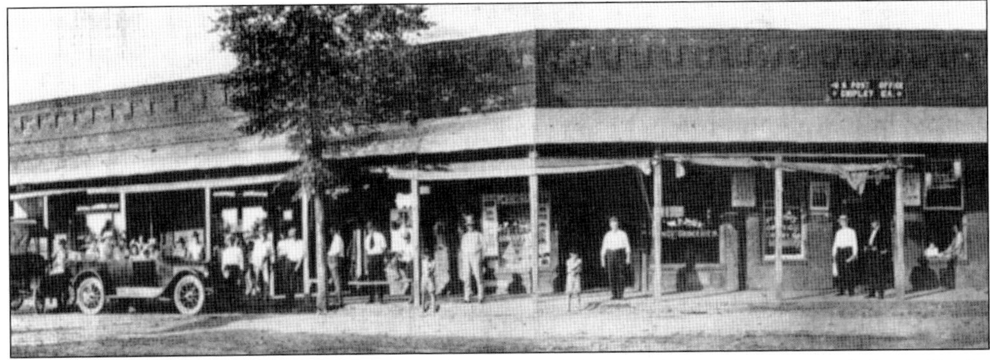

By 1925, the block next to the post office had expanded to include other stores. J. Pope Davis, a Chipley mail carrier, had bought out W.J. Key's store. There was an ice-cream store between Davis's store and C.W. Spinks's barbershop, where all the men are gathered in the photograph. The center stores on the block later became Builders Supply.

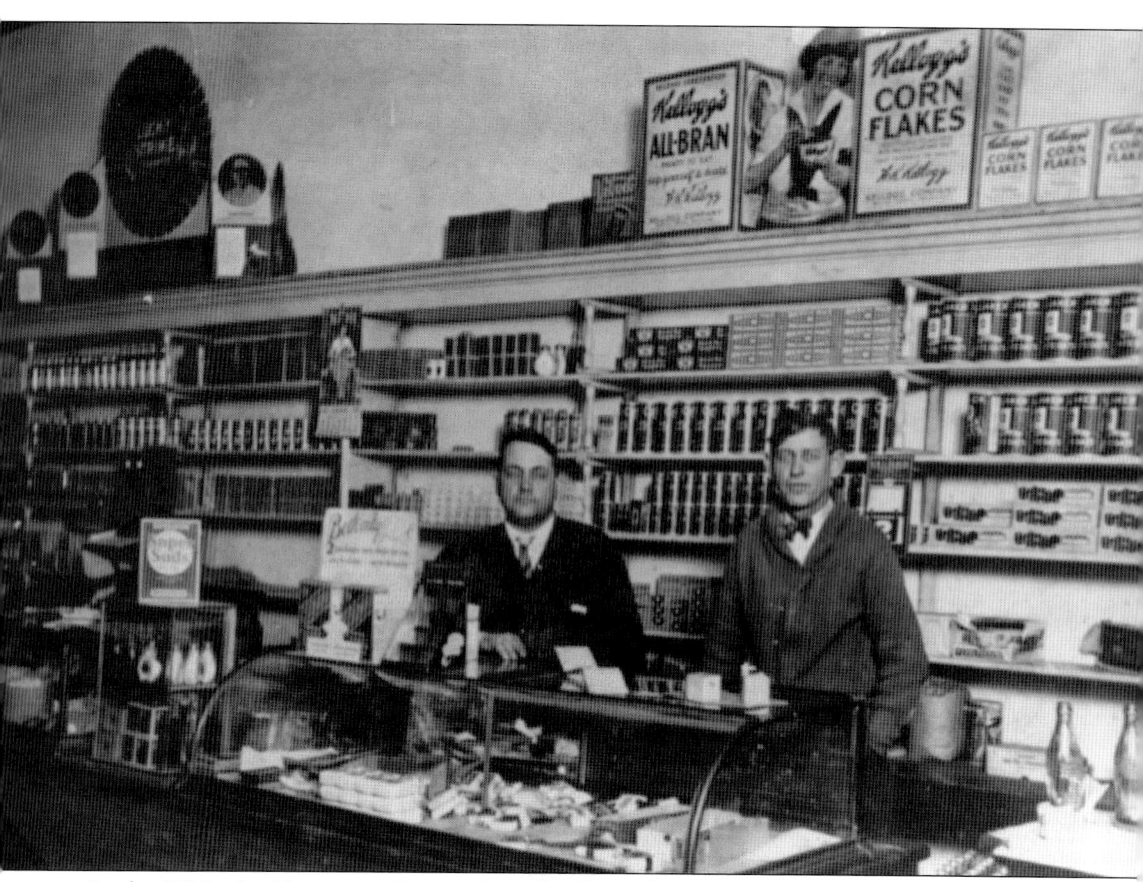

In the 1920s, the Champion Grocery Company, located on US Highway 27, carried groceries and fresh meat. The shelves were stocked with boxes and cans of popular brands, some of which are still in demand today. Local businessman Jesse H. Champion, on the right, owned and operated the store. Champion later managed the local Builders Supply store in Chipley, where Doggone Good Bargains is located today. On Champion's left is his brother-in-law, Jim Chambers, who was also involved in other businesses in town. He and his wife, known by townsfolk as "Miss Paul," lived above the store. In the 1940s and 1950s, she had a dress and millinery shop and sold piece goods. Many Chipley young folk also took art classes from Miss Paul at her shop. This building, which today houses the Pine Mountain Tourism Association, was constructed in 1904. (Bill Champion.)

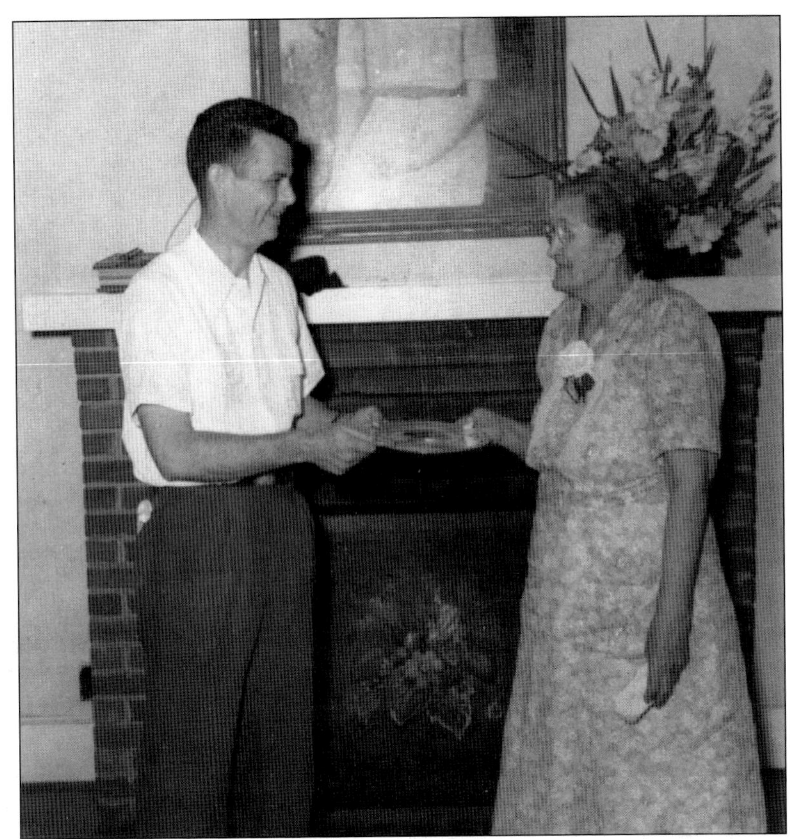

A.D. and "Miss Claude" Davis took ownership of the telephone company in January 1924. She connected callers to the correct home or business but frequently informed the caller that the requested recipient was not home. She also knew whom to call when a child asked to speak to "grandma." In 1952, Miss Claude received a silver tray in recognition of 28 years of service.

Telephone Directory

Chipley -:- Waverly Hall

SUMMER —:— 1952

In 1952, under the new Skelton ownership, a directory was available. Subscribers had individual numbers; however, many had party lines with distinct rings, such as one long and two shorts. Rates were based on homes with one line; a one-party line cost $2.50, but four parties on one line cost $1.75 each. Children were cautioned not to listen in on others' conversations.

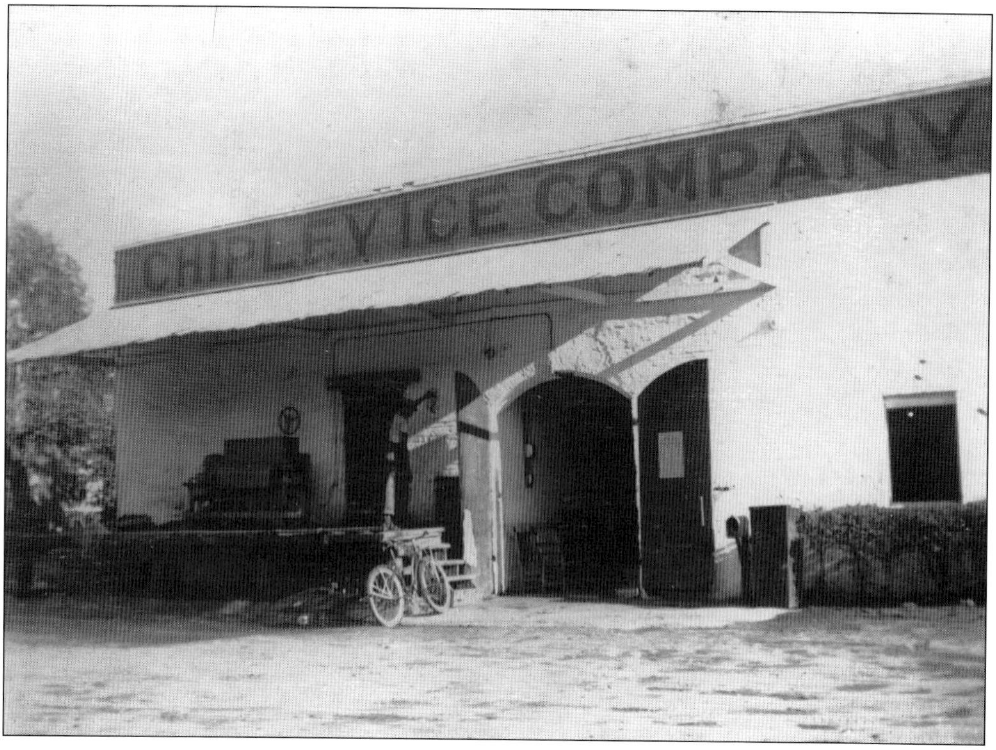

The Chipley Ice Building first served as a livery stable and then a cotton warehouse. In 1936, folks were pleased to have a new business in town that produced ice made with Kings Gap spring water. Ice packed in wooden boxes was delivered to Chipley homes. An additional service was the short-term storage of watermelons in the summer months. Folks would pick from their garden or perhaps purchase a melon during the week, carve the family name or initials on it, and pick it up on Sunday afternoon to enjoy in their backyards. Ice tokens were often purchased in advance to be used for the purchase of ice later. Also, since many homes were heated only with fireplaces, Chipley Ice Company also later sold coal. Coal was brought in on trains. Chipley Ice Company sold an average of nine to ten tons of coal annually. The building was razed in 1970.

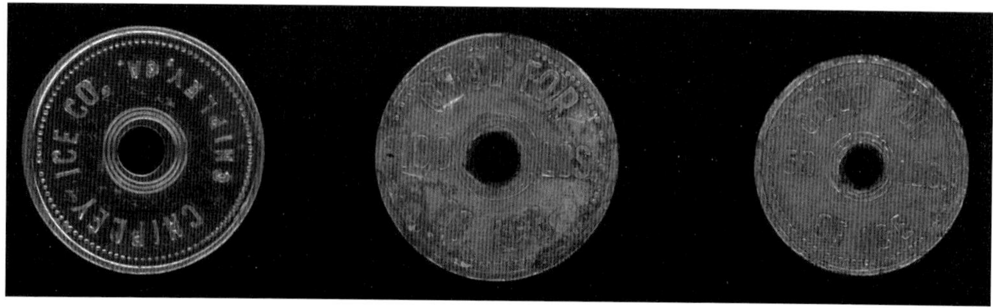

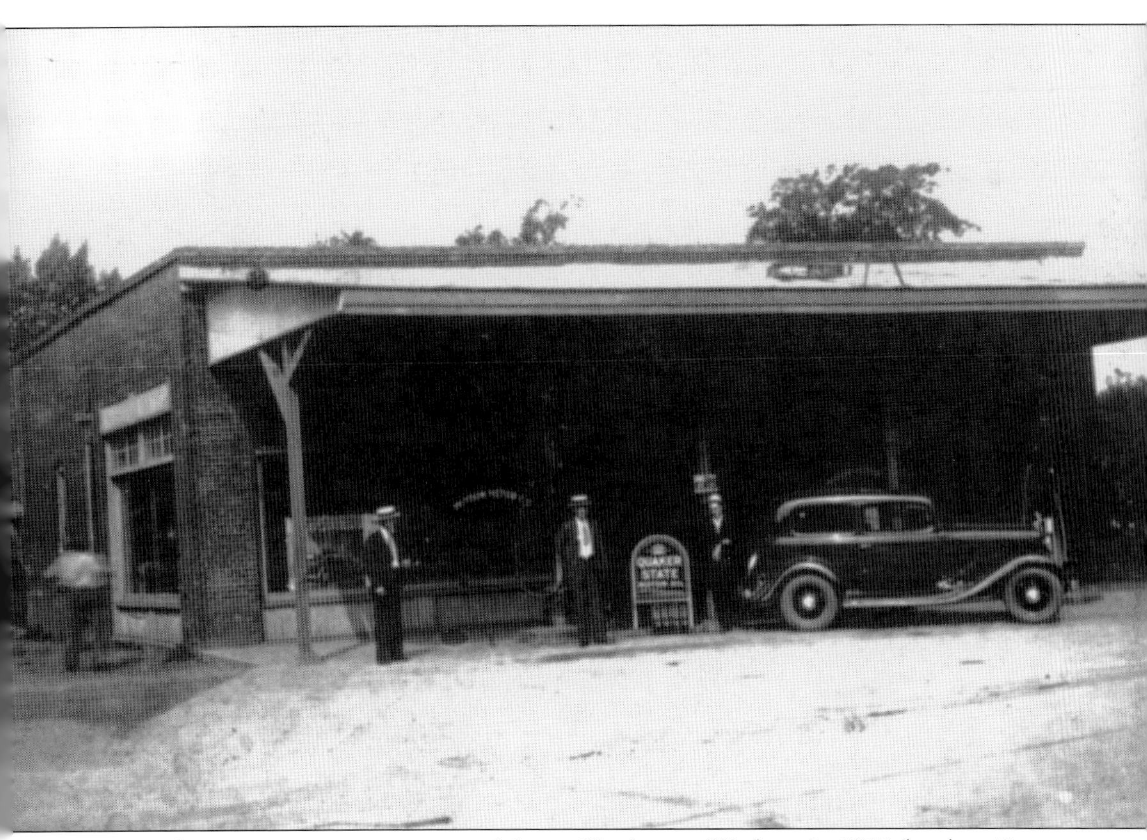

For years, the prominent name in automobiles in Chipley was Wisdom. In 1917, brothers Tom and Wiley Wisdom and Pearce Layfield opened Wisdom Motor Company for the sale of Fords, marketed as "the universal car." In 1933, the dealership announced its brand would now be Chevrolet, "the only low-priced car built in Georgia." Despite this change, the location of the business remained at the corner of Harris Street and US Highway 27, where Circle K is today. Wiley Wisdom died in 1957, after being in the automobile business in Chipley for 40 years. Delford Parker, who had worked for Wisdom, purchased the business and opened Parker Chevrolet at the original location. It remained there until 1957, when it moved to the US Highway 27 and Highway 18 split, where San Marcos Restaurant is today. The dealership finally closed, and new cars are no longer sold in Pine Mountain.

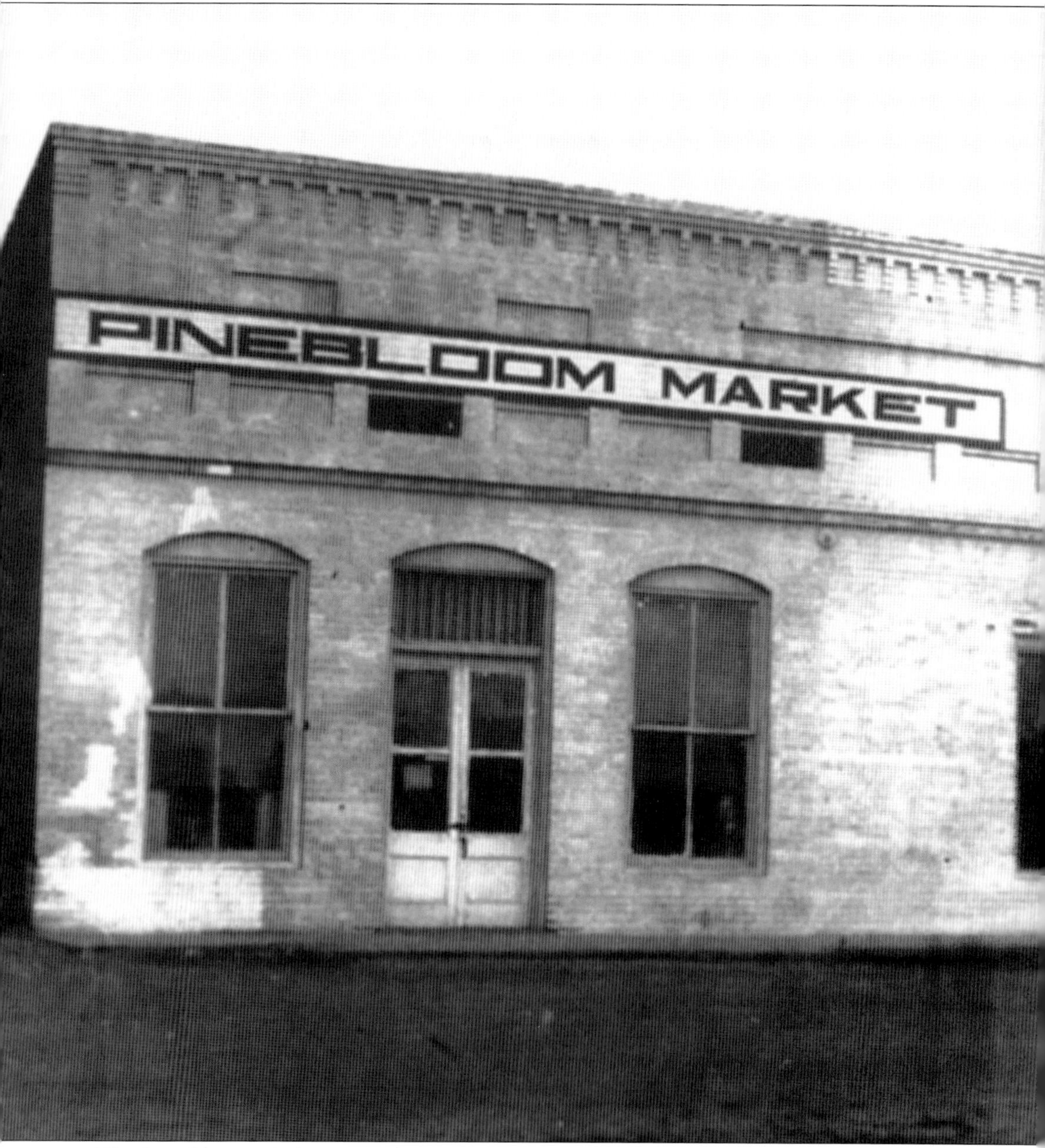

The Pine Bloom Market opened in September 1937. It was in the Layfield Building, which has been the location of several business ventures through the years. The Georgia Bureau of Markets was established at a time when Georgia's food crop production was quite high. Markets throughout the state were operated by local women on a commission basis to sell their farm, garden, and handmade products. Young boys also brought kindling and dressed rabbits for sale. The home economics classes at Chipley High School were regular patrons, often purchasing butter and eggs. Canned fruits and vegetables, preserves and pickles, cakes and candy, butter and eggs, and handmade items, such as quilts, were available. More recently, a towel outlet was located here; presently, Chipley and Main occupies this building. The building is across from First Peoples Bank. The Chipley mural on the opening page of this book is on the side of this building.

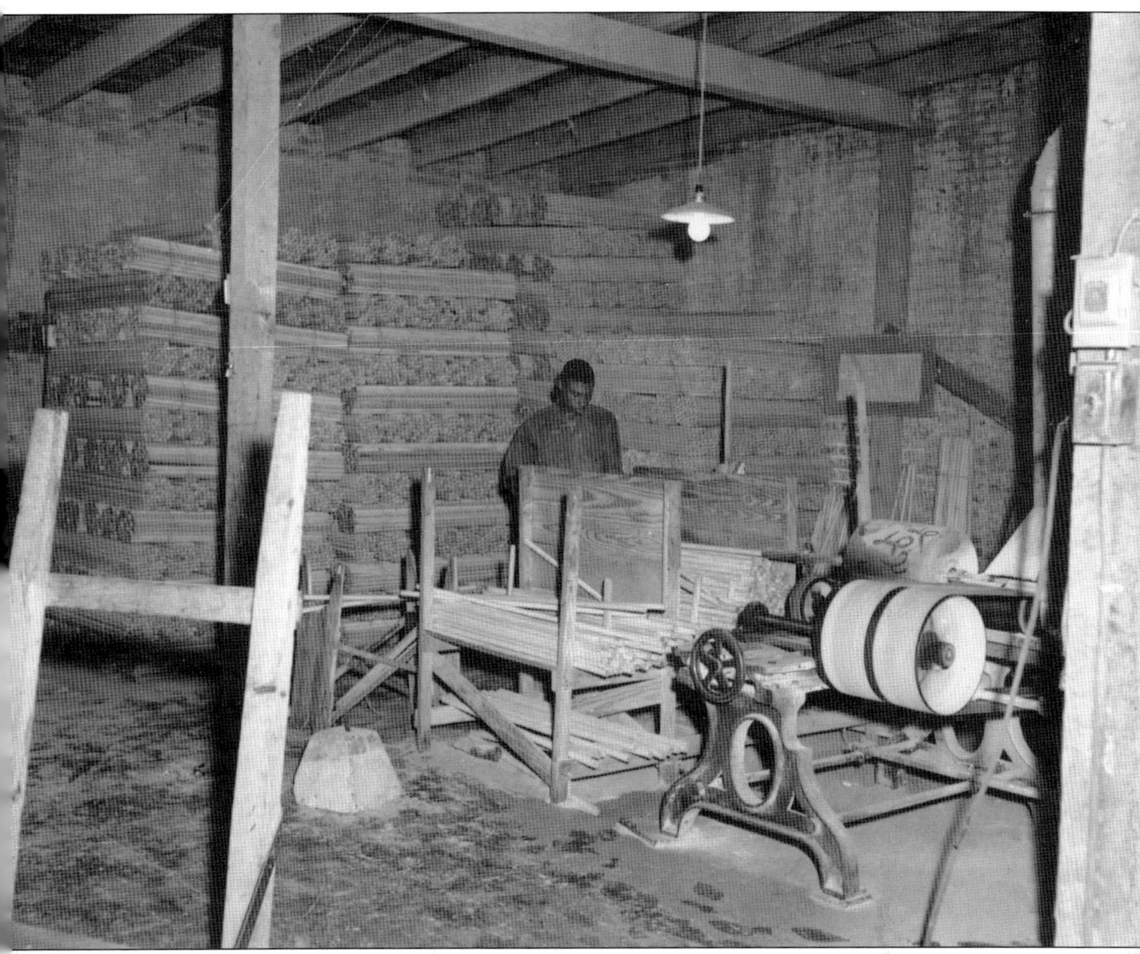

In the 1940s, a handle factory opened in Chipley where Chipley and Main is today. The first products were mop handles made for the US Navy. Jim Chambers was the owner-operator. Soon, the demand for mop handles waned, and in 1949, the company opened as the Chipley Handle Company, with J.O. Kimbrough as owner. The plant produced 25,000 mop and broom handles each week. Six months later, C.D. Horton purchased the business and employed five workers, each receiving a salary of $26 weekly. The next year, dentist Joe Miller and businessman John Whorton bought the factory and changed the name to the Mop and Broom Handle Company. The final owner was Abbie Shepherd, a Black businessman. He moved production to Davis Lake Road on the property where his home was located. Shepherd also operated a sawmill there.

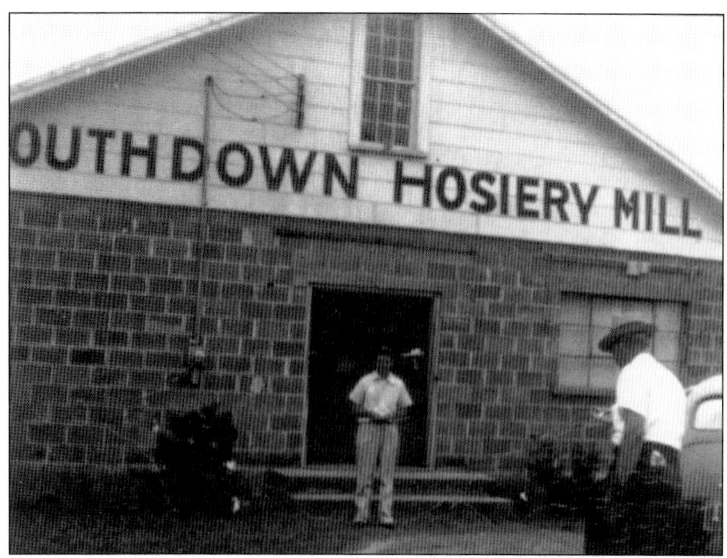

The earliest textile business in Chipley arrived in 1946 when Southdown Incorporated began production of fine knit hosiery for men. John Whorton's Southdown Hosiery Mill was the first of its kind in the United States. Whorton, shown here at the plant's door, brought this new industry to Chipley after spending three months in Canada learning the trade.

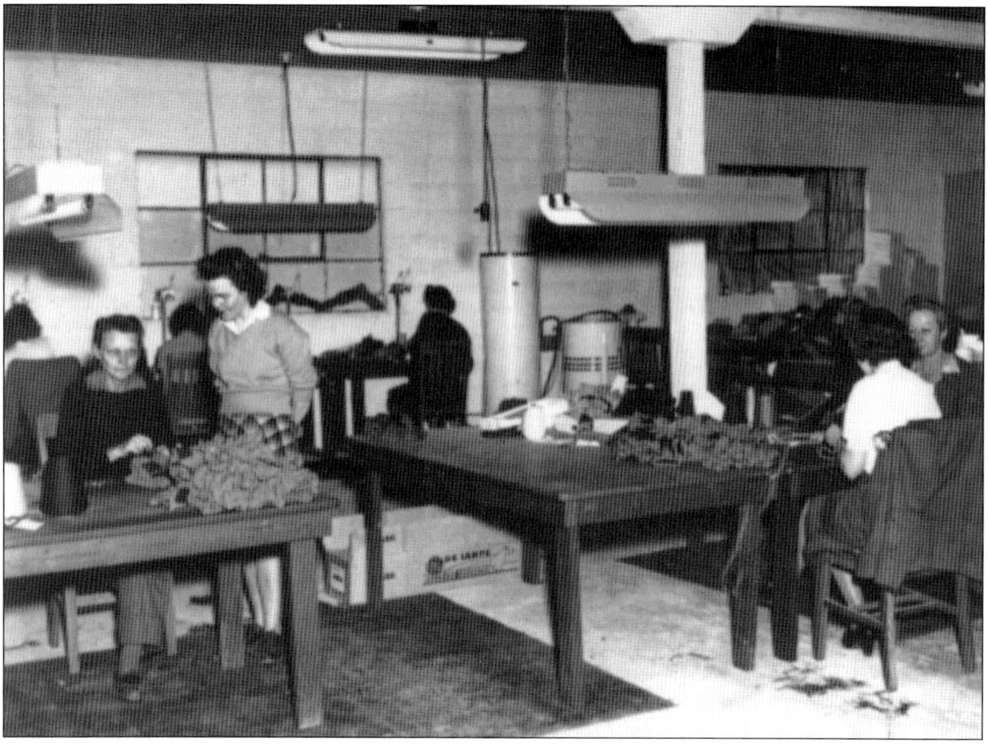

Southdown operated two shifts daily, five days a week. Forty-five women were employed at the "sock factory," the name locals gave to the mill. Each shift produced 200 dozen pairs of socks each week, a total of almost 5,000 pairs. Employees made the socks on small, individual machines operated by hand.

The Southdown label was well received in the South, which was home to much textile production. However, the socks labeled "Hand Knit Chipley, GA" had a short life. The business closed after 12 years when similar socks were produced in Atlanta on automated machines. The building later served as the Callaway Gardens print shop.

Local women were pleased to have steady employment in the brand new, if rather small, plant. The building was constructed by J.M. Dunn at the north end of McDougald Avenue, adjacent to his cotton gin. Dunn's business interests were varied; in addition to the plant and the gin, he also opened Chipley's first swimming pool on the same site.

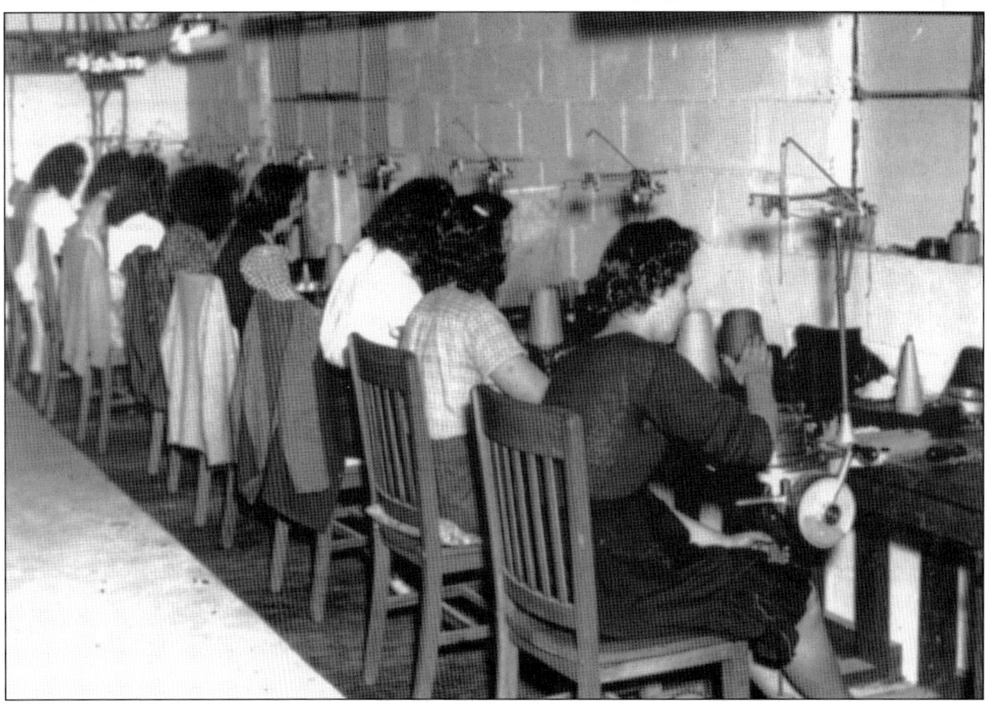

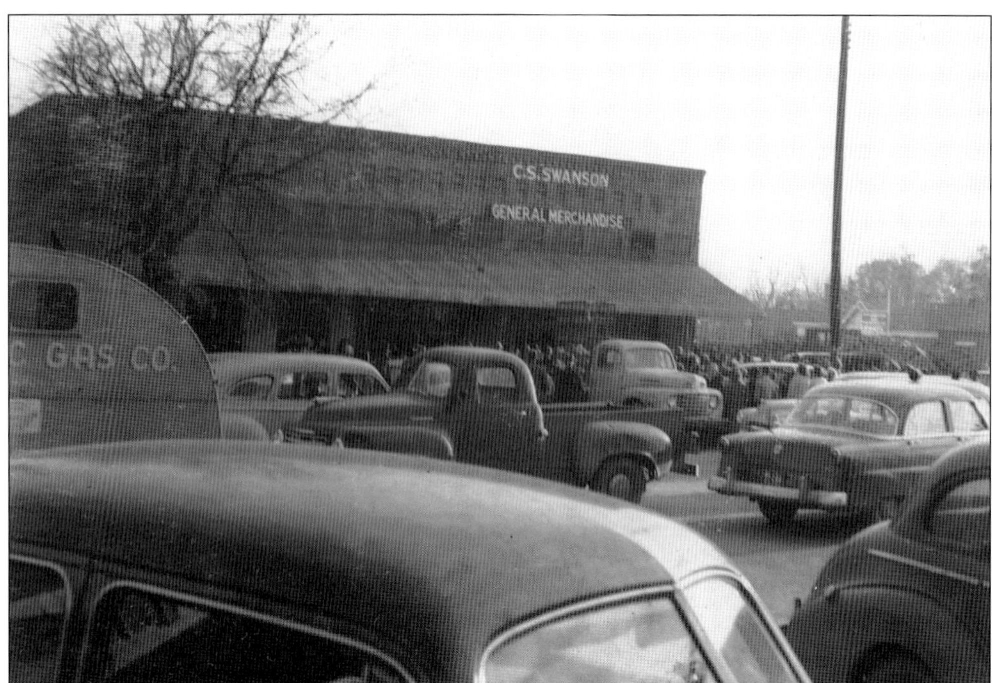

The C.S. Swanson General Merchandise store was one of several in Chipley in the 1940s, with loyal customers shopping there year-round. At Christmas, the store was perhaps busier than its competitors. Crowds came to Swanson's in greater numbers the week before December 25. Young and old alike held tickets for the annual turkey raffle to see who would take home the main dish at Christmas dinner. The drawing for the winners was held under the watchful eyes of employees of nearby Farmers & Merchants Bank. Proud winners crossed Broad Street to claim their prizes. Today, Wells Fargo Bank is at this location.

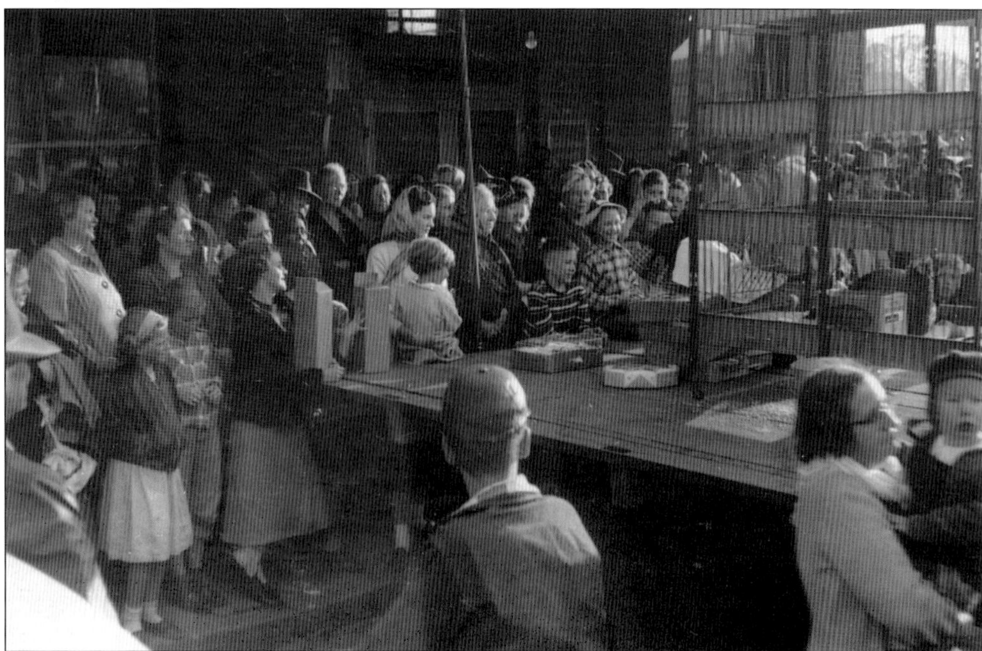

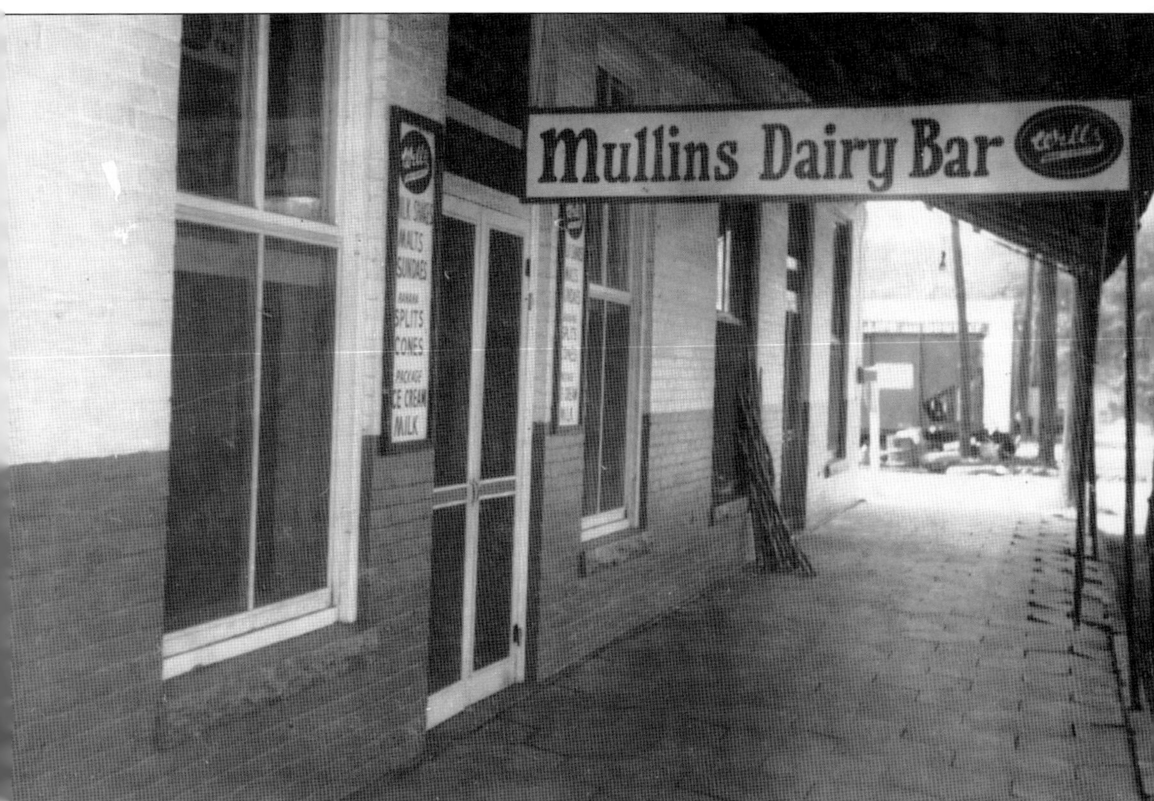

Alf Mullins purchased the Swanson store and opened his grocery store on the same site in the 1950s. It was well stocked with staples, had a meat counter with a solid butcher block in the rear, and carried hardware, tools, and Sherwin-Williams paint. Occasionally, farmers would bring local produce, fruits, and vegetables for barter or to be sold for a small profit for themselves. These seasonal items, such as stalks of sugar cane, were readily available. The front counter where the cash register was located often had various novelty items, sure to appeal to children; flavor straws and plastic bags of water with pairs of goldfish were especially popular. Late in November, some grocery items were reshelved, and a toy room was opened featuring stuffed animals, cars and trucks, and dolls, waiting for Santa to shop. The Dairy Bar was adjacent to the grocery store. It was especially popular in the summer months. All manner of ice-cream treats were available, as was a light lunch. Today, Wells Fargo Bank is on this site.

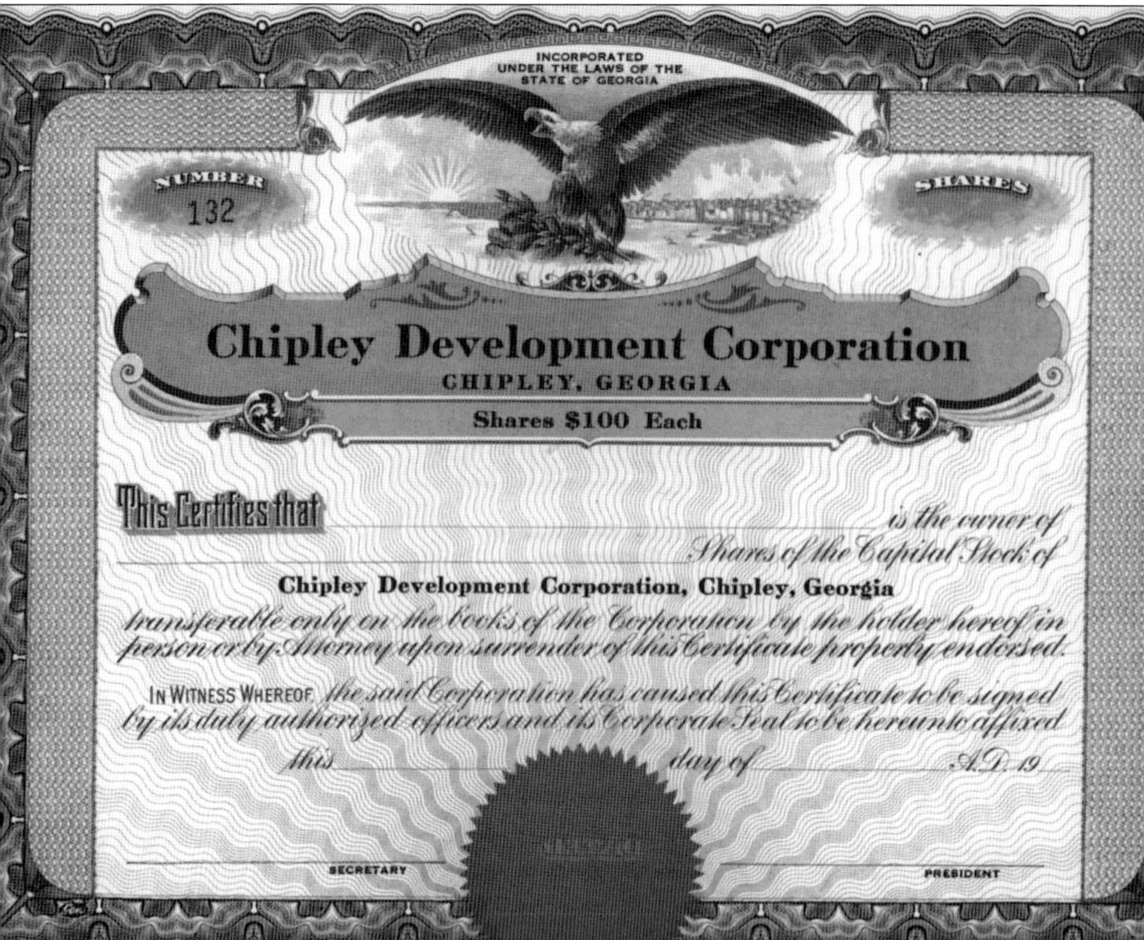

INCORPORATED UNDER THE LAWS OF THE STATE OF GEORGIA

NUMBER 132

SHARES

Chipley Development Corporation

CHIPLEY, GEORGIA

Shares $100 Each

This Certifies that ______ is the owner of ______ Shares of the Capital Stock of

Chipley Development Corporation, Chipley, Georgia

transferable only on the books of the Corporation by the holder hereof in person or by Attorney upon surrender of this Certificate properly endorsed.

In Witness Whereof the said Corporation has caused this Certificate to be signed by its duly authorized officers and its Corporate Seal to be hereunto affixed this ______ day of ______ A.D. 19__

SECRETARY

PRESIDENT

The Chipley Development Corporation was founded on July 1, 1947, by influential businessmen and citizens interested in attracting industry to the town; J.O. Kimbrough was president. Local folks bought a total of 164 shares in the first year for a total of $16,400. Town leaders recognized the need for a boost to the town's economy. There were certainly local businesses meeting the needs of its small population; however, employment was limited to local businesses or farm work. The first project of the corporation was a concrete block building completed in record time. On October 1, 1947, Schwobilt arrived and began operations in the new building. Two other groups have been instrumental in promoting the economy of the town. The Chipley Chamber of Commerce was active beginning in the early 1940s in supporting local merchants. Later, as Callaway Gardens began to attract visitors and businesses catering to them, the Pine Mountain Tourism Association was founded.

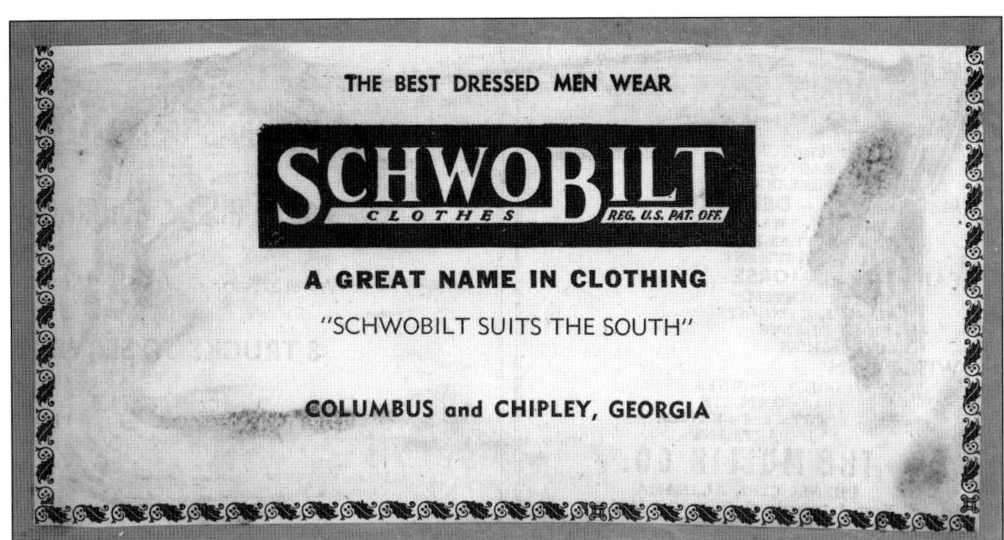

With its headquarters in nearby Columbus, Georgia, the Schwobilt trade name was well known in Chipley. The men's suits and outerwear of the Schwobilt Manufacturing Company now bore a "made in Chipley" label. The company came to Chipley in 1947 and was a significant contributor to the town's economy until 1957, when it ceased operations because of the death of Jacob Schwob.

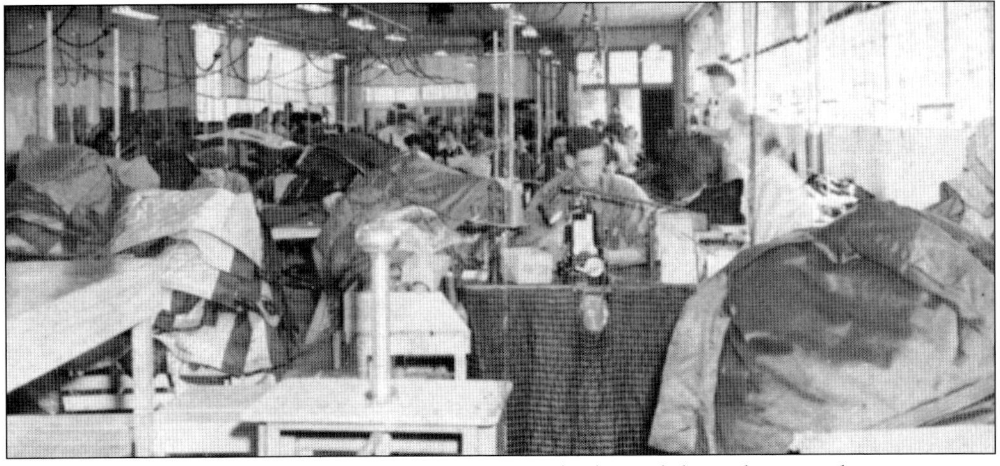

The plant was also a factor in household income in Chipley. While working conditions were not ideal and were rather crowded when production was at its highest, the company provided welcome employment opportunities for local folks. Schwobilt regularly upgraded its equipment to increase production, which in turn provided more job opportunities.

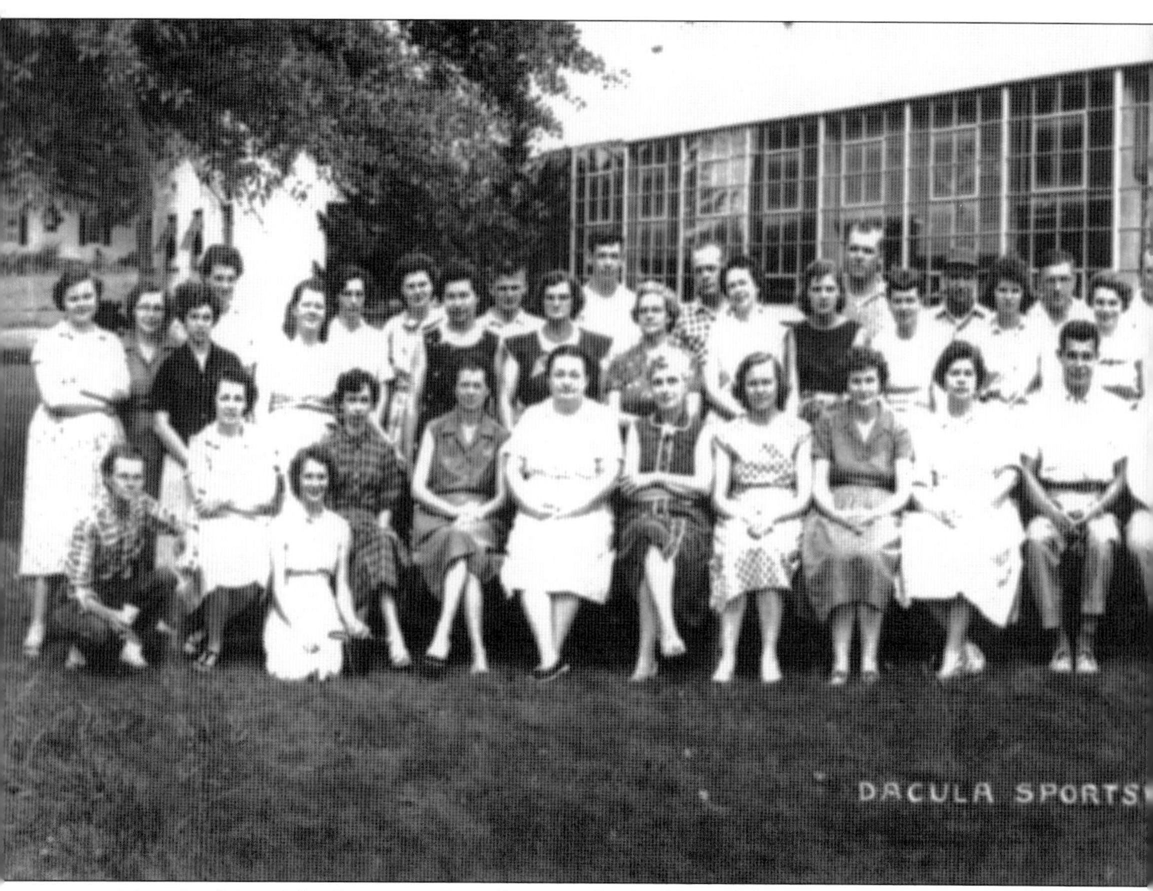

After the Schwobilt plant ceased production, the building did not stay vacant for long. Dacula Sportswear was the next tenant. In addition to the new signage, improvements were made inside the plant, and more space was made available for additional workers, including a larger parking lot. Approximately 80 employees worked at Dacula, and most of the employees are pictured here. The Dacula product was men's sports jackets, and the Chipley plant made, on average, 5,000 jackets

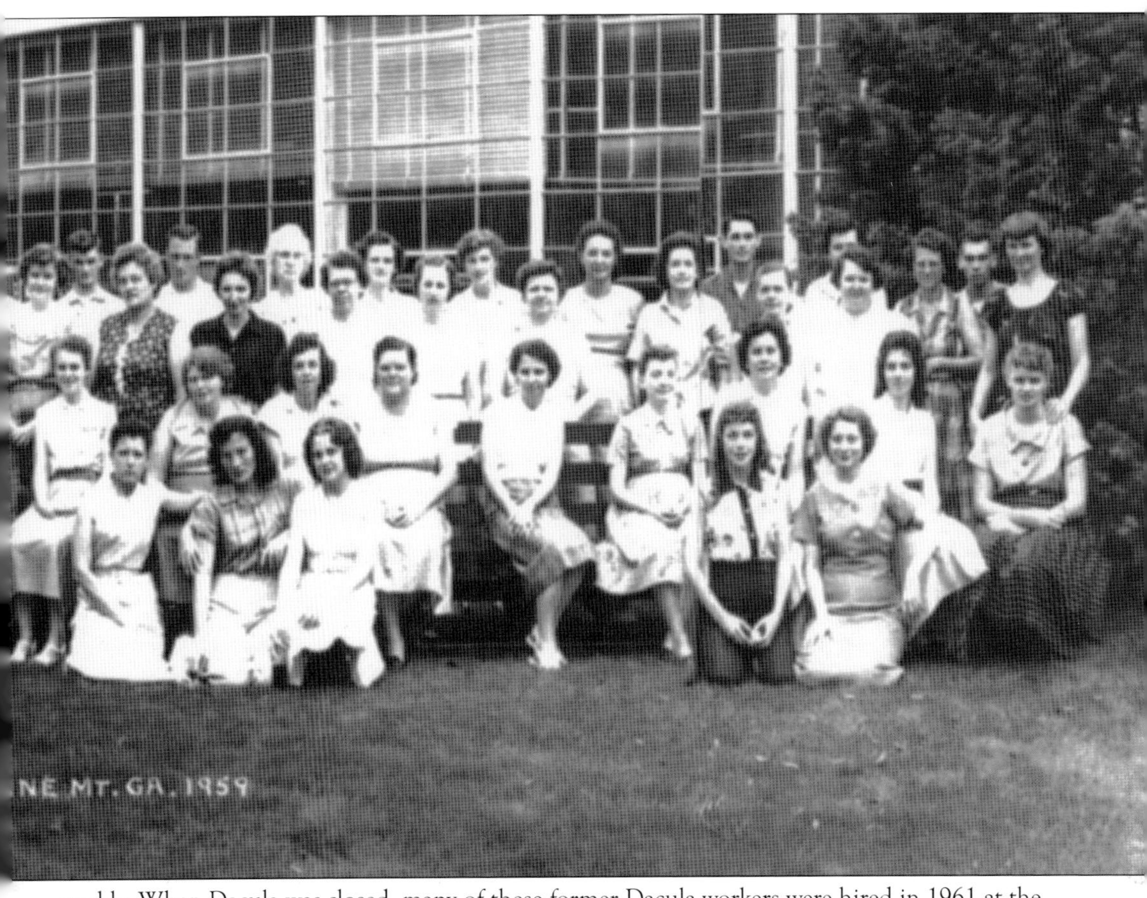

weekly. When Dacula was closed, many of these former Dacula workers were hired in 1961 at the same plant by Chipley Outerwear to make jackets. Of the four textile industries in Chipley/Pine Mountain, Dacula had the largest workforce. However, failure to pay taxes caused Dacula to close suddenly in 1960. Today, it is home to Maverick Transportation and Pocket Change ministry.

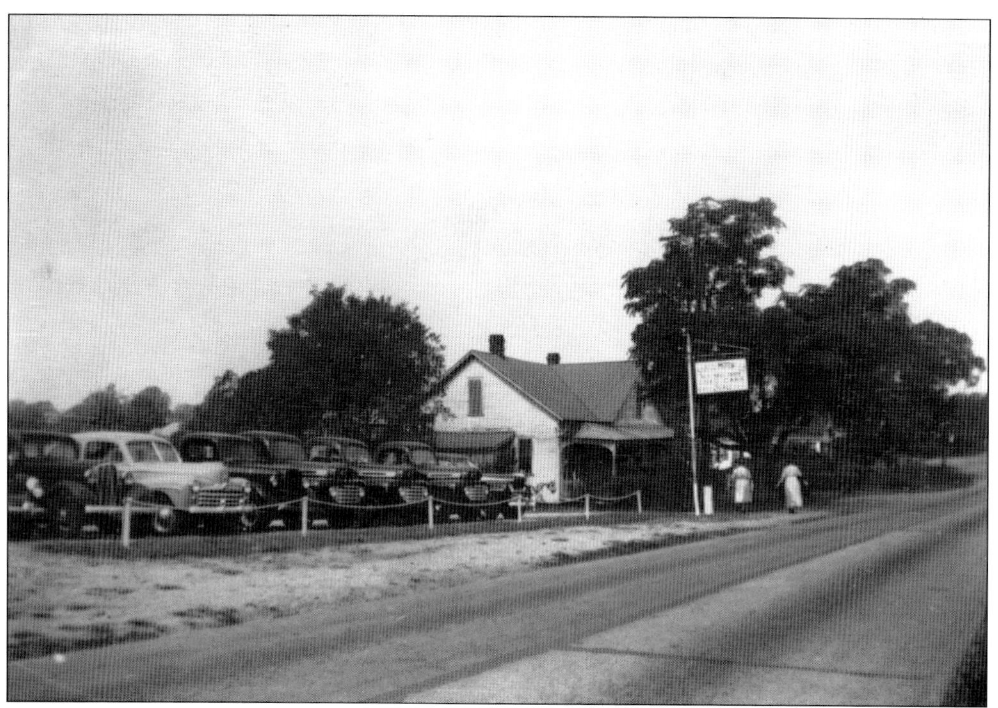

This photograph shows Durand Sivell's used car lot at the present site of Three Little Pigs restaurant. Earlier, in 1951, he had renovated a two-story warehouse on Blevins Street, one-half block off US Highway 27, for his Ford dealership, which today is the vacant lot behind Pure Chipley. That business had offered new vehicle sales, all maintenance services, and an upholstery shop for custom seat covers.

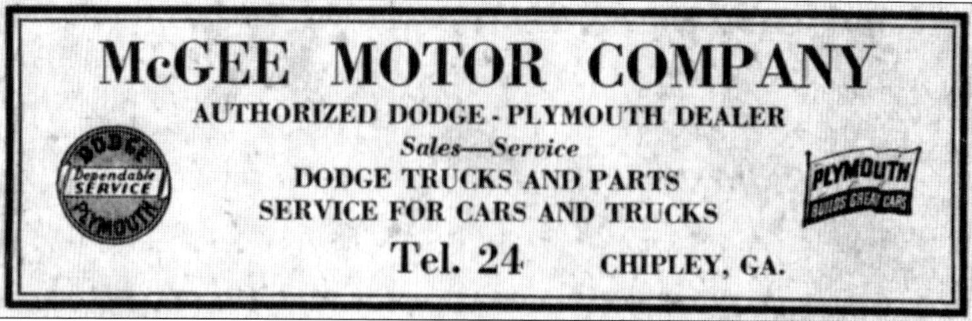

The automobile business boomed in Chipley in the 1940s and continued well into the 1960s. Jesse McGee opened his Dodge dealership in April 1945, where the Pine Bloom Market had been located earlier. It is now home to Chipley and Main. Previously, at this same location, sometimes called the Layfield Building, Jim O 'Neal sold Ford automobiles.

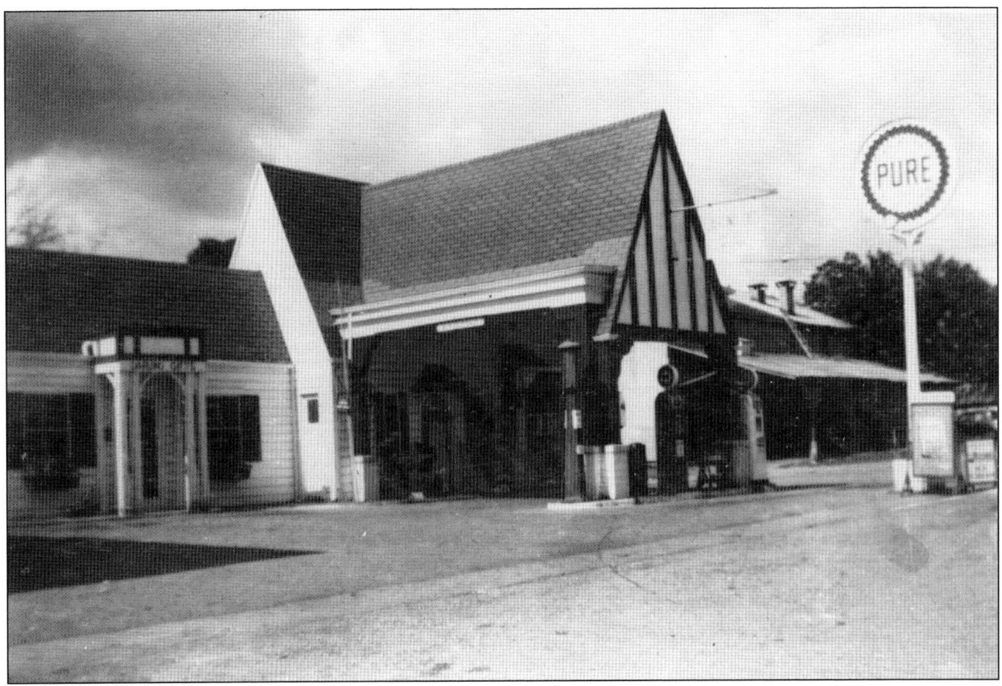

The Pure Oil Service Station was originally a Woco Pep Station. .Pure Oil sold fuel, but it was also a sporting goods store, primarily with items for fishermen. While a Woco Pep store, there was also a tea room, which became a gift shop under the Pure name. Today, the building is still in use, housing a retail establishment named Pure Chipley.

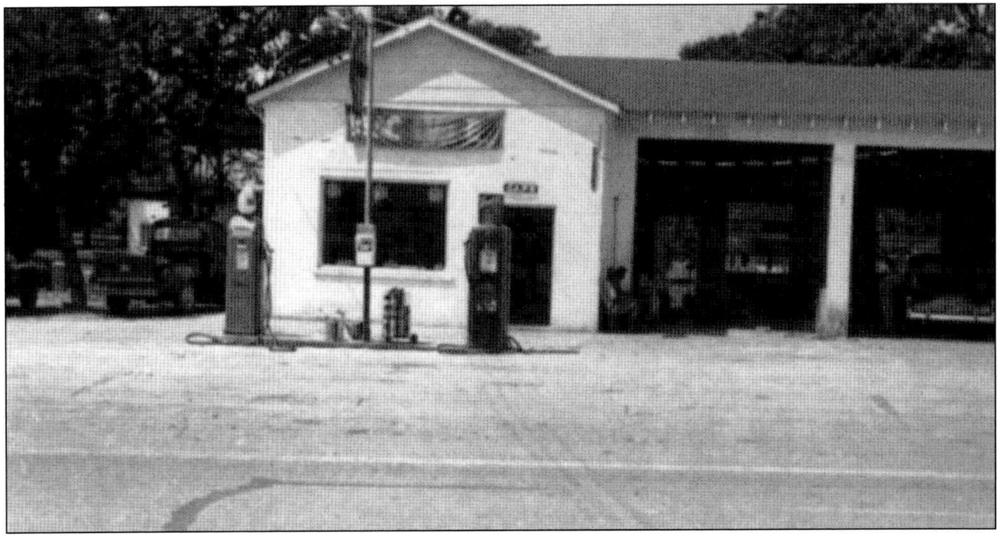

Another service station was Cook Brothers, which was opened in 1948 by Robert and Glover Cook. Their first building on US Highway 27 was demolished in 1952 and replaced by a concrete block structure. Today, at the same location, in the new building, Steve and Adam Cook, the son and grandson of Glover, operate Cook Auto Supply.

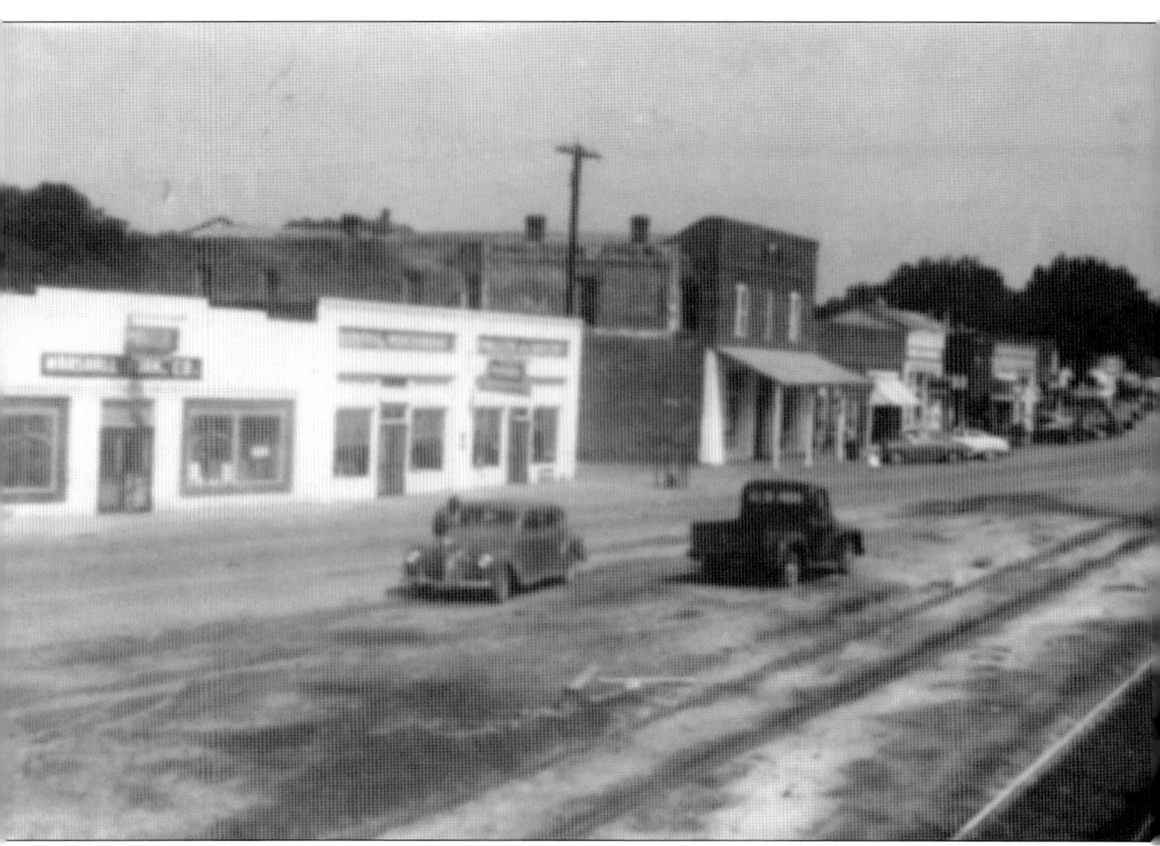

The heart of the retail district in Chipley was the lineup of locally owned stores on Main Street, offering everything from furniture to gas and oil. There was a drugstore, a movie theater, and a café. The main rail line and sidetracks were directly across the highway, and the arrival of either passenger or freight trains would bring crosstown traffic to a halt. Freight trains, especially, divided the town and impeded commerce for as long as it took to drop off or pick up boxcars or flatcars. Notice the entry to "cotton alley" between the white building and the two-story structure. The two-story building was the home of Kimbrough Brothers, cotton agents, and in the fall, there were processions of mule-drawn wagons and pickup trucks bringing cotton bales from the two gins to be weighed and stored for shipment, often along the side of the alley itself. Today, there is no locally grown cotton and no train, and the procession of wagons is just a memory.

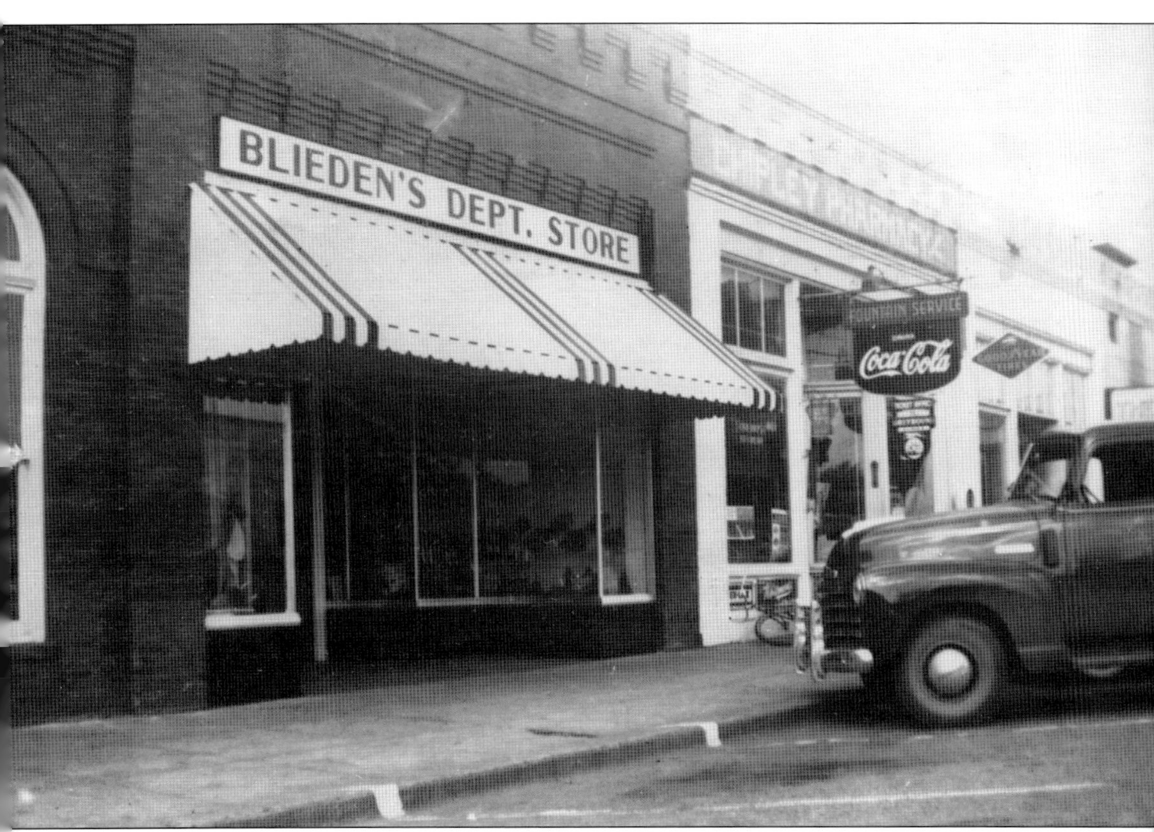

Blieden's Department Store and the adjacent Chipley Pharmacy on Main Street are shown in this photograph from the early 1950s. Blieden's was more a ready-to-wear clothing store than a department store by today's standards. It included some piece goods and notions but was stocked primarily with ladies', children's, and men's and boys' apparel. That building is now the site of Absolutely You. The Chipley Pharmacy next door was owned and operated by J.O. Kimbrough, who had bought the business from Hopkins and Wisdom in 1917. It had been established on Broad Street next to the Farmers & Merchants Bank. Kimbrough had worked there as a young man, had decided to pursue a career as a pharmacist, and had eventually bought the business. He moved it to the site on Main Street in 1930. By the 1950s, it featured a soda fountain that was very popular with high schoolers. With the town's name change in 1958, it became Pine Mountain Pharmacy. Subsequent owners/pharmacists were Jack Taylor and then Charles Storey. It is now U-Save-It Pharmacy.

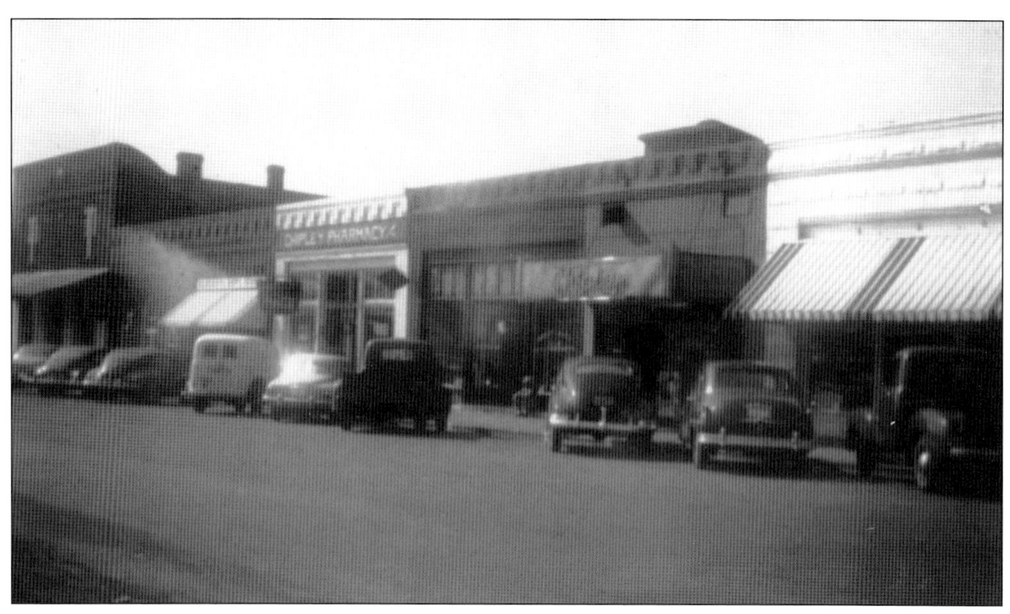

Chipley's main street, formerly called West Railroad (US Highway 27), had a vibrant business section in the 1950s. The photograph above shows, from left to right, Kimbrough Brothers; Patrick's Grocery; Blieden's Department Store; Chipley Pharmacy; Chipley Variety; Chipley Theater, billed as the "only movie theater in Harris County;" and Chapman's Grocery, later Strickland Market. The photograph below extends the view past the grocery to include the City Café and a glimpse of the gift shop attached to the Pure service station, previously Woco Pep, that filled out the block. The café was operated through the years by different families and was the go-to place for lunch. The nature of some of the businesses and their ownership changed a number of times and are quite different now from those in the 1950s, but the buildings still line US Highway 27 today.

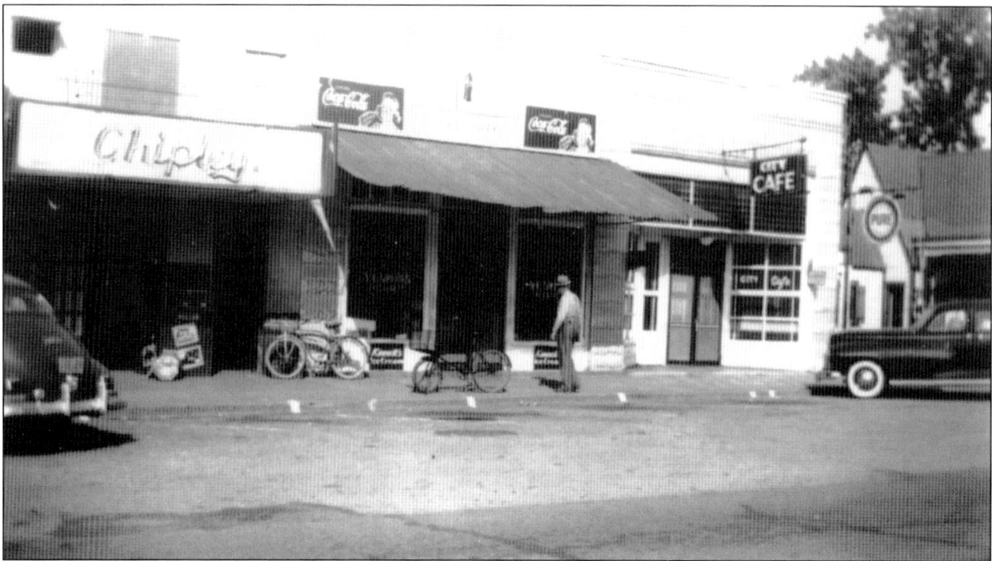

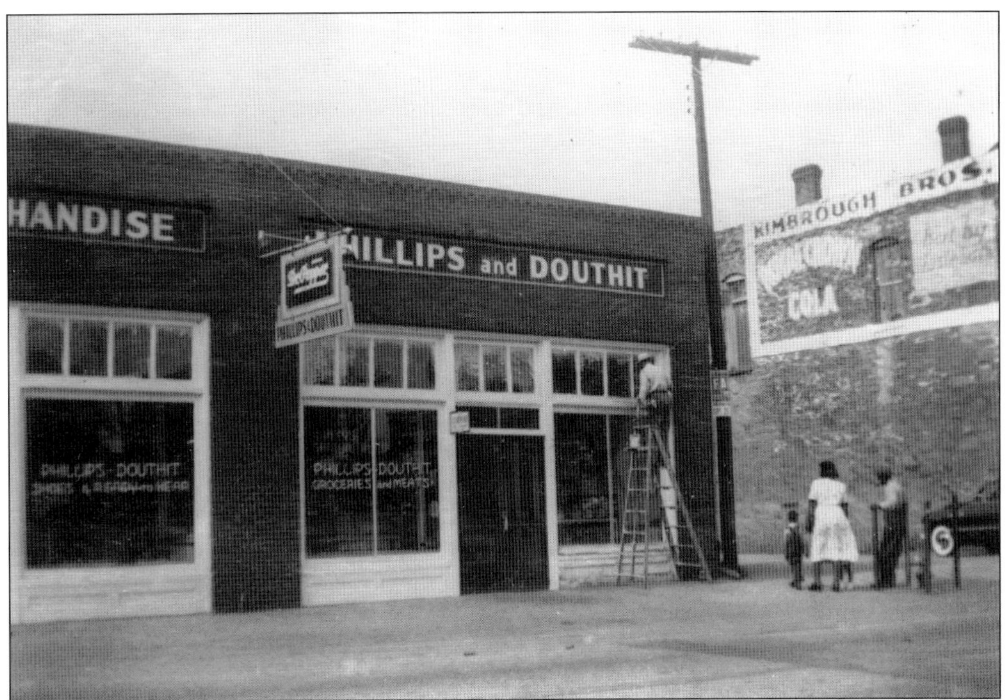

Phillips and Douthit was established in the mid-1940s by Earl Phillips, who purchased the building from Durand Miller. Phillips's father-in-law, Max Douthit, later became a partner. The store handled canned goods, fresh meats and produce, shoes, ladies' hats, cloth cut to order, delivery of telephone orders, and credit on a monthly basis.

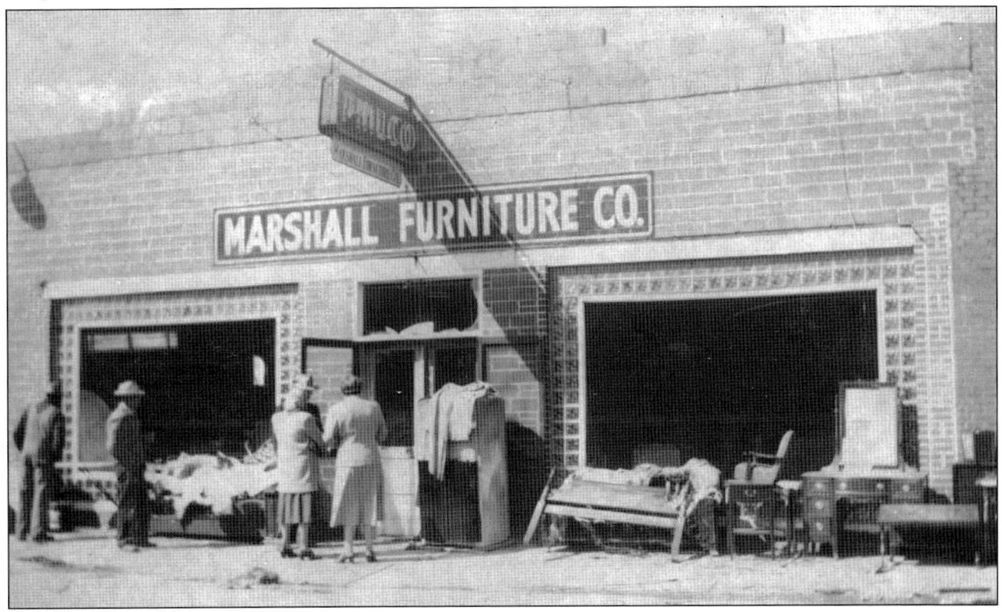

Marshall Furniture store was one of the very few specialty stores in town. It was located south of Unique Expressions today. Its inventory, payment on credit, availability, and delivery service were greatly appreciated by local folks. A fire in 1950 damaged the building and its contents; however, it reopened 40 days later. The fire sale held two weeks later was its biggest single sale of the year.

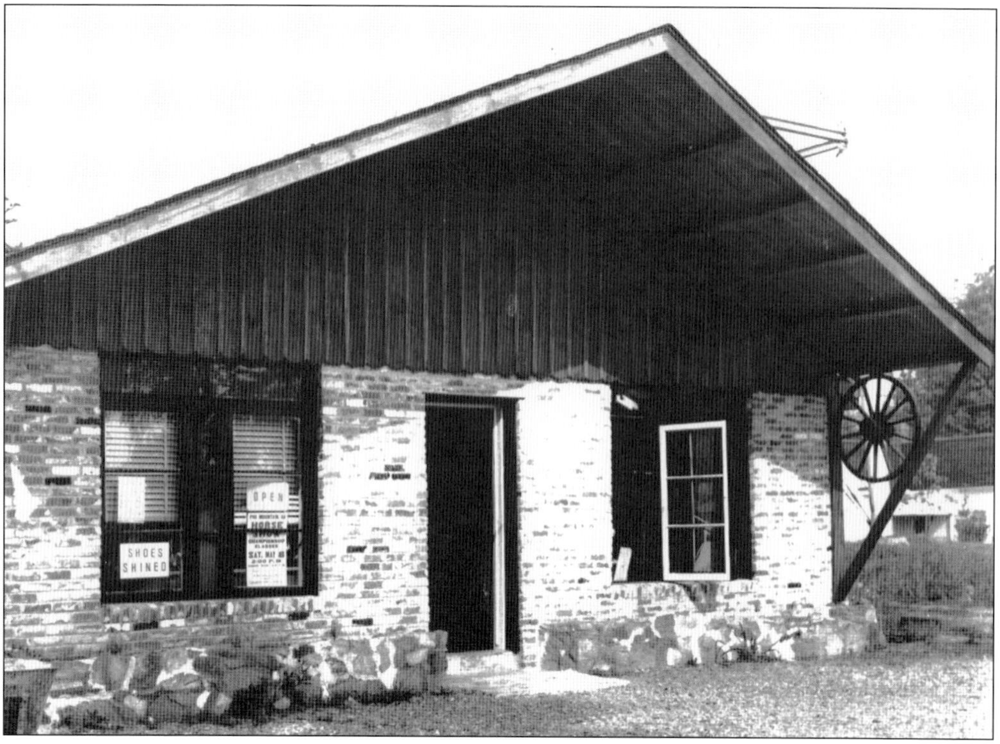

A vacant lot is now at this location on McDougald Avenue across from the post office and beneath the water tower. At one time, it was home to a plumbing business. Later, this building provided a home for dry cleaning and shoeshine services. It also served as the bus station, and folks could pay Georgia Power and telephone company bills here.

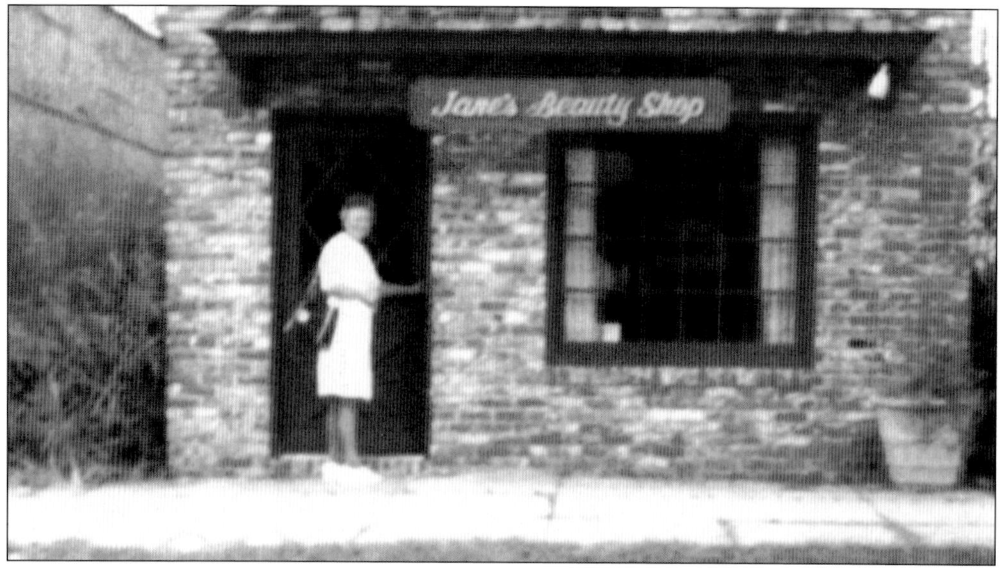

Around the corner was Jane's Beauty Shop. Ruth Parker is shown here in the white uniform and shoes, formerly worn by hairdressers in the 1950s. Those ladies worked in beauty shops, not salons, and were hairdressers, not stylists. Her business had several locations before its final location on Broad Street. Her shop was always named after her daughter Jane.

Seven

Activities and Leaders

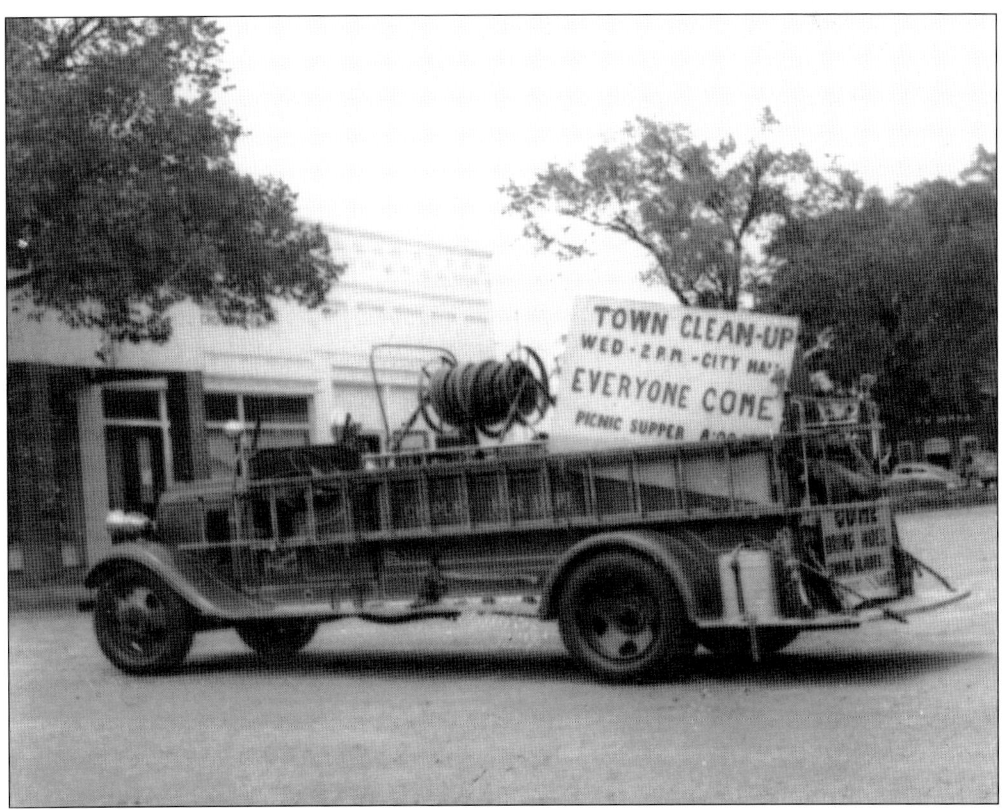

When Chipley entered the Georgia Power Champion Home Town contest in 1952, a concentrated effort was made to "spruce up" the town. Since social media was nonexistent, the firetruck parked on Broad Street advertised the event. The cemetery was a focus of some of the work, along with sidewalks and the playground. Members worked on the grounds of their churches throughout Chipley.

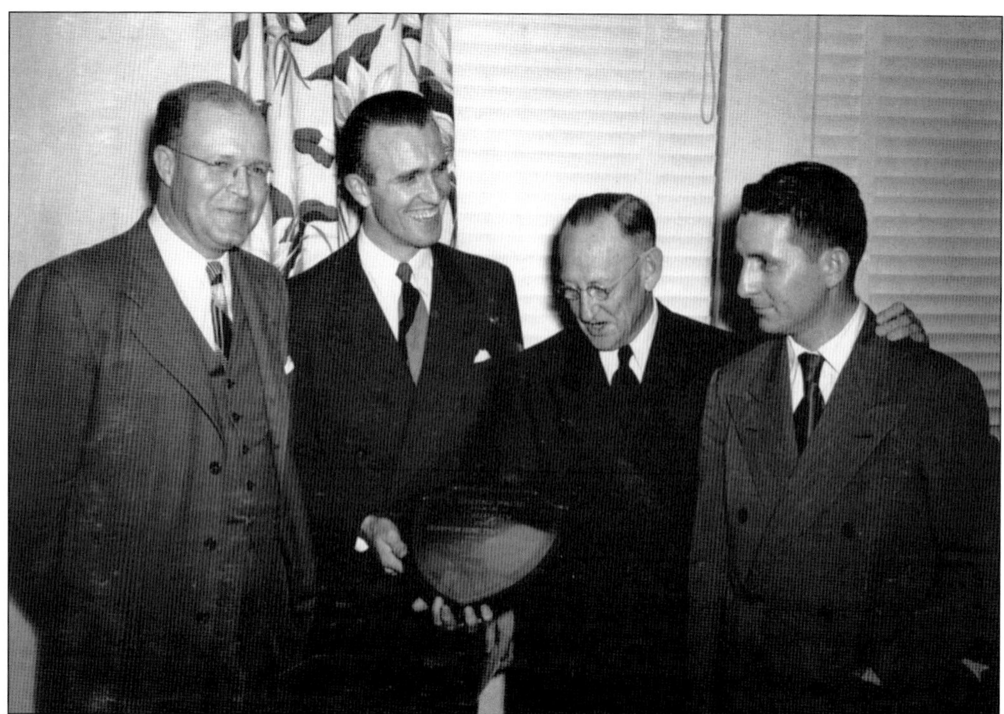

From 1949 through 1953, Chipley entered the Georgia Power Champion Home Town contest. Chipley was in group two, towns with populations of 750 to 3,000. The contest required submission of scrapbooks describing town activities and achievements on topics such as business and industry; education, culture, and religion; Negro report; and municipal development. Each chapter had an introductory narrative and many illustrative snapshots. (Many pictures in this book are from those scrapbooks.) Townsfolk were organized into committees for each chapter. In 1949, Chipley won second place, receiving a check for $750. In 1950, the town won an honorable mention and won another second place in 1951. Chipley won no prize in its last year of participation, but townsfolk surely agreed with the Georgia Power vice president that the effort showcasing the town's achievements proved there was "no better place in which to live and work." Above are, from left to right, unidentified; Comer Brownlow, pastor of the Methodist Church; C.A. Collier of Georgia Power; and unidentified.

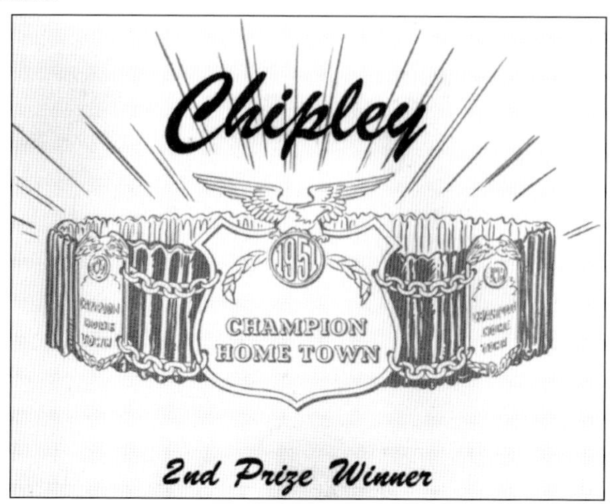

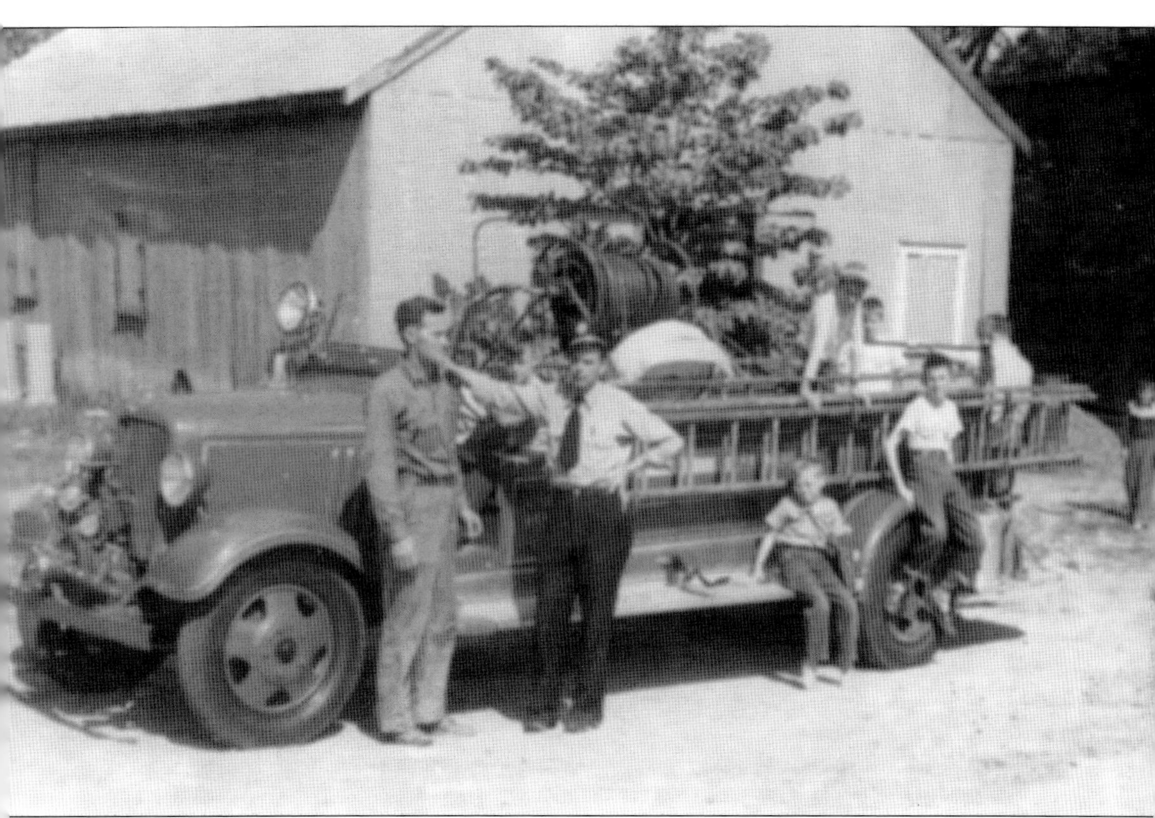

Chipley was served by a volunteer fire department (as Pine Mountain is today). Townsfolk, especially the firefighters and young boys, were glad when a fire truck arrived in 1953. Earlier that year, after a late-night fire at the Marshall Furniture store, the town hired a night watchman, primarily as a precaution against fire. No town funds were paid to the volunteers; however, the town council voted to pay $725.85 from the town treasury toward the total cost of $1,200 for the firetruck. Chipley citizens were asked to contribute, and $424.16 was raised. A fireman's ball was held, which raised $97.20. The firetruck was paid for, with a little left over.

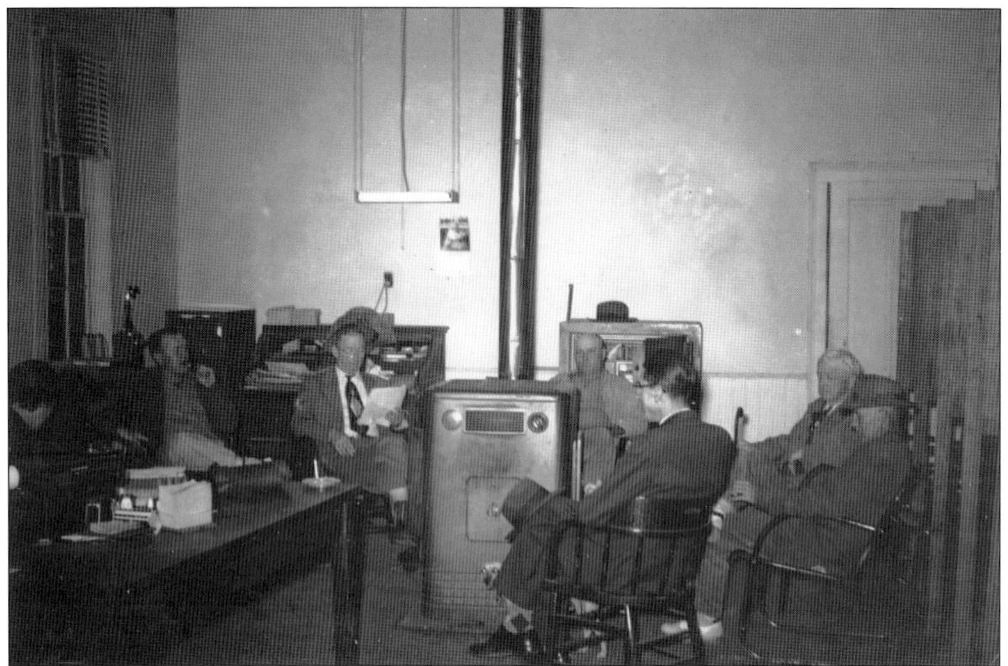

The original city hall building was constructed in 1906 and is listed in the National Register of Historic Places. It includes two jail cells, complete with graffiti written by inmates. The town council has always met in the city hall. The first city hall was replaced in 1978 and became part of the Chipley Historical Center, which now includes a second building added in 2021. In this 1952 photograph are, from left to right, Mary Askew (clerk), Earl Phillips, J.B. Patrick, A.H. "Buck" Anderson, Louis Askew, J.W. Caldwell (mayor), and Albert Dunn. Over the years, seven women have served on the town council. Since 1924, Chipley/Pine Mountain has had eight mayors.

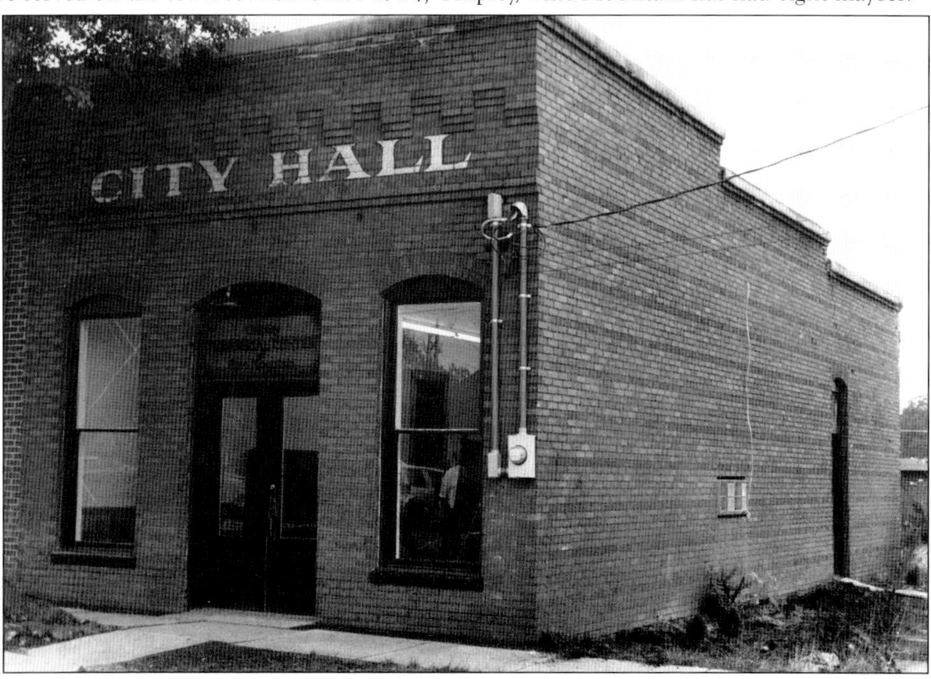

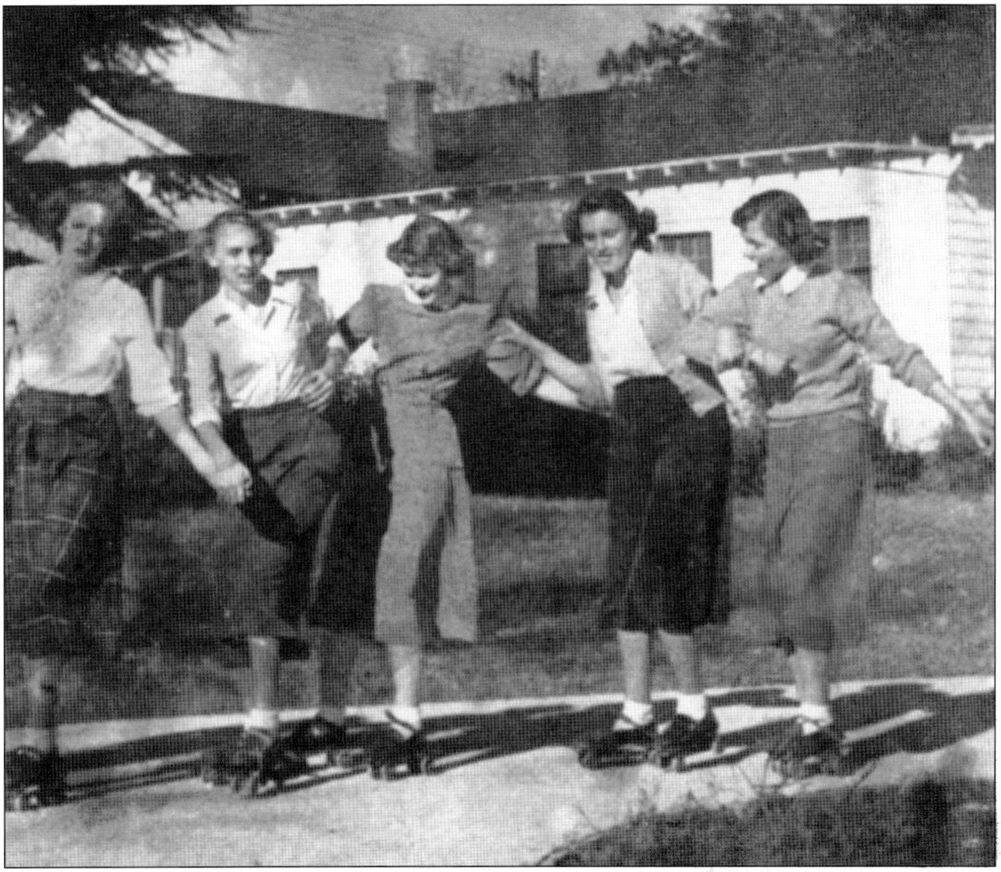

Free recreation opportunities were available courtesy of the Chipley Woman's Club. In the 1940s, Chipley children enjoyed the concrete oval skating rink, walking from all over town to try out their four-wheeled metal skates attached to their shoes with skate keys. Also located on the property were tennis courts and a baseball field used for pick-up games and organized Little League games. Evidence of the skating rink remains today.

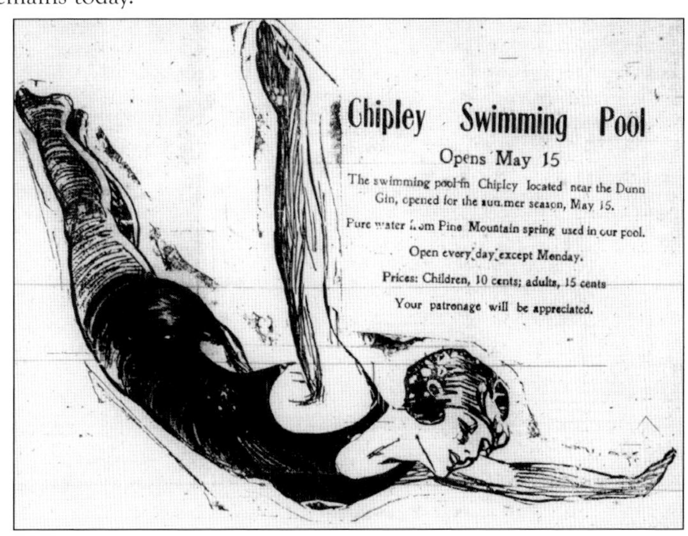

Although there was no formal recreation program in Chipley in the 1930s, there was a swimming pool for local young folks to enjoy. The pool was a basic rectangular cement structure, no vinyl, no tiles, and certainly no diving board. However, it was a spot for gathering and cooling off. The pool was located at the north end of McDougald Avenue.

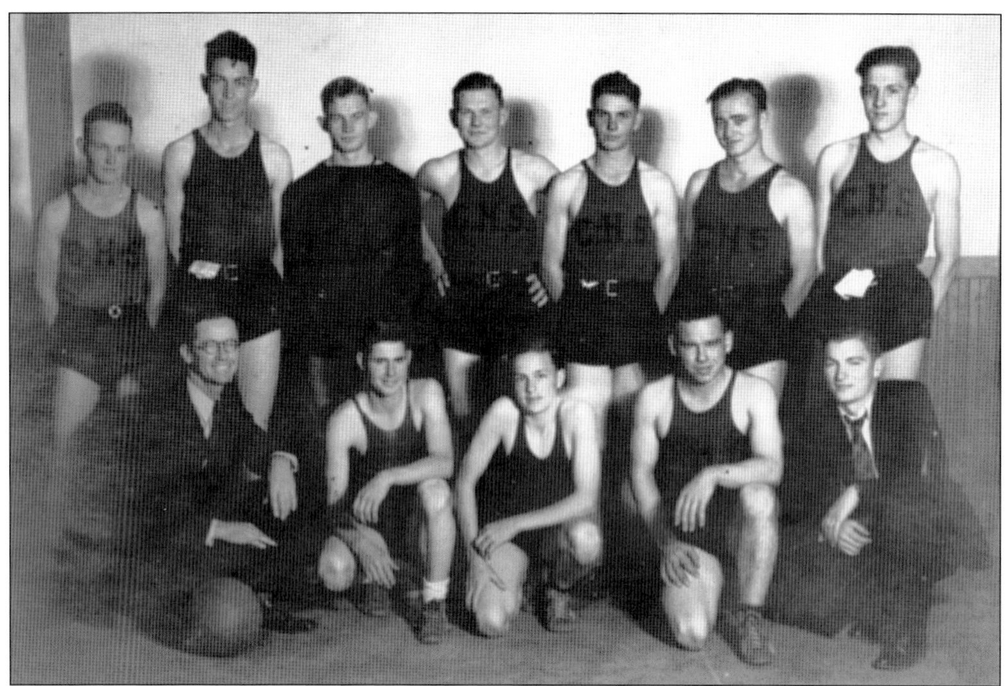

The 1938 Chipley High School men's basketball team is shown here. They are, from left to right, (first row) Coach J.B. Patrick, Gillet Champion, Billy Cornett, Dick Crawford, and Roger Treadwell; (second row) Julian O'Neal, Leroy Gresham, Alf Mullins, Edwin Marsh, James O'Neal, Watson Stevens, and Ted Ellis. There were no professional sporting events in Chipley, so townsfolk came out to support the high school teams.

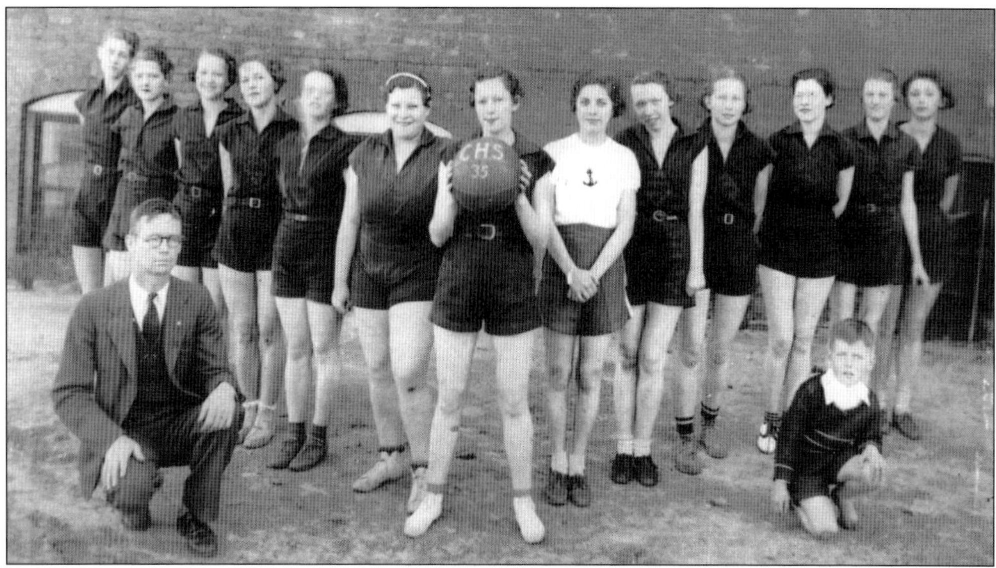

J.B. Patrick, Chipley High School principal, teacher, and coach, is shown here with the 1935 women's basketball team. The members are, standing from left to right, Sara Allen, Mary McGee, Janet Miller, Erin Sivell, Annie Florence Armstrong, Hazel Royal, Dorothy Hadley, Mildred McDaniel, Marguerite Woodruff, Bonnie Cornett, Alice Askew, Nancy Stripling, and Annie Myhand. The young mascot is unidentified.

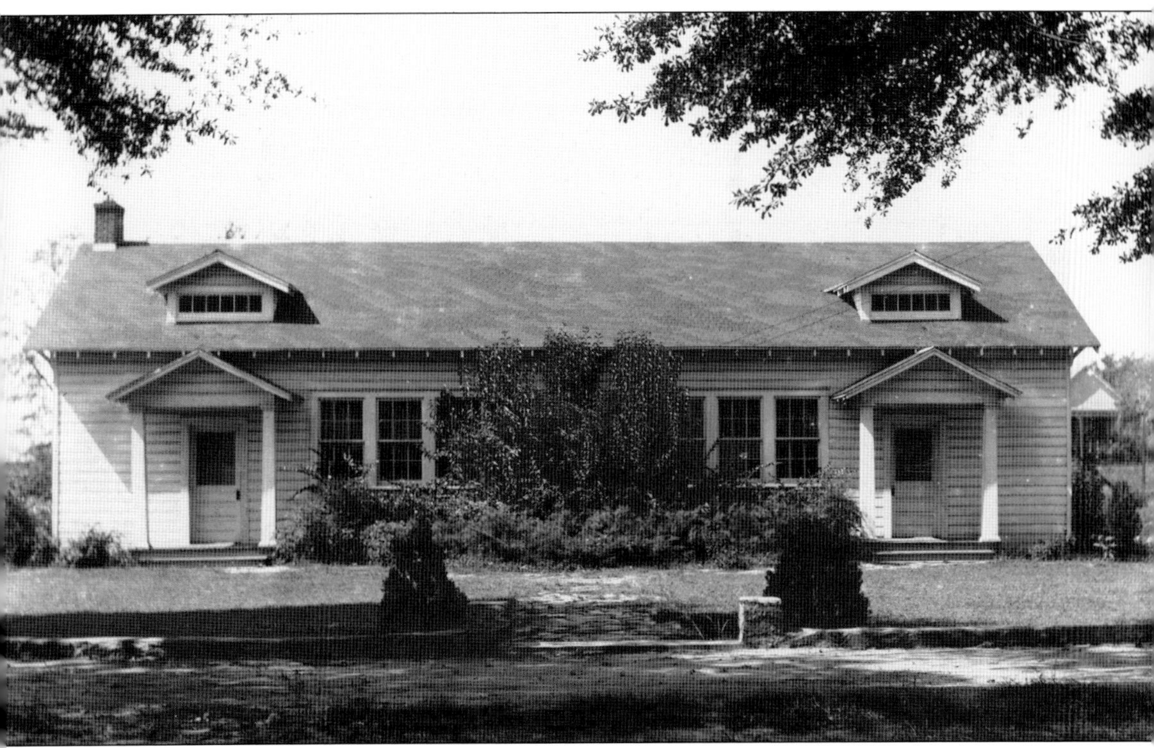

First organized as a civic league in 1913, the Chipley Woman's Club became a garden club in 1916 and a member of the Federation of Women's Clubs in 1919. Early on, the club aided in the formation of the Harris County Extension Home Economics Program. The club made a down payment in February 1927 on the two-acre lot and paid it off in 1928. Construction began on the building during the Great Depression in 1932, and it was paid off by 1934, thanks to many talent shows, bazaars, and cake sales. The club also built a playground and skating rink for community use. Today, the Woman's Club hosts a variety of activities, including wedding receptions and family reunions, in addition to the club's own monthly meetings. The club also sponsors a scholarship program for local high school students.

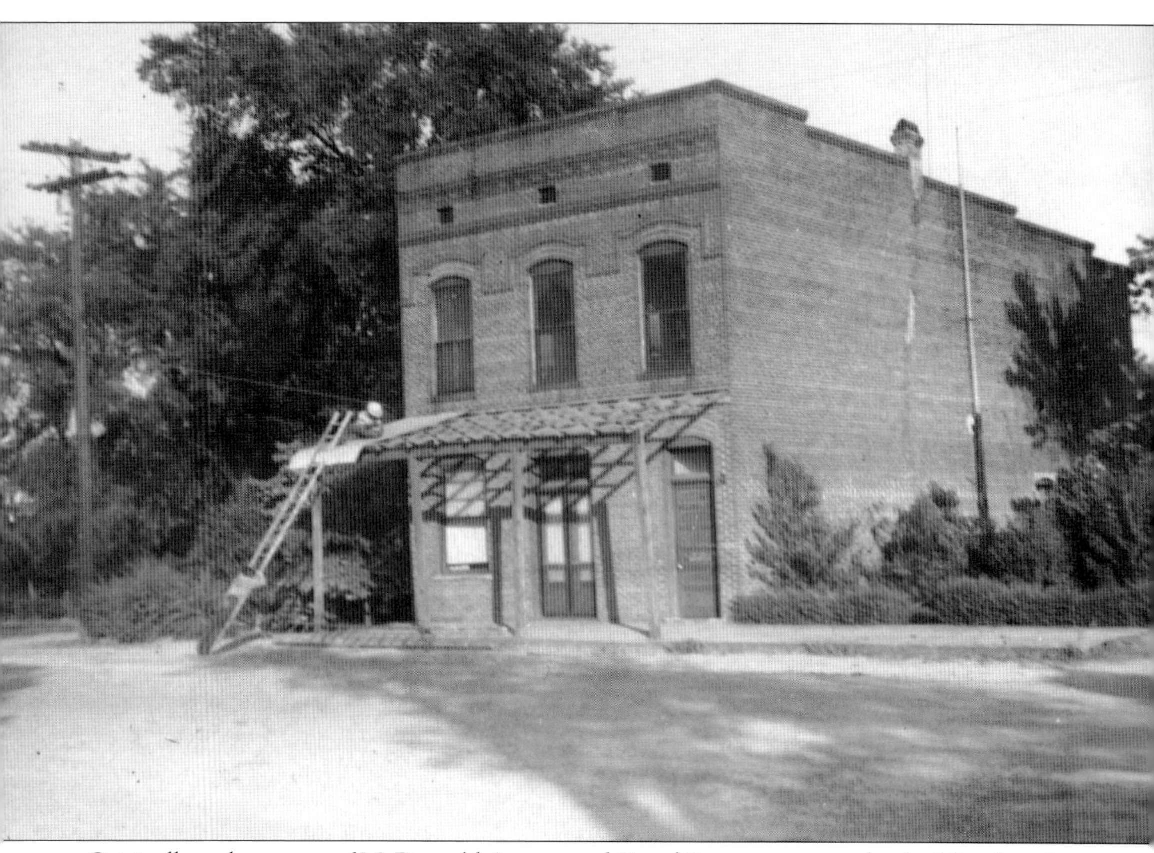

Originally at the corner of McDougald Avenue and Broad Street was a wooden building housing a general store and livery stable owned by the Murrah Brothers, who relocated their business from Hood to Chipley in 1883. On the front step of this brick building is a metal plate with the date 1905; the side entrance has a similar plate with 1904 on it. The structure is known today simply as the Masonic Lodge, home to Chipley Lodge No. 40 Free and Accepted Masons, which purchased the building in 1936. One of the oldest continually used buildings in town, several retail stores, notably a candy shop, a toy store, and two florist shops owned by the Mitcham family, have all been located on the first floor. In the 1950s, the second floor was the dentist office of Dr. Joe Miller. Today, Over Yonder on Broad with antiques and collectibles is at this site.

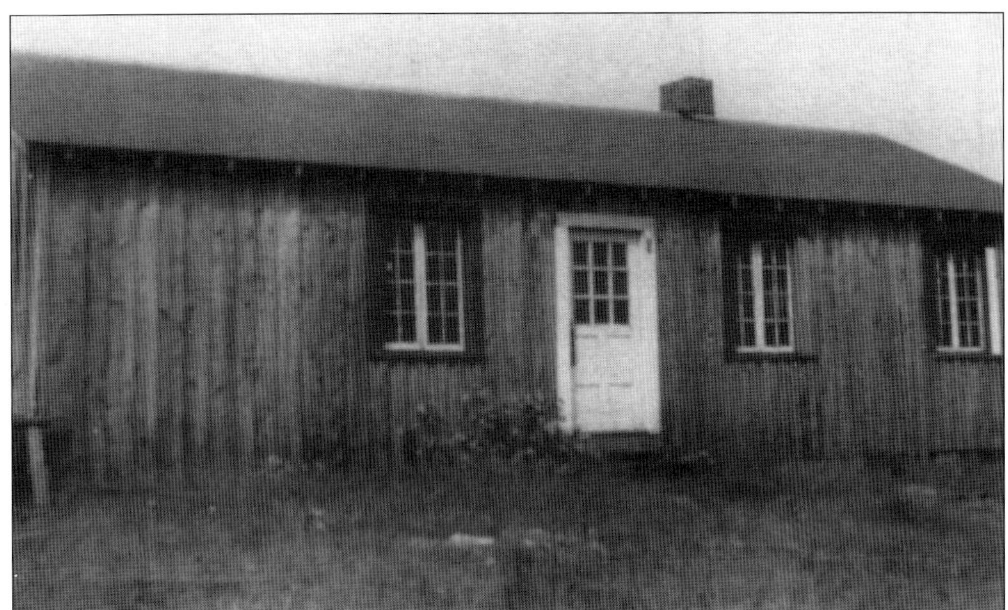

Scouting for boys and girls has a long history in Chipley/Pine Mountain. Boy Scouts were present as early as the 1920s, but it was not until 1944 that local Troop 40 became active, and it has remained so until today. Charles White was the troop's first Eagle Scout; his uniform and badges are displayed at the Chipley Historical Center. There have been approximately 70 Eagle Scouts from Troop 40. The Boy Scouts meet in the Scout Hut built in 1952, above, and have been sponsored by the chamber of commerce and the Methodist Church. In contrast, Girl Scouts, such as the group below, and the Brownies for younger girls, have been organized and led primarily by mothers, although the Chipley Woman's Clubs sponsored them at one time. These girls' organizations are no longer active in Pine Mountain.

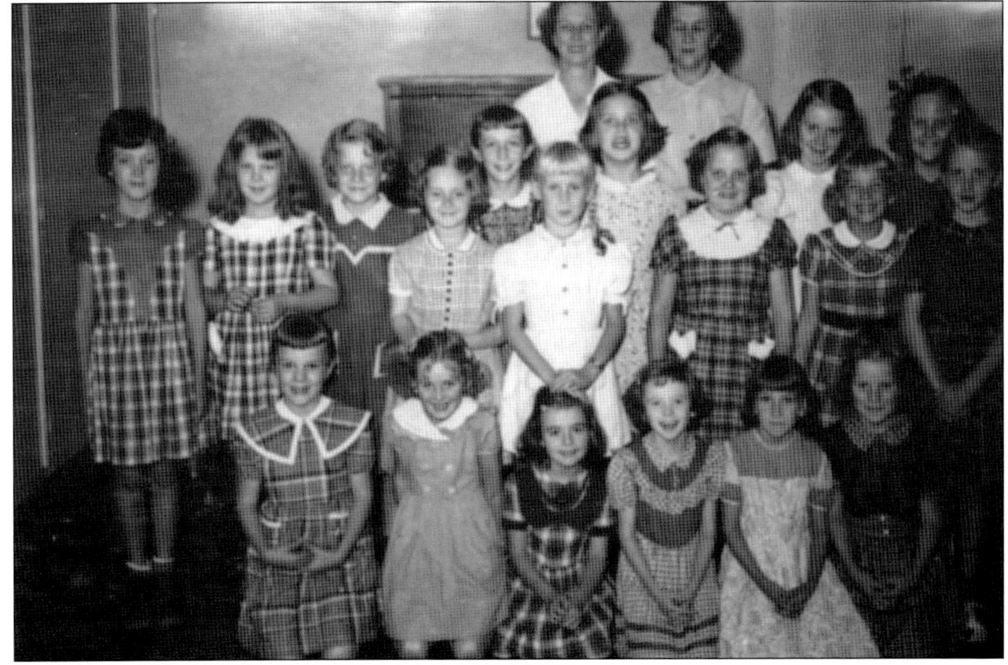

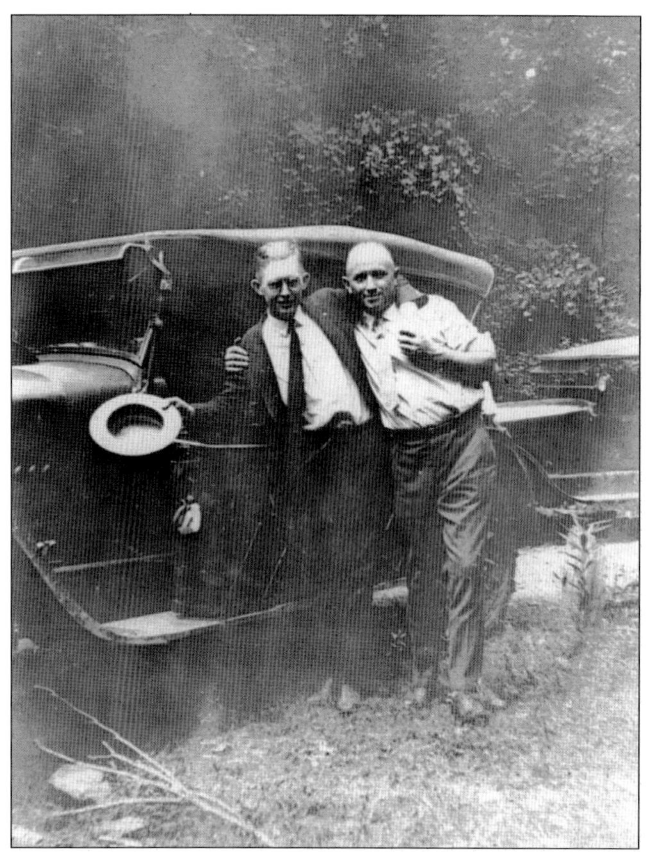

John Wallace (in the left image on the right) may be the most famous (or infamous) person from this area. Wallace lived across the Meriwether County line, but he had many friends in Chipley. His story is found in the 1979 book *Murder in Coweta County* by Margaret Anne Barnes and in the 1983 movie of the same name. Wallace was a farmer but made moonshine on the side; he was executed in 1950 for the murder of one of his workers. However, for all his vices, many people remember Wallace as a good man, "as long as you didn't cross him." In the photograph below, J.P. Davis Sr. presents the deed for 80 acres of land from the Wallace estate to D.F. Parker. Wallace deeded the land to the Boy Scouts just three days before his death. (Below, Dot Moore.)

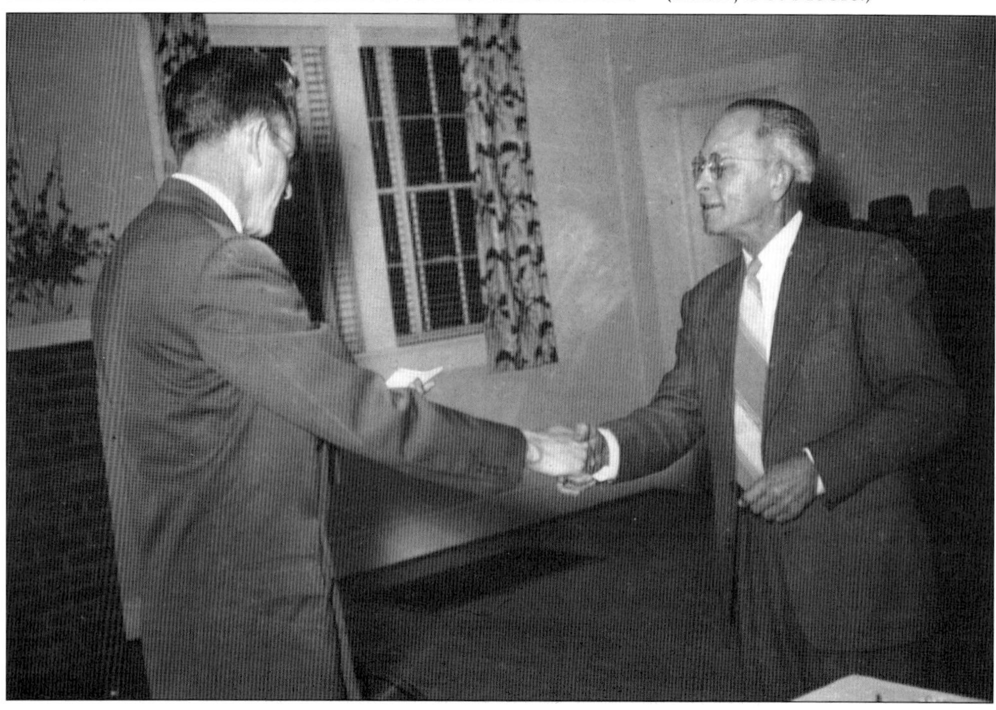

J.W. Caldwell served as Chipley's mayor for 20 years. He is remembered as an early promoter of tourism in the area and was president of the Taft Memorial Highway. Later, he was elected president of the US Highway 27 Association, which worked to promote commerce and tourist travel from the Midwest through west Georgia to Florida.

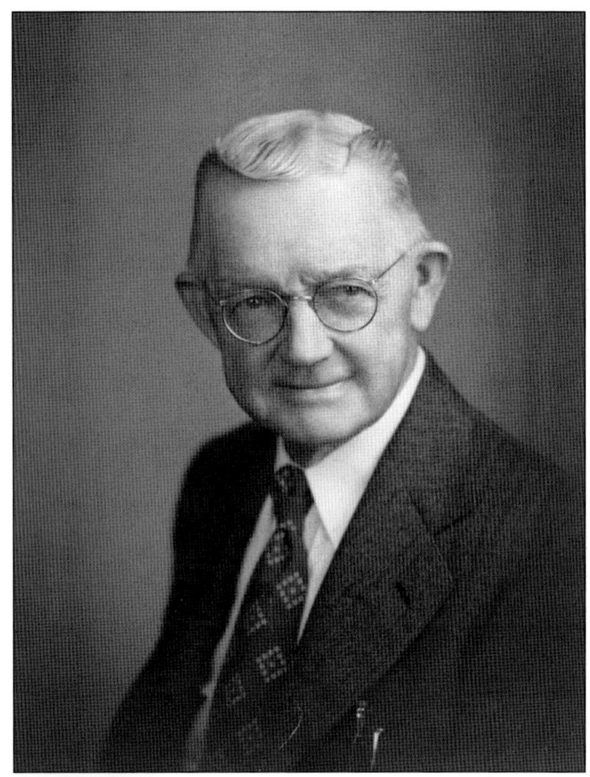

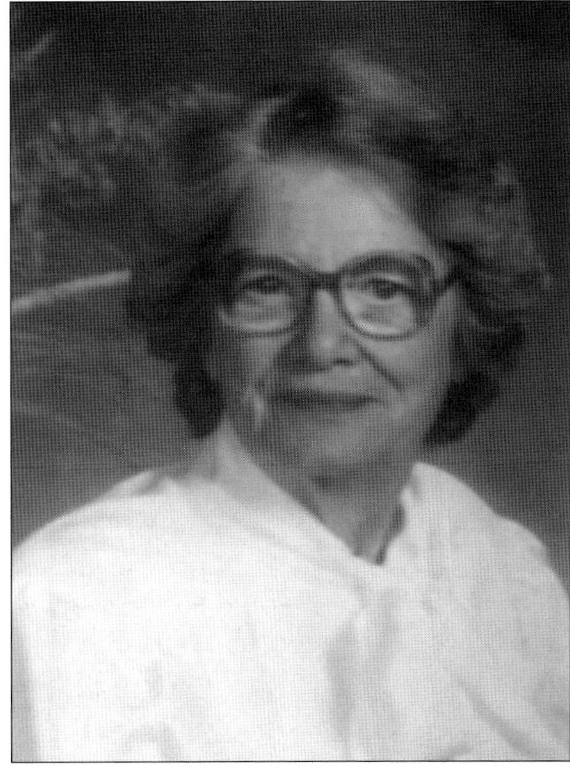

Mary Carlisle Askew, born near Oak Mountain in Harris County, married Louis Askew and moved to Chipley in 1939. She was Mayor Caldwell's neighbor. When visiting him at home, she saw that he was handwriting town water bills and volunteered to help, and a 34-year career was born. Her service as town recorder (later clerk) began in 1947. She retired in 1981.

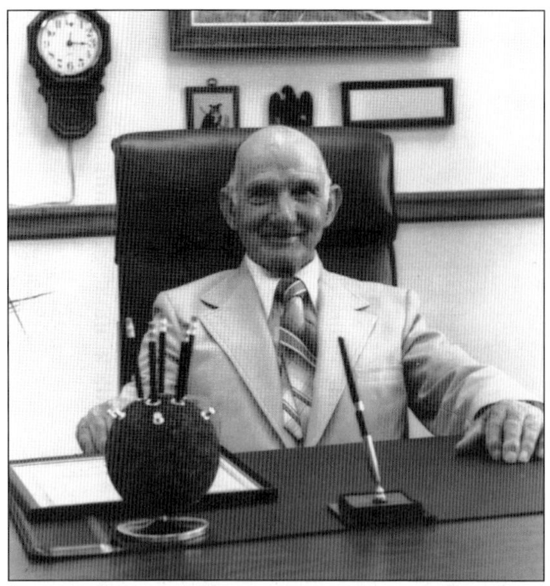

O.E. "Brer" White, a lifelong resident of Chipley/Pine Mountain, served as a city councilman and was mayor from 1962 until 1984. He was a dairy and cattle farmer and also owned a feed and seed store for a time. He was active in the local chamber of commerce, a fire department volunteer, and a founding member of the Chipley Historical Center. Nickname source is unknown.

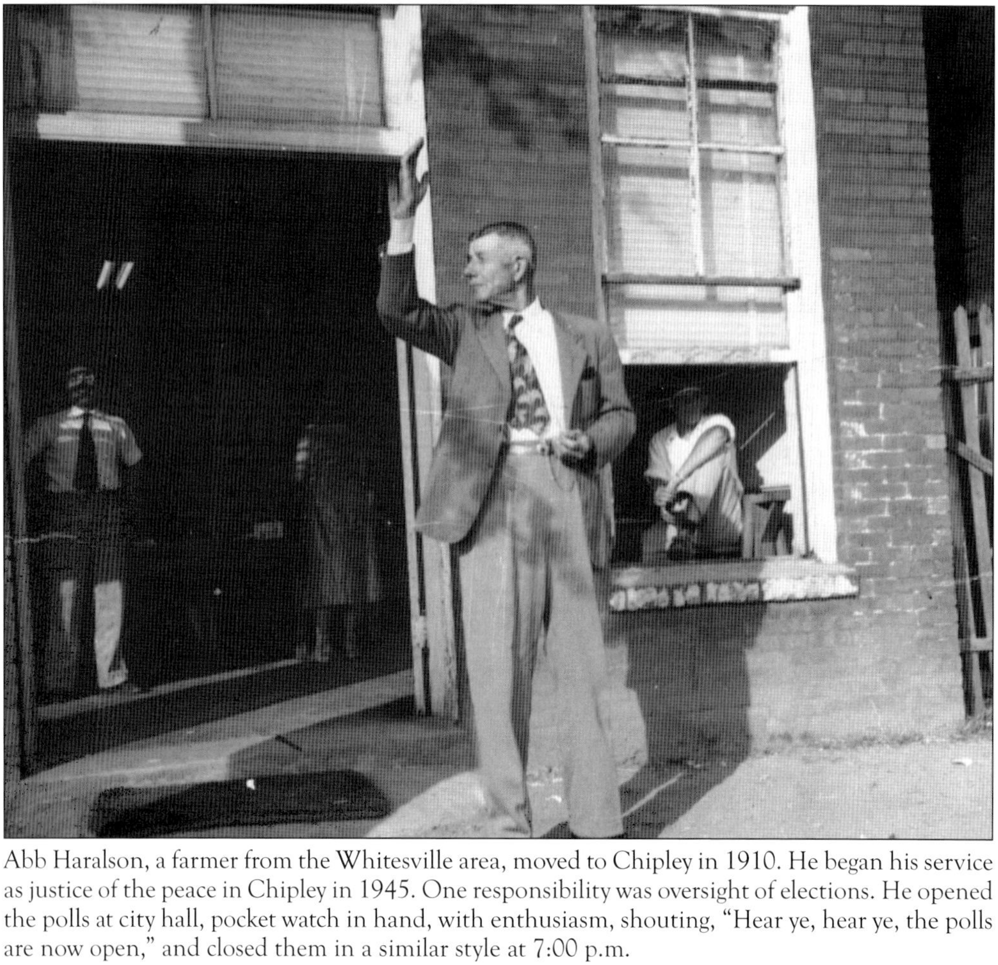

Abb Haralson, a farmer from the Whitesville area, moved to Chipley in 1910. He began his service as justice of the peace in Chipley in 1945. One responsibility was oversight of elections. He opened the polls at city hall, pocket watch in hand, with enthusiasm, shouting, "Hear ye, hear ye, the polls are now open," and closed them in a similar style at 7:00 p.m.

Earl Phillips's work as a civil engineer helped to improve and modernize Chipley, and his grocery store helped fill the community's daily needs. He was mayor for 10 years and, as a lifelong member, taught Sunday school at Pine Mountain Methodist Church. Perhaps his greatest contribution to this community was his leadership of the peaceful integration of Harris County schools as chairman of the school board in the 1960s. (Bob Phillips.)

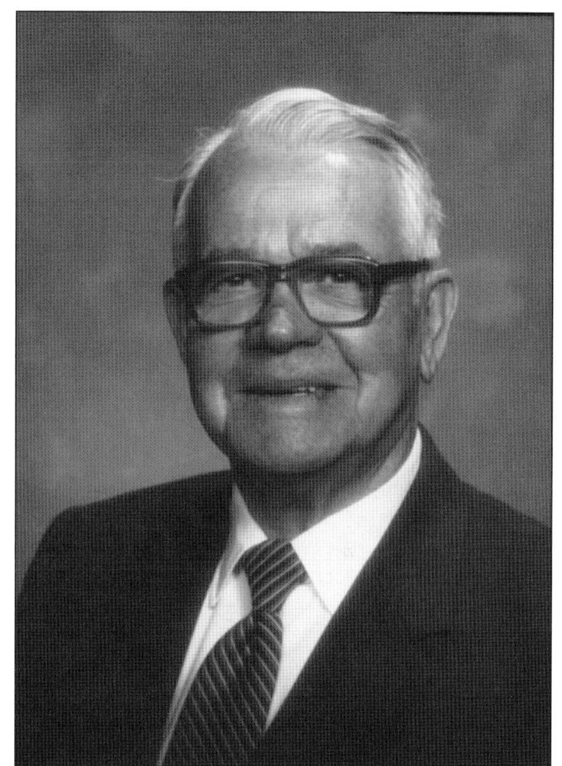

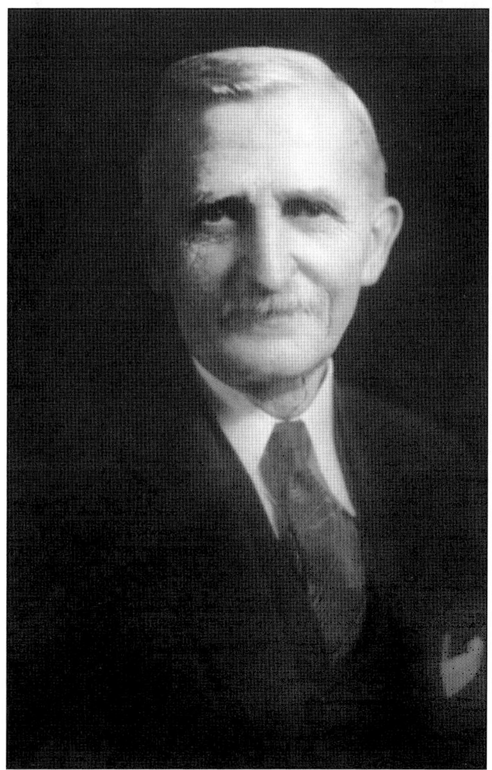

Henry C. Kimbrough, known affectionately in Chipley as "Uncle Henry," was the patriarch of the large Kimbrough family in Chipley; descendants still live in Pine Mountain today. He was the epitome of a public servant, serving locally on bank, school, and church boards and as a state legislator. He is perhaps best remembered as a friend to Franklin Roosevelt, who visited with him when he came to Warm Springs. (Jerry Jones.)

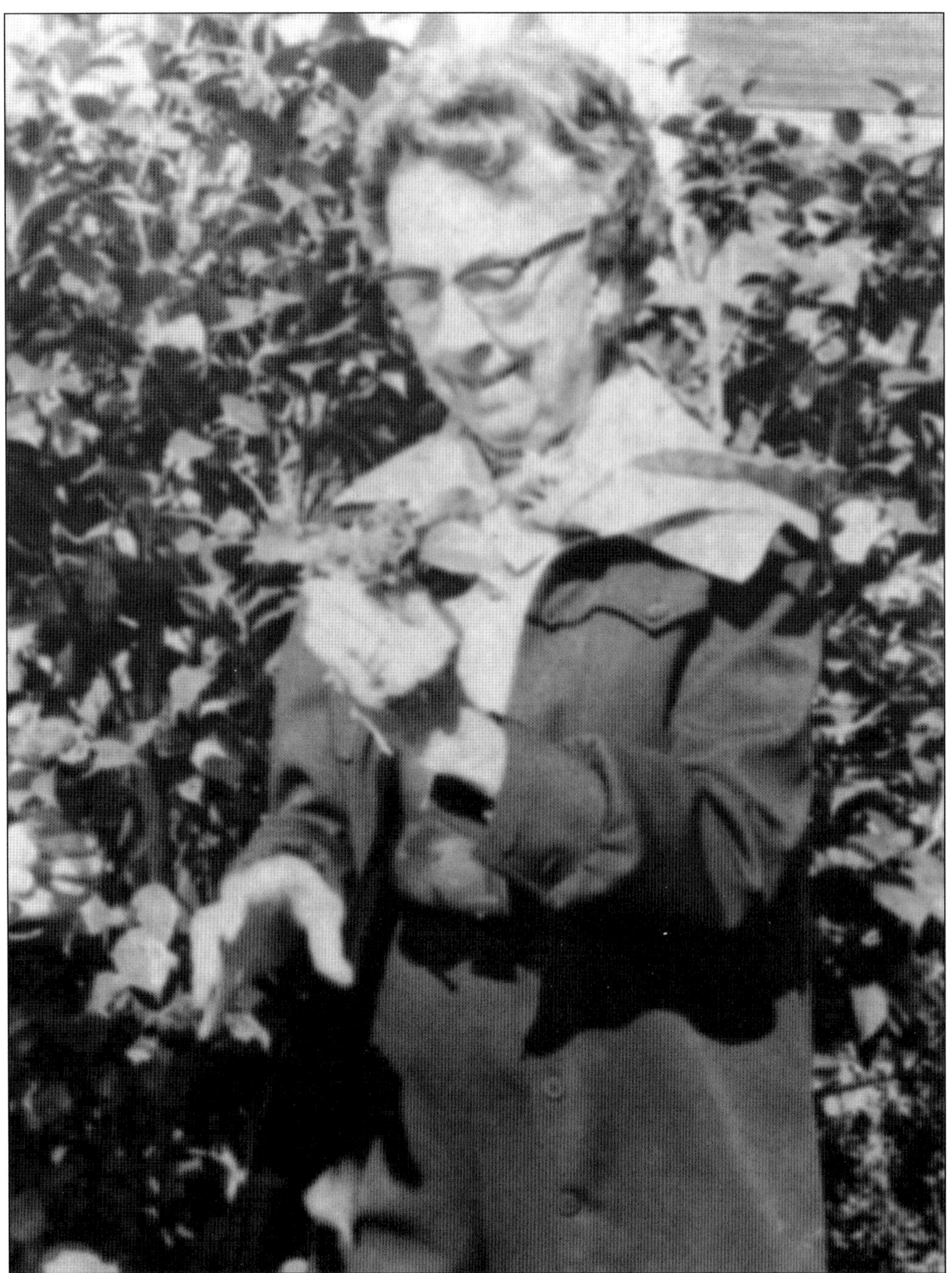

Janie O'Neal Layfield, a lifelong Chipley/Pine Mountain resident, is fondly remembered as a teacher. She taught for 25 years at Chipley High School and chaperoned the senior class trips. She ended her teaching career as the visiting teacher for Harris County schools. She also taught each summer, directing the Vacation Bible School at her home church, Chipley Methodist.

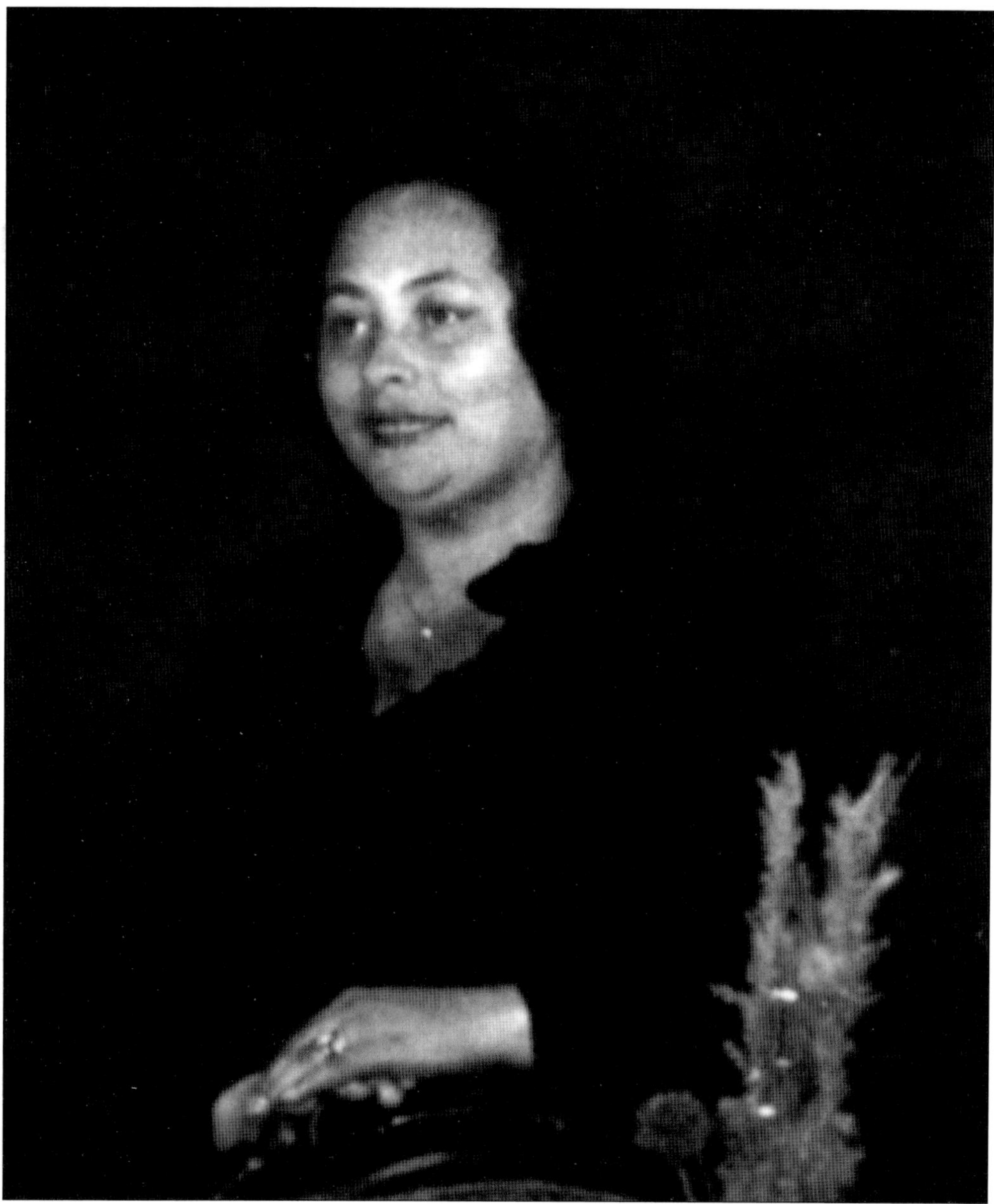

Jarvis Moss, a native of LaGrange, Georgia, moved to Pine Mountain when she married Willie Shepherd. She quickly became an active member of her community. She taught first at Dunbar Elementary School, then at three others, and was also a school counselor. She was the first Black person elected to the town council. While serving, she restarted annual Christmas parades and initiated the numbering of buildings in town. (Marva Copeland.)

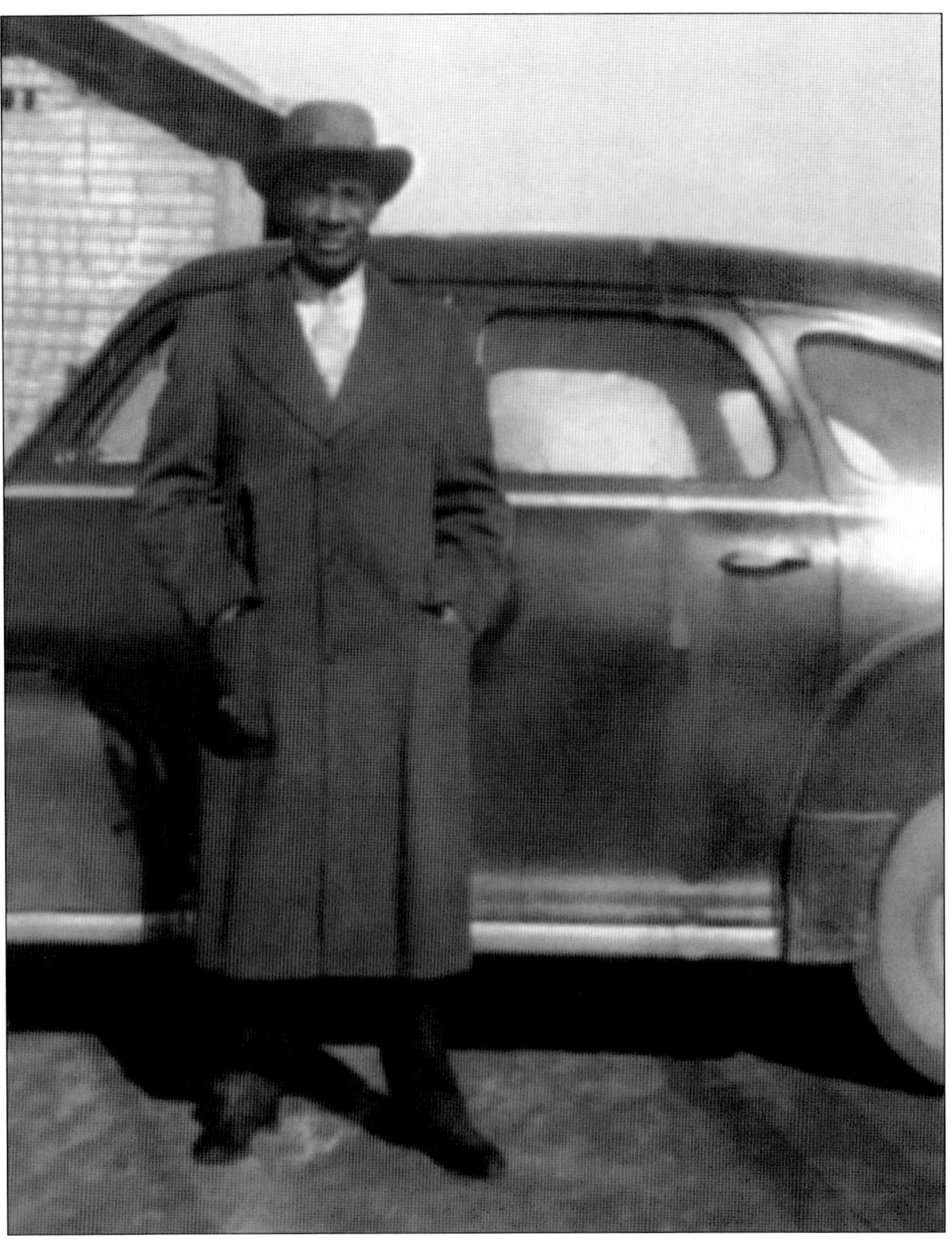

Fairfield McGee, known by most as "Bud," was a lifelong Chipley resident. He had many jobs, among them farming, driving a school bus, and blacksmithing. Many folks appreciated his caring service as a funeral home director. He was a master syrup maker, and he had a unique singing voice often heard at Ebenezer Baptist Church, where he served as a deacon. Many relatives live in Pine Mountain today. (Marva Copeland.)

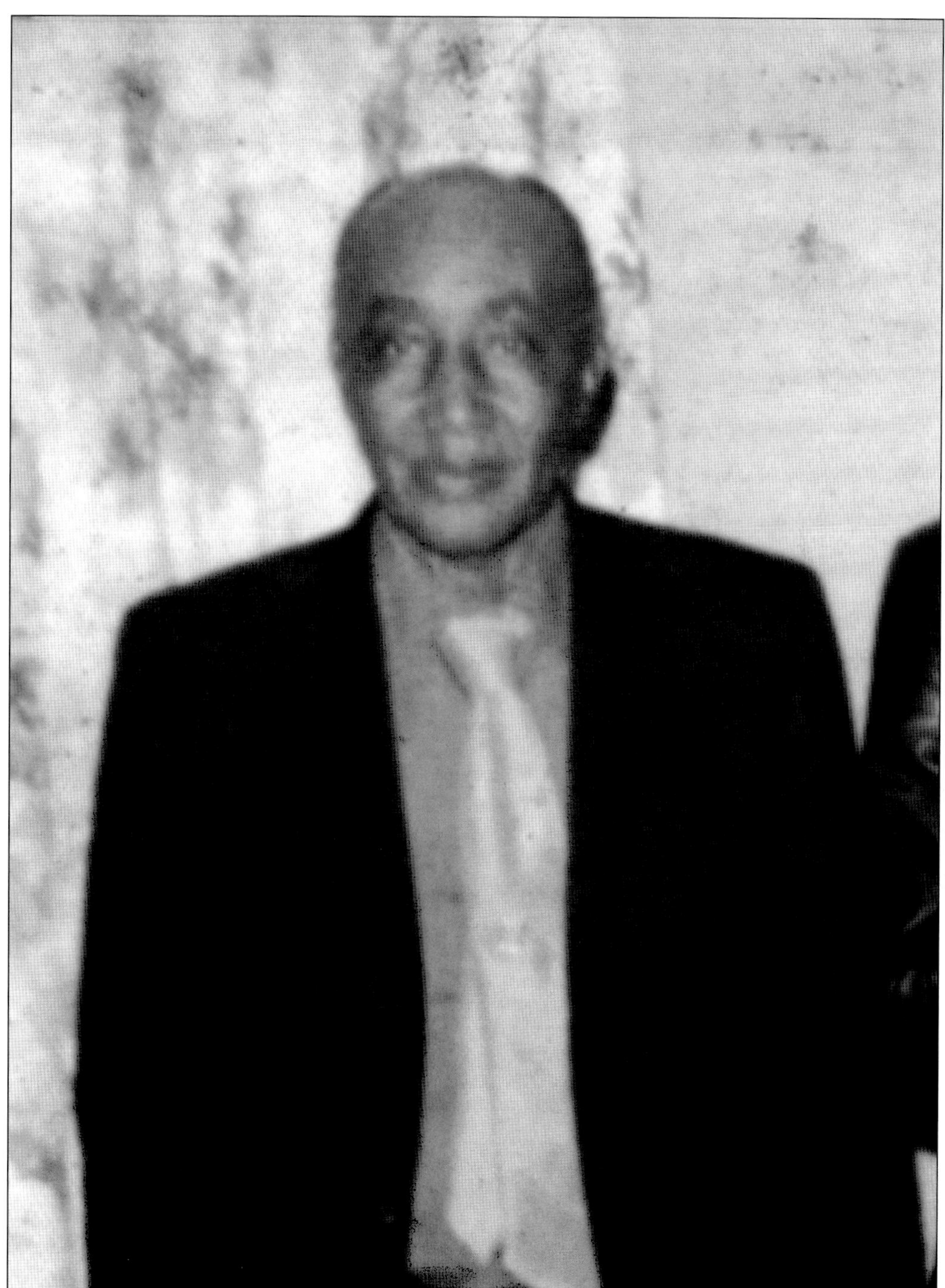

Abbie Shepherd was the final owner of the handle factory in Chipley, which began in the 1940s. He bought the business in 1957 and added a sawmill operation two years later. He is perhaps best remembered by many folks, Black and White, for his expert service at his television repair shop. Both the factory and shop were by his home on Davis Lake Road. (Dorothy Williams.)

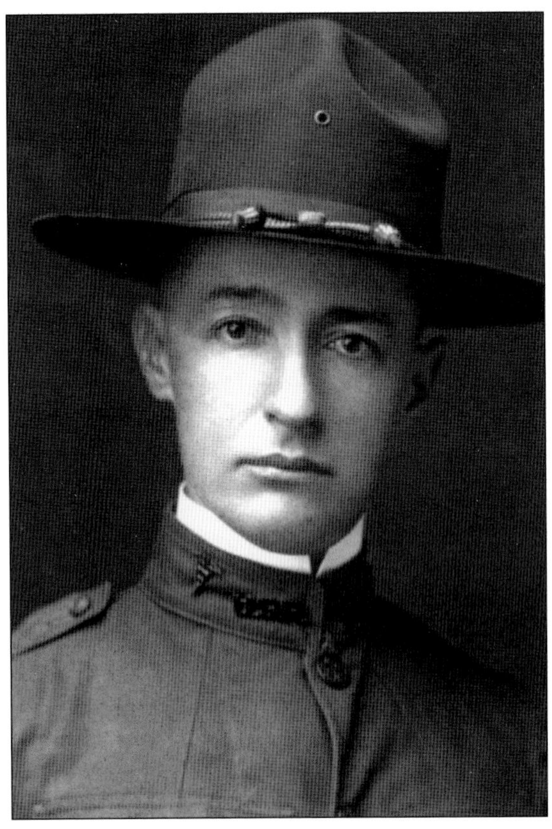

Dr. William Phelps Ellis was the beloved doctor for Chipley folks for 35 years. Graduating in 1906 from Atlanta Medical School, now Emory University, he served in World War I. Soon after, he and Dr. V.H. Bennett established a practice in Gay, Georgia. When they learned that nearby Chipley needed a doctor, they flipped a coin to decide who would move. Dr. Ellis lost, but Chipley won. He established his practice here in 1929. He saw patients daily in his office on Broad Street, regularly made house calls, and even accepted patients in the evenings at his King Avenue home. He was the physician for Camp Kimbrough, the local Civilian Conservation Corps (CCC) camp; was a city councilman; and worked with the Harris County Public Health Department. Dr. Ellis died in 1966. His relatives still live in Pine Mountain today. (Both, Minnie Whitaker and Jeri Bishop.)

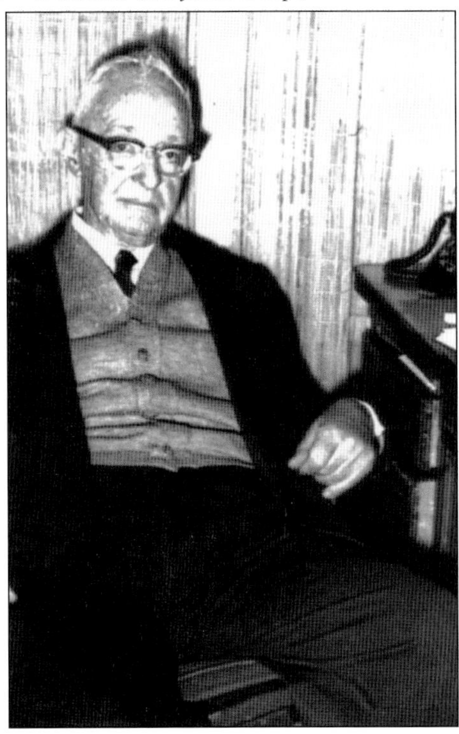

Eight

Tourism

Chipley was promoting itself as a tourist destination as early as the 1930s and 1940s, as this map from the Chipley Chamber of Commerce shows. The Taft Memorial Highway ran directly through Chipley, following US Highway 27. Named for US president William Howard Taft, the highway stretched 1,900 miles from Sault Ste. Marie, Michigan, to Fort Myers, Florida. An effort was made to improve the road quality to attract travelers.

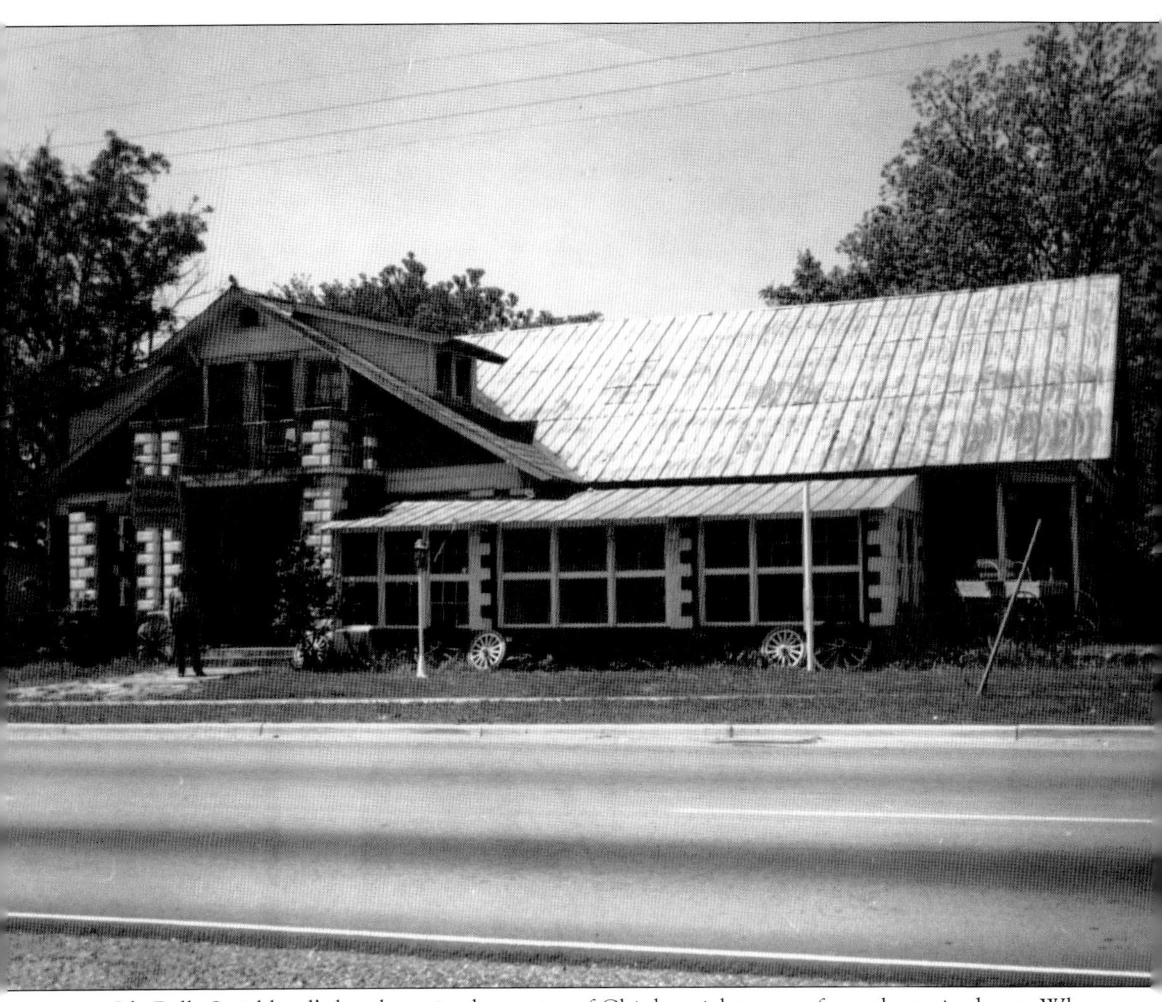

Ida Belle Strickland's hotel was in the center of Chipley, right across from the train depot. When it opened in the early 1940s, it had eight rooms and was a renovation of one of the earlier hotels located at this site. In 1949, an additional 12 rooms were added. The hotel boasted a coffee shop open for breakfast and a "recreation" room.

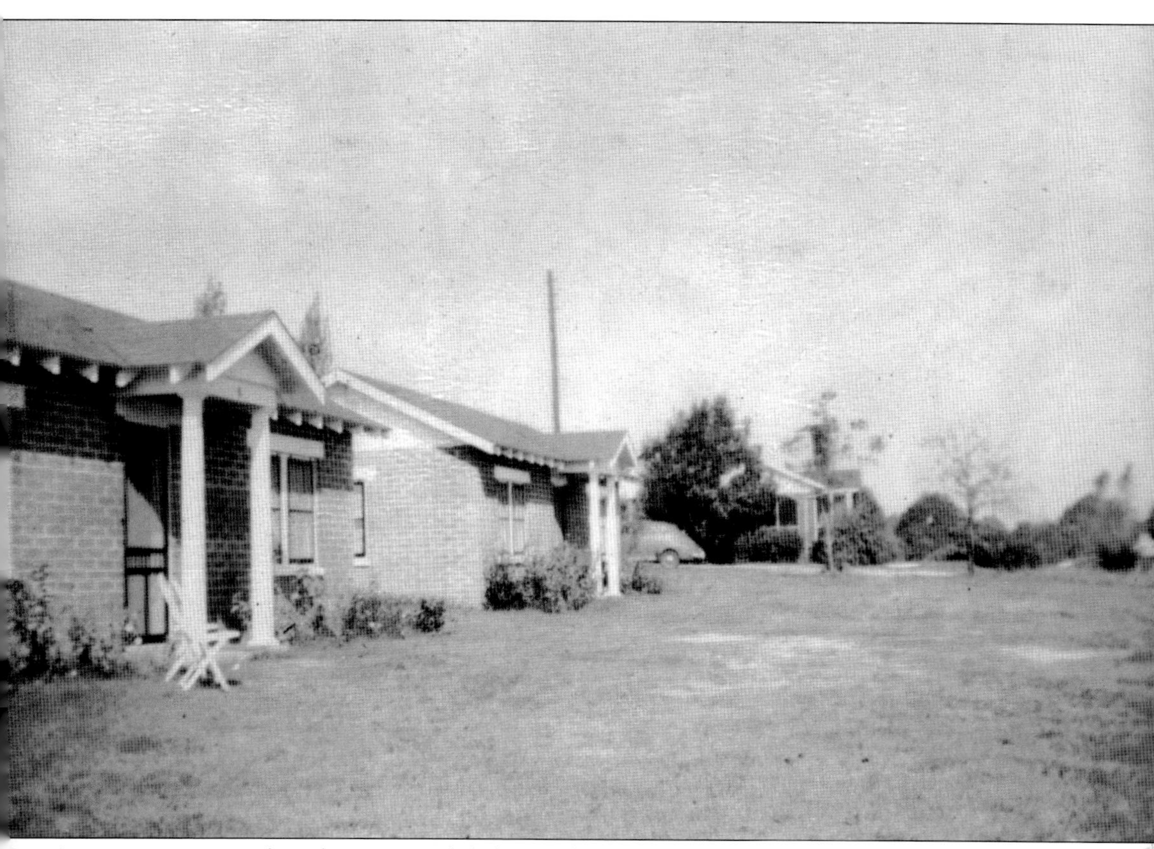

As tourism increased in the area, so did the need for lodging. D.C. and Lucille Bonner Royal opened their Royal Cottages in Chipley in 1949. Construction costs for these accommodations totaled $7,000. When Callaway Gardens opened in 1952, the cottages were often full. The Royals would then call Dester Neal, whose home on McDougald Avenue had spare rooms. She graciously welcomed unexpected travelers for a night or two.

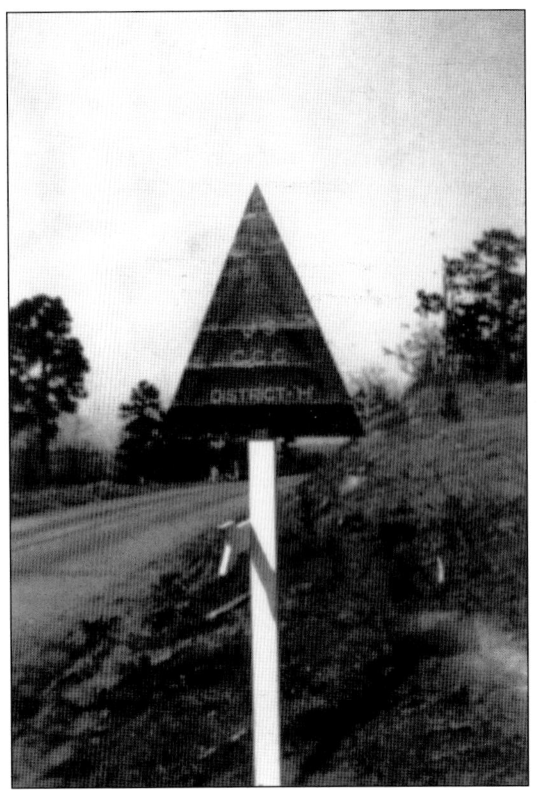

The United States was in the throes of the Great Depression when Franklin Delano Roosevelt became president in 1933. He immediately began an effort to help the American people with his New Deal program. In April 1933, he established the CCC, designed to improve the lives of young American men through conservation work and building programs. Groups of about 225 young men, trained and supported by the US Army, were organized into companies and housed in hundreds of "camps" around the country and assigned to "emergency conservation work"—planting trees, soil conservation, and developing state and national parks. One of these, Camp Kimbrough, was the home to CCC Company 4463, whose enrollees developed F.D. Roosevelt State Park. Young men were paid $30 per month, $25 of which was sent home to their families. Seen at left, the distinctive sign points the way to the camp. Below, members of No. 4463 SP-13 stand at attention for a flag-raising ceremony.

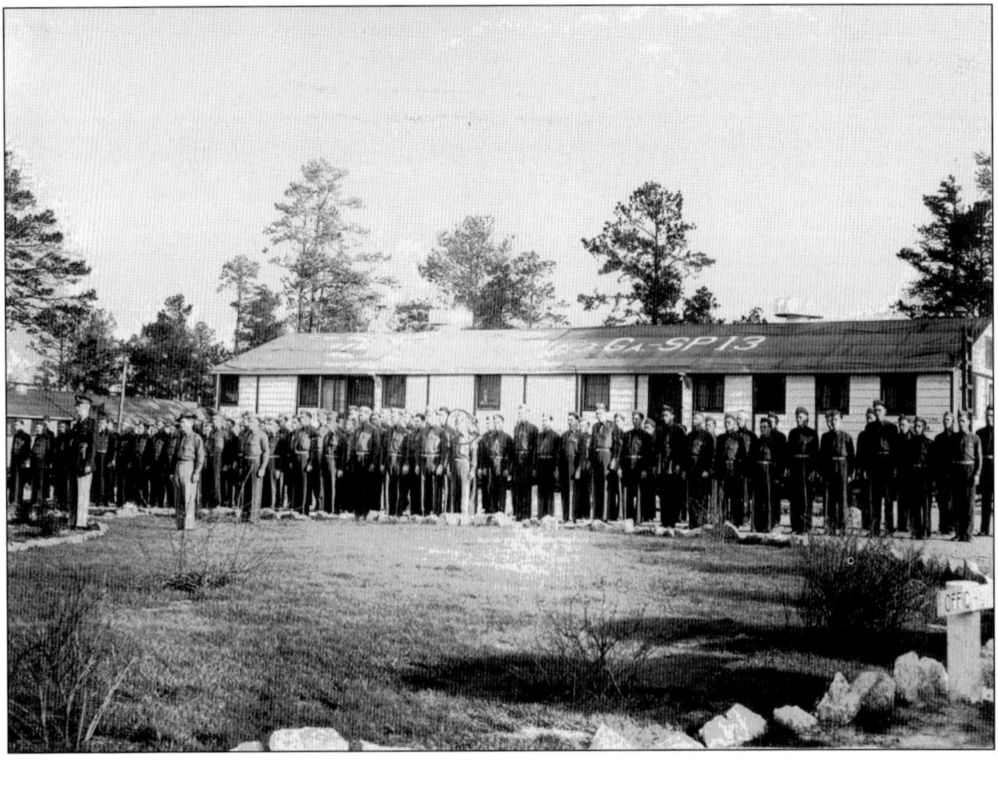

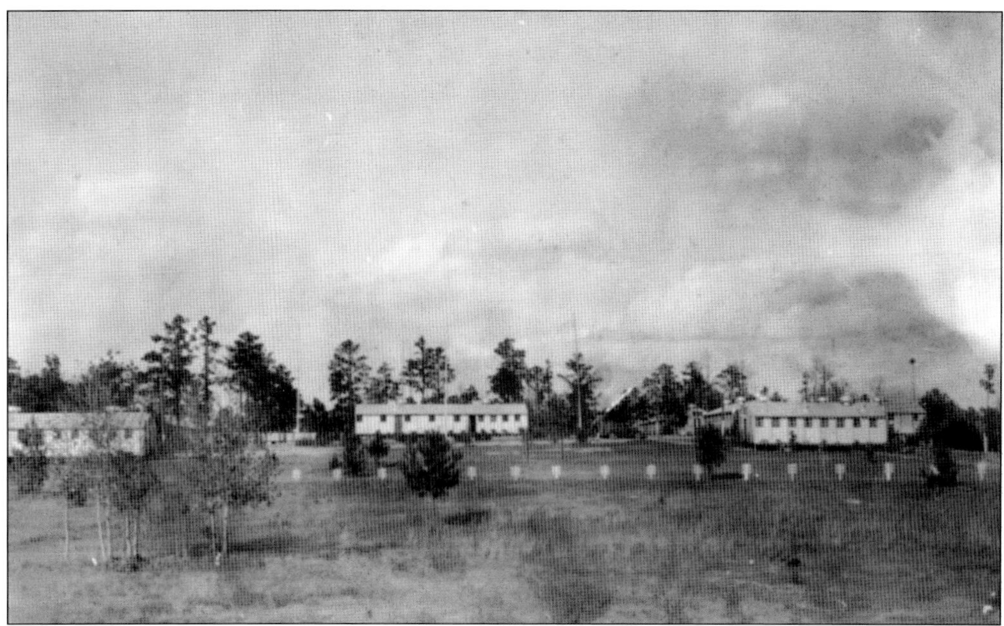

CCC "enrollees," as they were called, worked on assigned forestry projects and lived in Army-designed barracks, shown above, and were furnished with uniforms, food, hot showers, health care, and sports activities as well as educational and vocational opportunities. Weekly inspections looked for the cleanliness of both the barracks and the boys. By today's standards, the pay was low, but during the Great Depression, the $25 that each boy sent home helped to keep their families fed. The boys spent their days in long, hard physical labor, including building structures at what would become the F.D. Roosevelt State Park. Below, Cecil Caldwell (center) and his crew are building one of the many rustic park structures, several of which still exist today. In 1999, a monument was erected for the CCC boys outside the park headquarters in honor of their hard work.

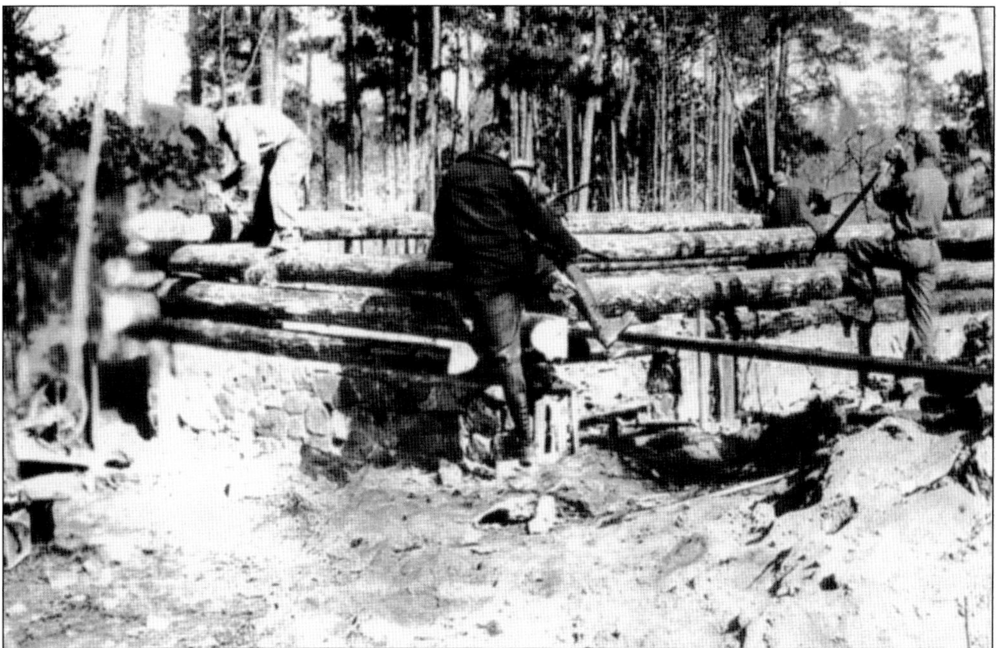

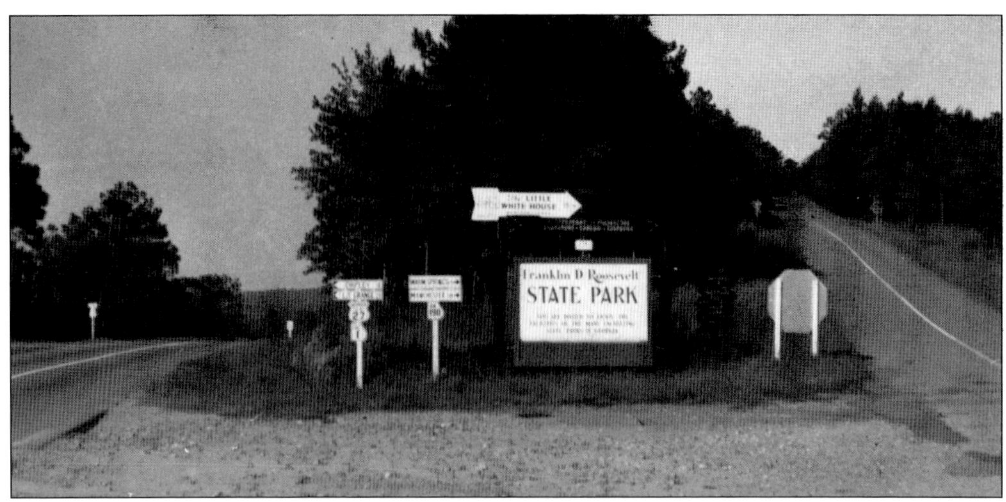

Both of these photographs point the way to F.D. Roosevelt State Park. As the image above indicates, the park can be reached by traveling up Highway 190. There is also a back entrance on Highway 354. The main office for the park is located on Highway 190 at the top of Pine Mountain. The sign in the image below still refers to the park office as the "Inn." When it first opened in 1938, the current park office was called the Inn and later the Tavern. It provided accommodations and served meals. Several longtime residents of the area remember eating there on special occasions.

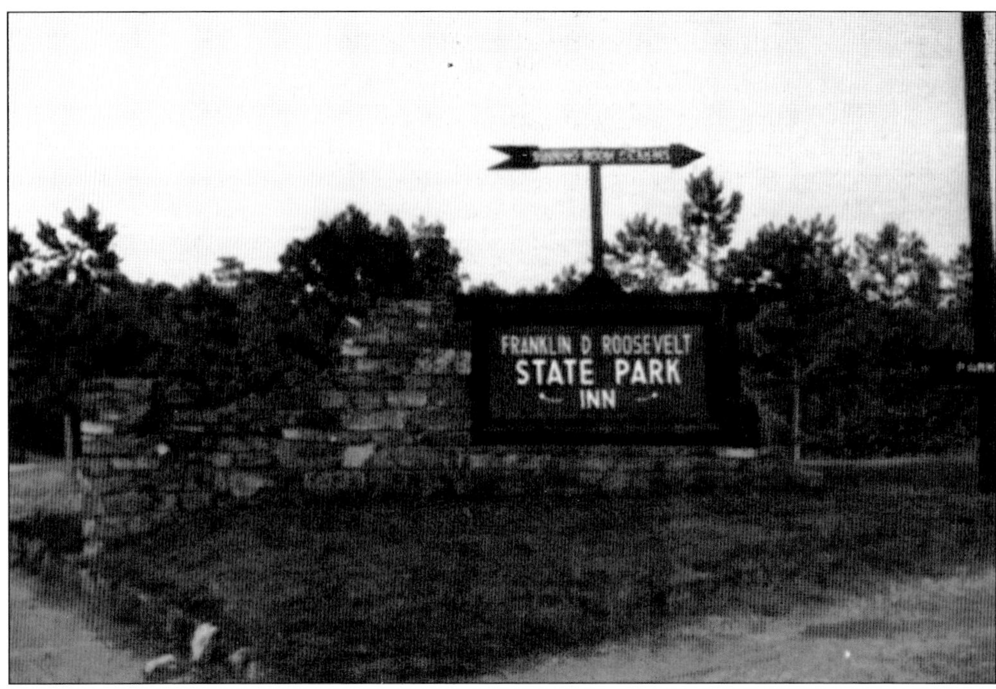

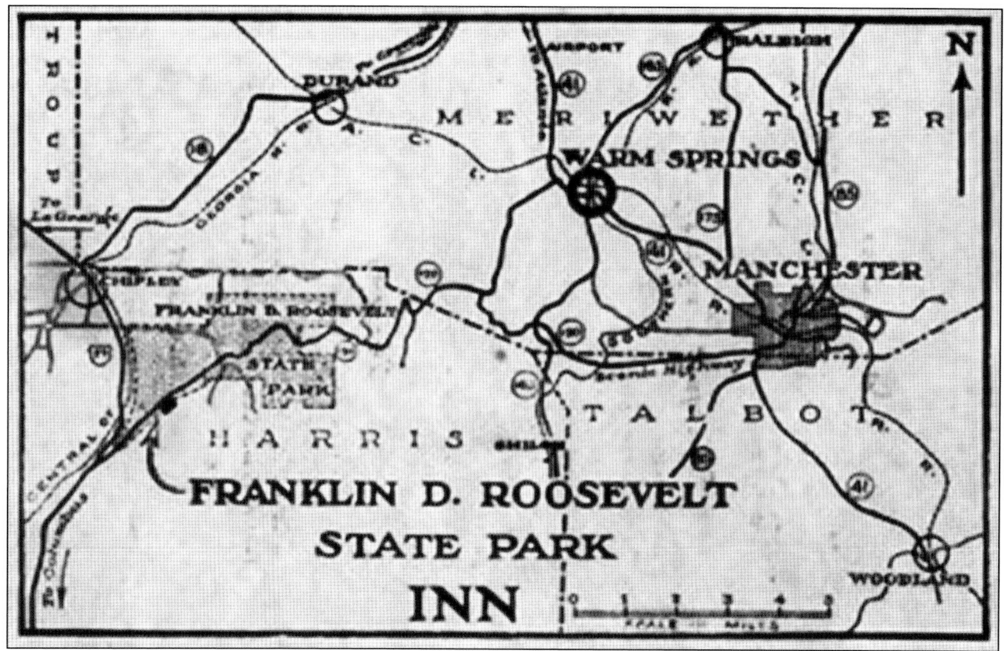

President Roosevelt visited both CCC camps at Warm Springs and Chipley on a regular basis. One of his favorite activities was driving his hand-controlled car around the countryside and talking to the farmers. Roosevelt purchased Dowdell's Knob (pictured below), a favorite picnic place and now part of F.D. Roosevelt State Park. Local businessmen also purchased property and deeded it to the State of Georgia. Today, it is the largest park in the Georgia system, encompassing over 9,000 acres, much of which lies along Pine Mountain Parkway (Highway 190) that follows the crest of the mountain from the Chipley/Pine Mountain area to Manchester.

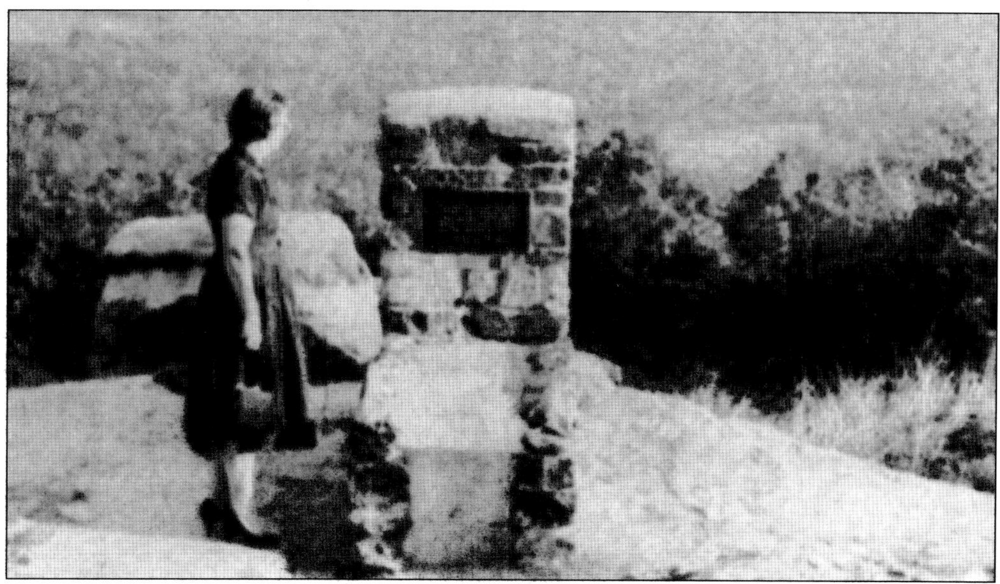

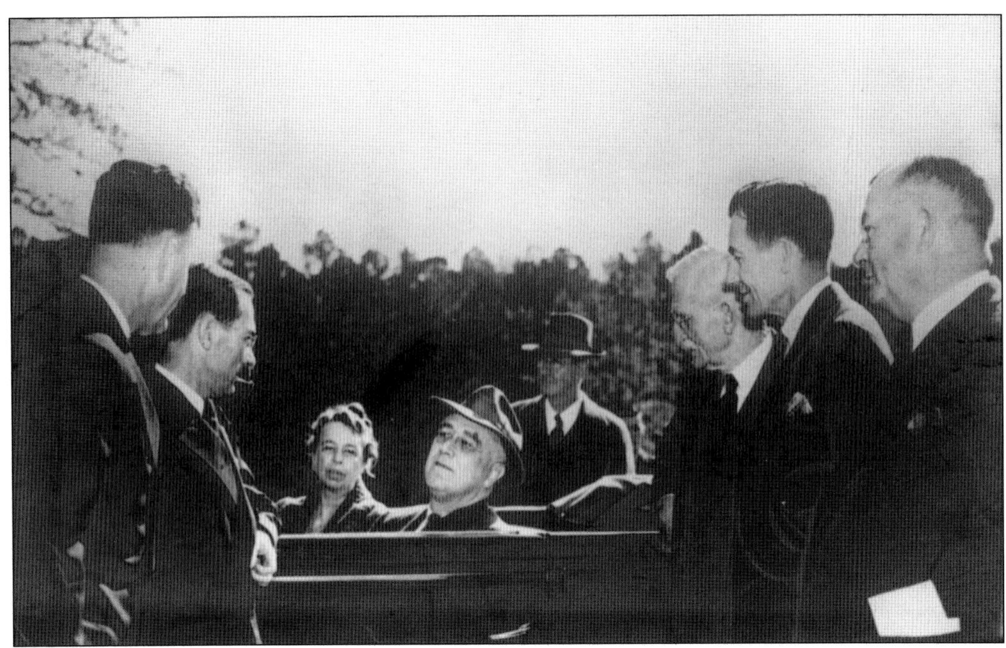

President Roosevelt was also a frequent visitor to Chipley, often driving over from the Little White House in Warm Springs, Georgia. Here, Roosevelt is shown in his car with First Lady Eleanor Roosevelt. Among the people gathered around the car are, from left to right, Tap Bennett; Jim Gillis; Edmund Starling; Henry Kimbrough, owner of the Kimbrough Brothers store in Chipley; W.L. Miller, chairman of the Georgia Highway Commission; and Clem Wright. President Roosevelt took a particular interest in the construction of the nearby state park that would eventually bear his name. When it was under construction, he remarked that the pool was shaped like the Liberty Bell. Builders added a shallow "baby pool" as the bell clapper, and the Liberty Bell pool was born. (Above, Kaye Minchew; below, John Croom.)

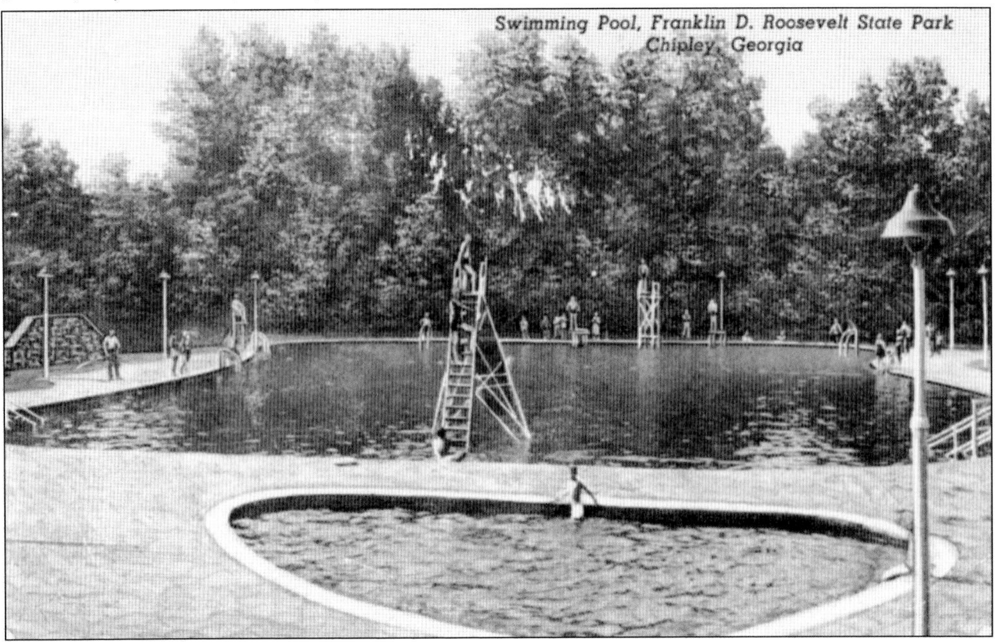

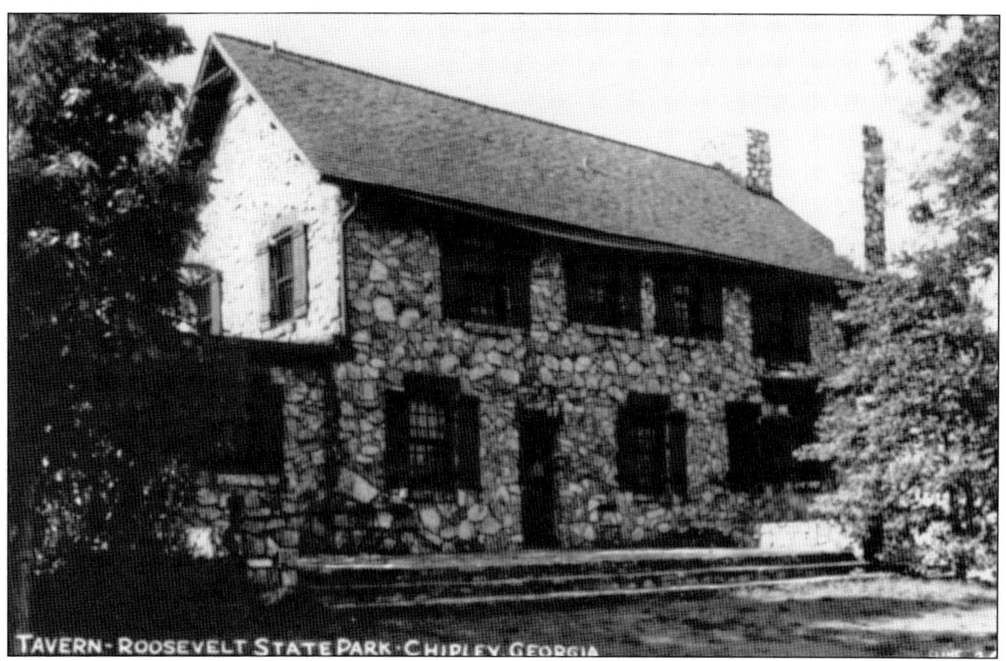

CCC work can still be seen throughout F.D. Roosevelt State Park, originally called Pine Mountain State Park. Examples include Lake Deleanor, the historic stone bridge over Highway 354, Highway 190 itself, the stone building now used as the park office and check-in station, the Liberty Bell pool, and several of the cabins at the state park. The stone building used as the park office was originally known as the Tavern or Inn. It featured lodging, a dining room, and even dancing on the outside terrace. In 1938, the federal government asked towns to submit a stamp, called a cachet, to promote the advent of air mail by the US Postal Service. Chipley's cachet featured the Inn at Pine Mountain State Park.

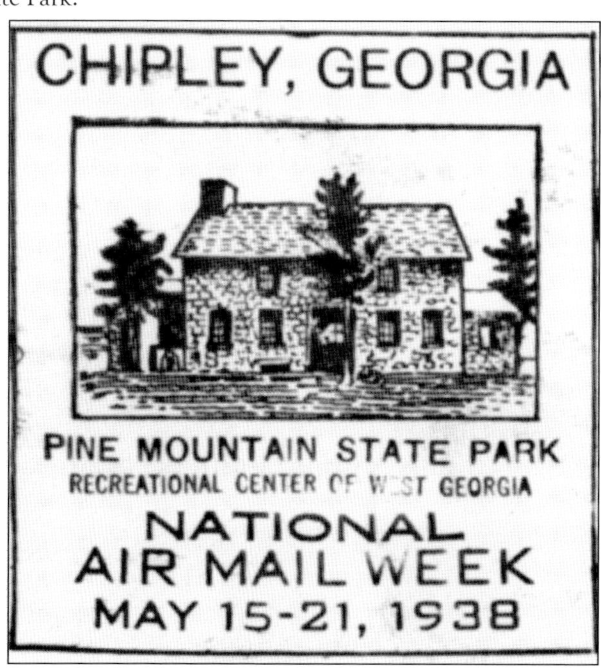

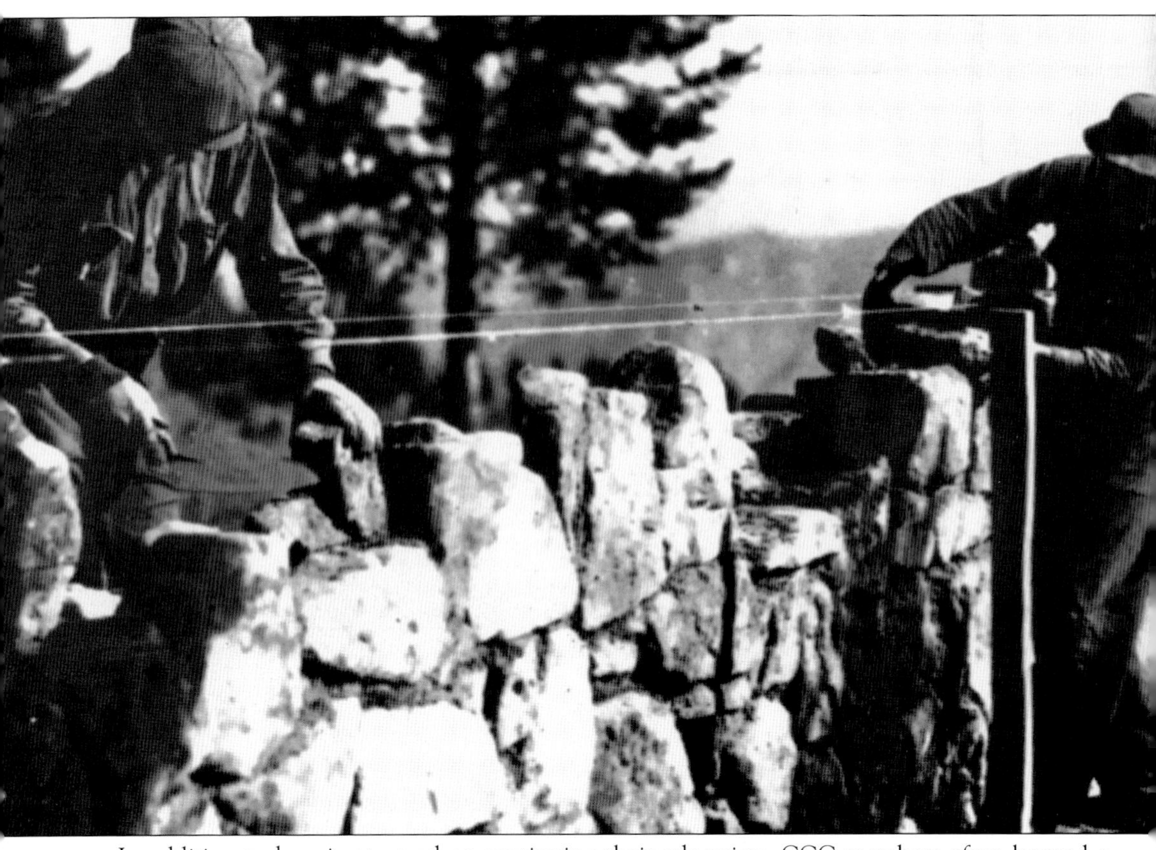

In addition to learning to read or continuing their education, CCC members often learned a trade while at camp. Carpentry and stone masonry were taught by master craftsmen who worked as overseers. In this photograph, two men work on laying the rock foundation for the Inn. Most of the structures built at the park feature some sort of rock component since it was plentiful in the area.

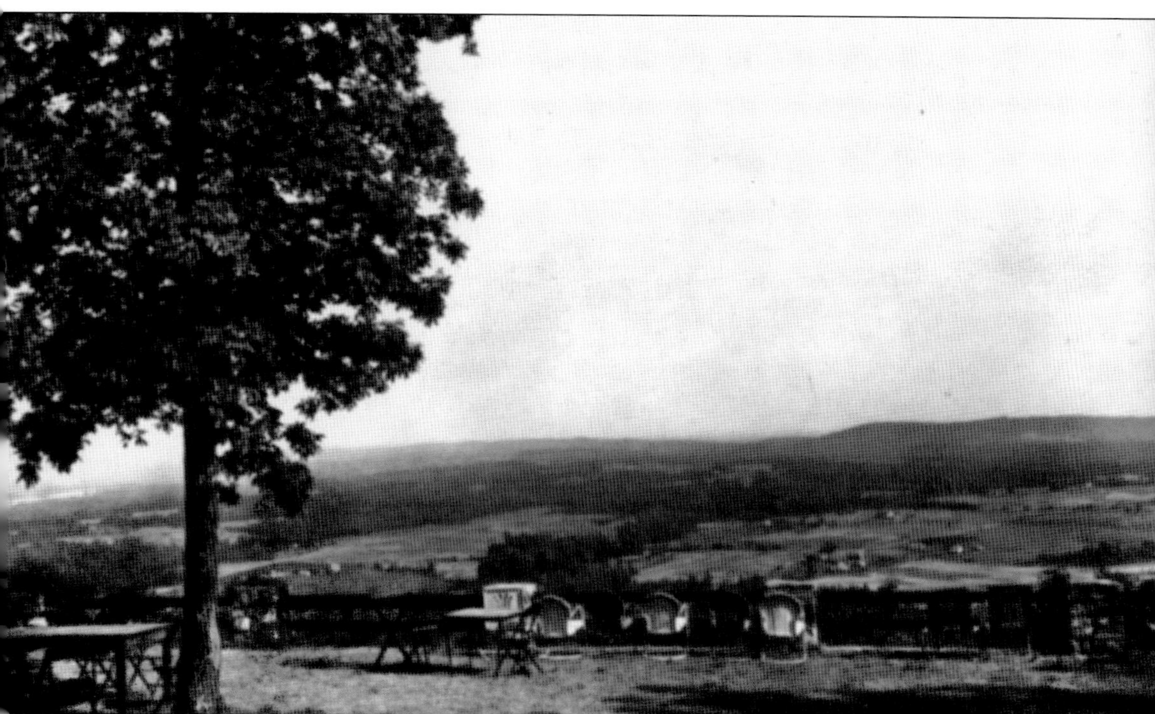

Visitors to the Inn could enjoy the view from the terrace overlooking Pine Mountain Valley. This was the site of the Pine Mountain Valley Resettlement project during the Great Depression. Like his other Great Depression programs, President Roosevelt conceived the idea to give people a chance for a fresh start. Selected families were provided housing, work, and education in the valley. Descendants of some of those families still live in the area.

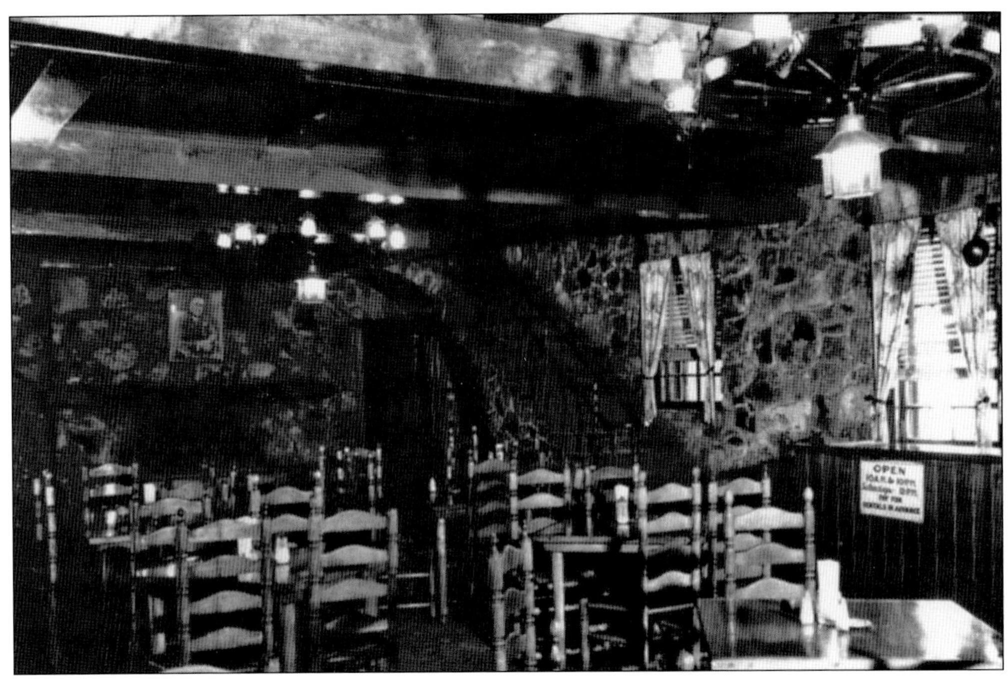

As shown in the photograph above, the dining room at the Inn was rustic but comfortable. A large stone fireplace anchored one end and featured a portrait of Franklin Delano Roosevelt. The terrace, pictured below, has been used for many activities over the years, including dancing and yoga. Today, the Inn serves as the park's headquarters with check-in for camping and hiking, along with offices for the staff. There are over 40 miles of trails in the park, including the 23-mile Pine Mountain Trail. Park rangers also offer a wide range of educational programs, including archery, scavenger hunts, and ranger-led nature walks.

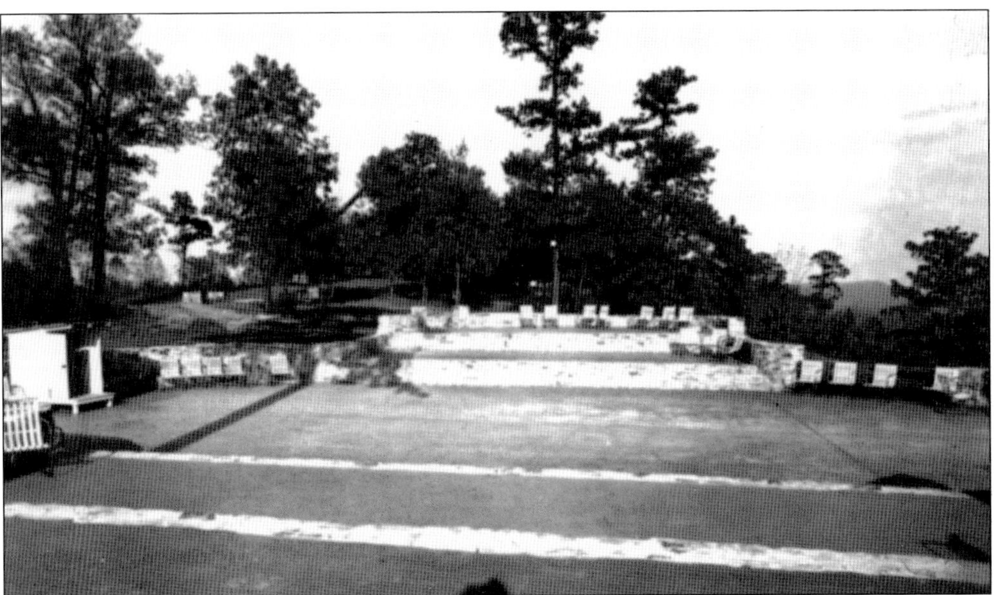

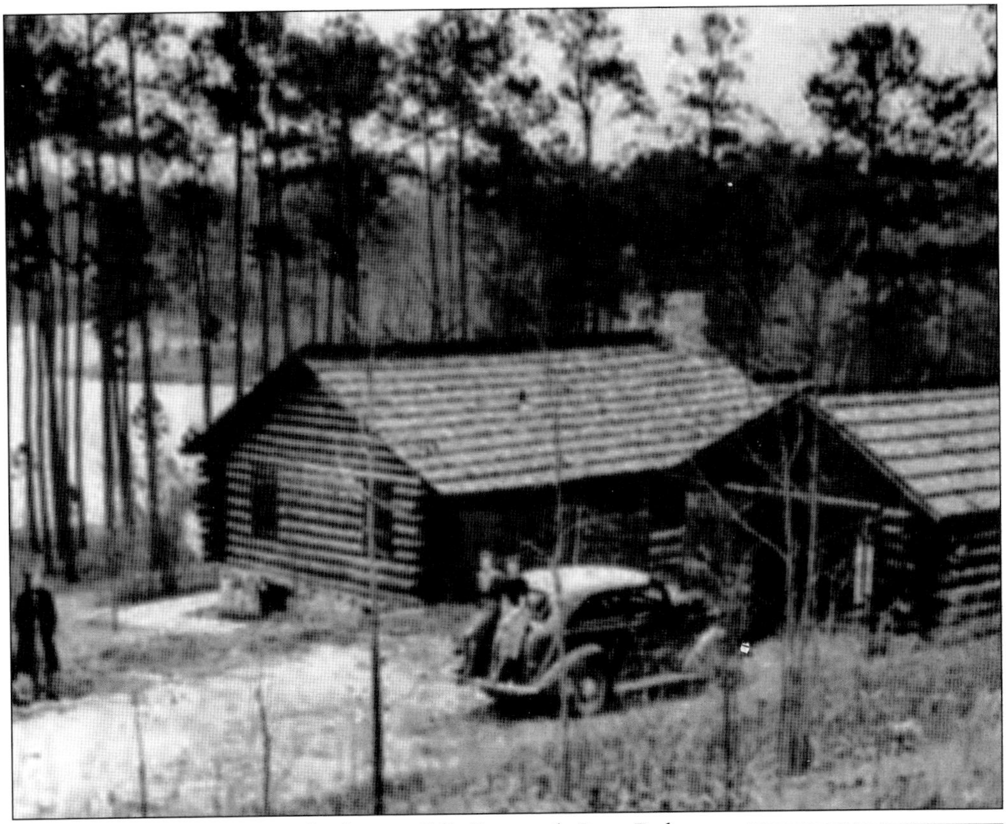

The CCC constructed several cabins in F.D. Roosevelt State Park. Many encircle Lake Deleanor, a name derived from a combination of President Roosevelt's middle name, Delano, and First Lady Roosevelt's name Eleanor. The name selected for the lake was the result of a contest held by the *Atlanta Constitution* in 1939. Fishing is allowed in this tranquil setting at the heart of the camping area. Other activities in the park include hiking, swimming at the Liberty Bell pool, horseback riding, archery, or attending one of the many programs conducted by the park rangers. Local volunteers hold American Frontier Days twice a year in March and November, which include demonstrations of early pioneer life. Then and today, as the matchbook cover at right says, F.D. Roosevelt State Park is "a congenial spot you'll like a lot."

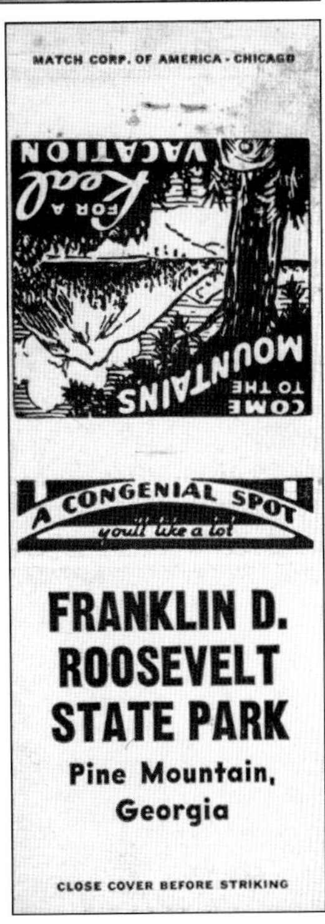

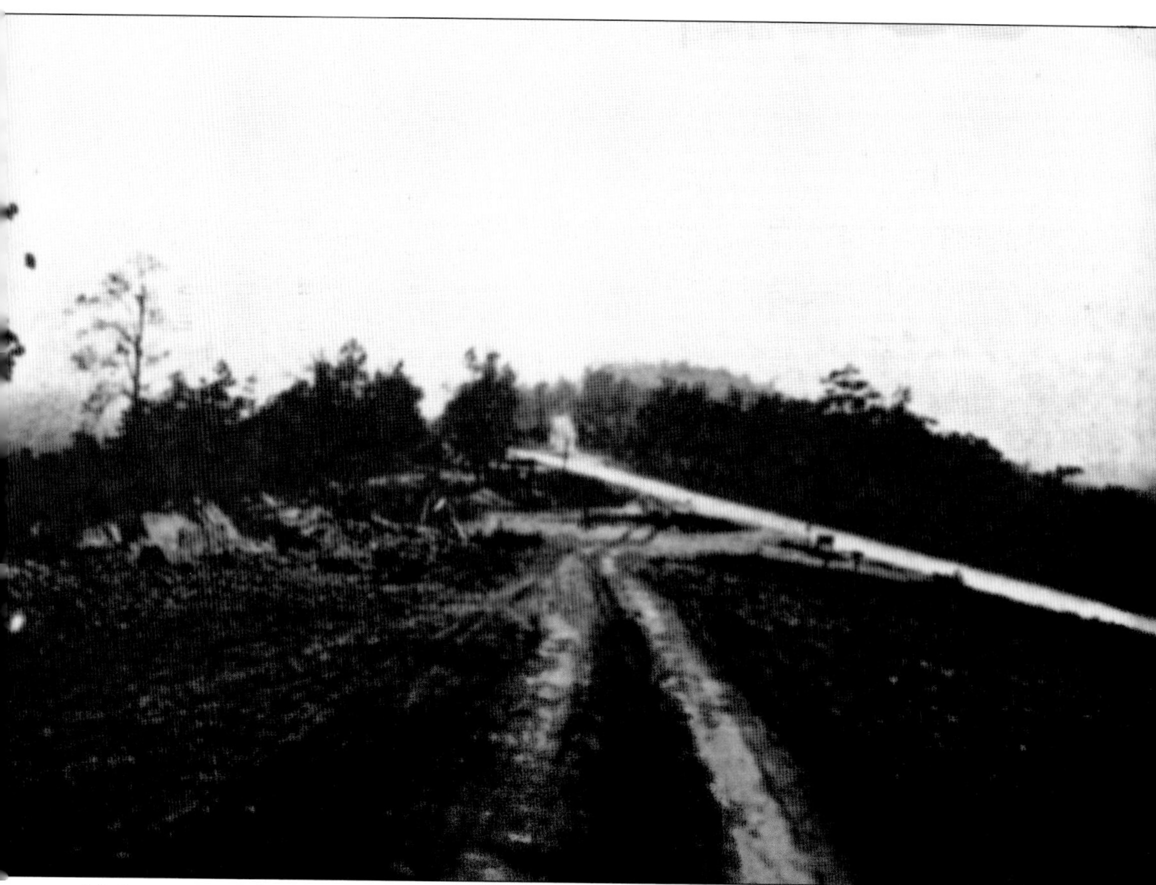

Highway 190, a very popular scenic route, runs along the crest of Pine Mountain to Manchester, Georgia. There are five scenic pullover spots looking down from the mountain into the valley below. The CCC constructed this highway from 1933 to 1937. This photograph shows the future Highway 190 heading toward the intersection with US Highway 27. The future site of the Callaway Gardens Country Store lies directly ahead.

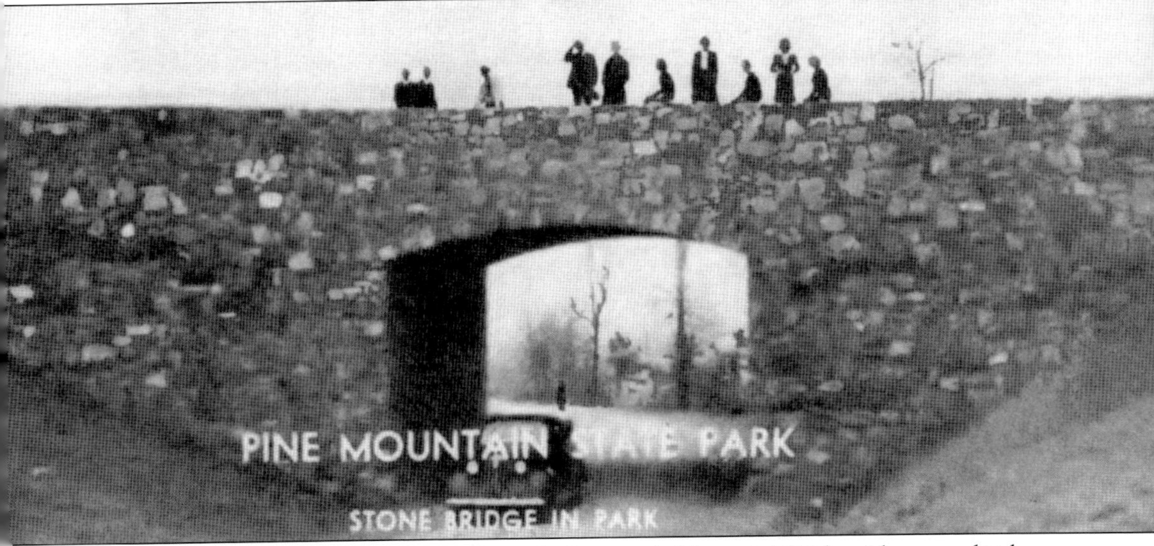

Highway 190 passes over Highway 354 via the Roosevelt Memorial Bridge. The stone bridge was another CCC project and was completed around 1937. Note that in this photograph from around 1938, the park is referred to as Pine Mountain State Park. The name was changed to F.D. Roosevelt State Park on April 17, 1947, with Eleanor Roosevelt's blessing. (Georgia State Department of Natural Resources.)

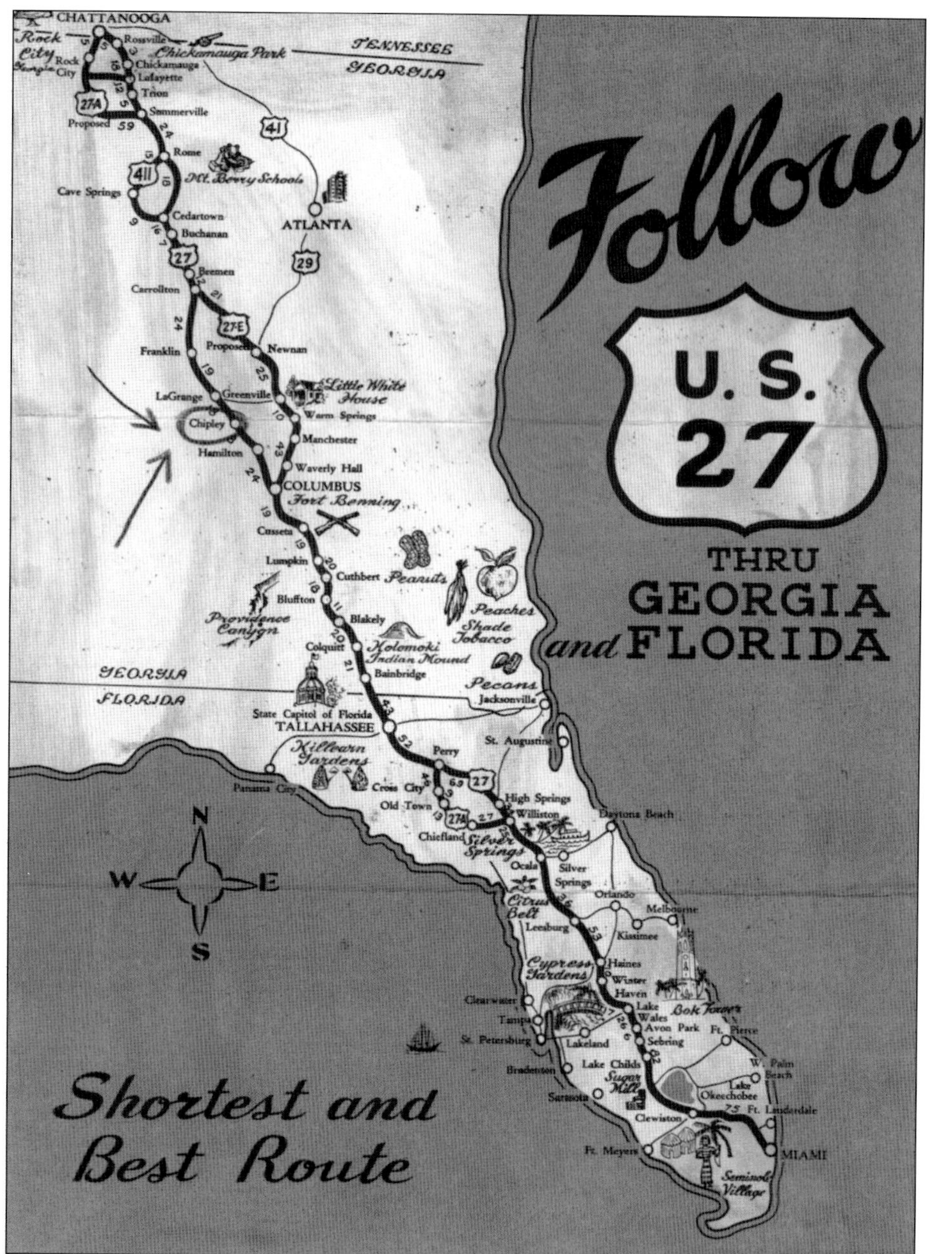

The eventual route of US Highway 27 was only slightly different from that of the Taft Highway described at the beginning of his chapter. It passes through the heart of Georgia and Florida and is the most direct route from the Great Lakes to Miami. It passes through many small- and medium-sized towns and has always given travelers from "up north" an authentic look at the Deep South. Notice that there are a number of alternate routes in both states, marked as 27A, often giving visitors directions to sites of interest not on the main route, such as the Little White House in Warm Springs. It seems, however, that most travelers now are more interested in arriving than traveling and sightseeing and choose the interstate over US Highway 27. Even so, many Chipley/Pine Mountain visitors over the years have discovered that a little side trip off an interstate can be quite worth their time.

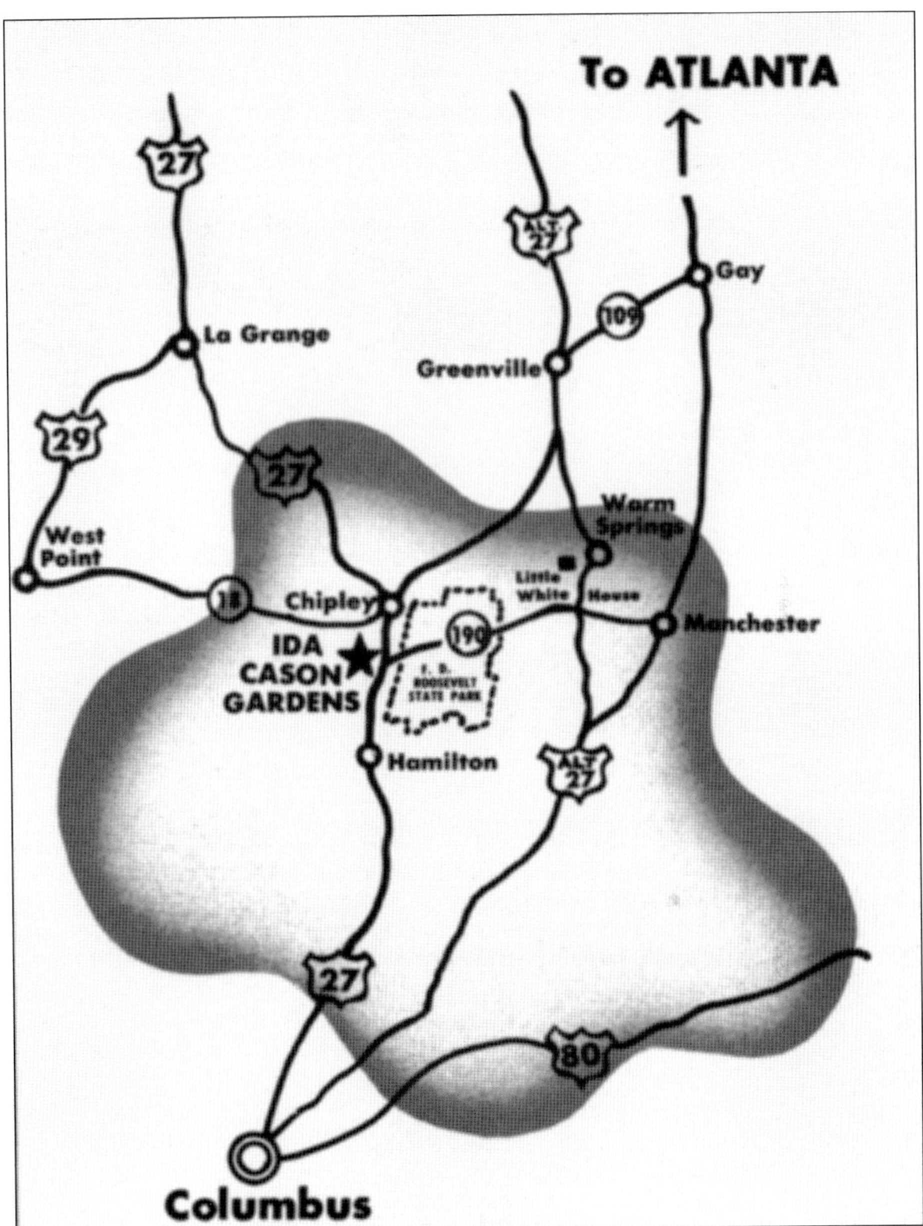

Another tourist attraction, Callaway Gardens, began as a dream of Cason Callaway and his wife, Virginia Hand Callaway, to showcase the natural beauty of the Pine Mountain area. Cason Callaway, a textile industrialist from LaGrange, Georgia, began purchasing land in 1930 in Harris County near Chipley as a retreat from the burden of his hectic life at the textile mill. He discovered a native azalea, *Azalea prunifolium*, growing there and determined to share its beauty with the world. In 1949, he began construction on what would become Callaway Gardens. Initially naming it Ida Cason Callaway Gardens after his mother, Callaway planned a recreational area in the Mountain Creek valley at the base of Pine Mountain. His vision included golf, fishing, swimming, and roads where visitors could enjoy the natural beauty of the area. Virginia Callaway designed an overlook and other viewing areas using seedlings of the *Azalea prunifolium* cultivated from those they had found on their property, along with hollies, magnolias, and rhododendrons.

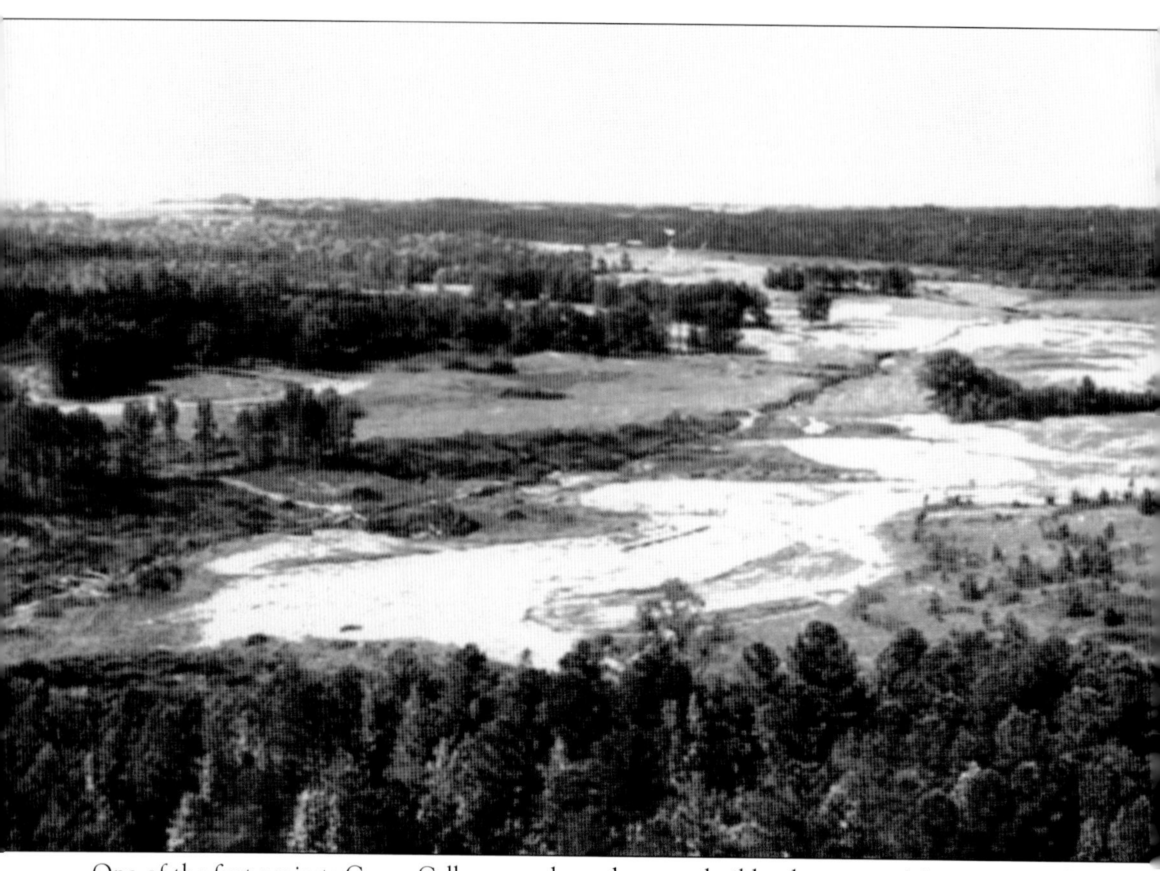

One of the first projects Cason Callaway undertook was to build a dam across Mountain Creek. Mountain Creek Lake, pictured above while under construction, is the largest lake in the gardens. The first golf course wound around the lake and included an Old English–style clubhouse on the south shore. Fishing is allowed on the lake. There is another championship-caliber course away from the big lake.

Ida Cason
Callaway Gardens
Chipley, Ga.

25c E. Pr. .2427
St.Tax.0073

CHILD

129057

IDA CASON
CALLAWAY GARDENS
Chipley, Ga.

E.Pr. .2427
S. T. .0073 25c

ADMIT ONE CHILD

129057

Ida Cason Callaway Gardens opened on May 21, 1952. Fifteen hundred visitors attended the first day, along with dignitaries, including Georgia governor Herman Talmadge. The *Harris County Journal* wrote, "We doff our hat in respect to Cason J. Callaway–a man who could [have] had it all for selfish self but gave it to all humanity to enjoy."

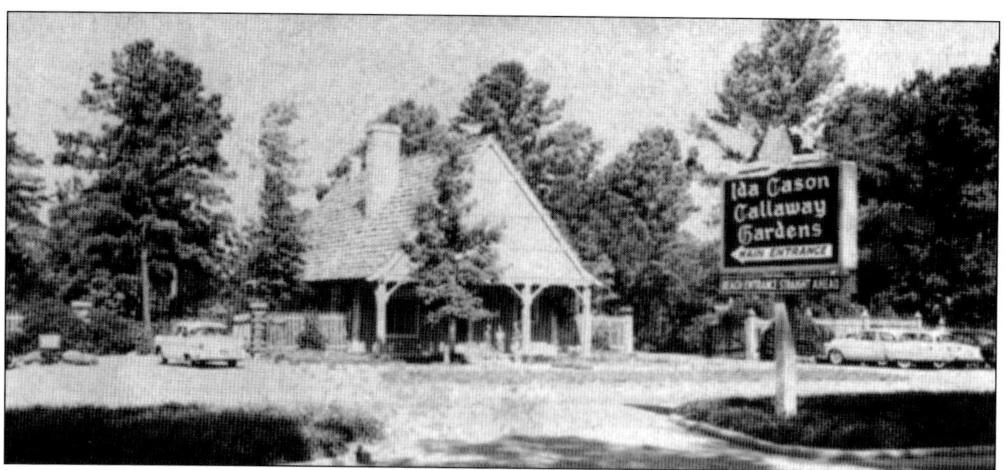

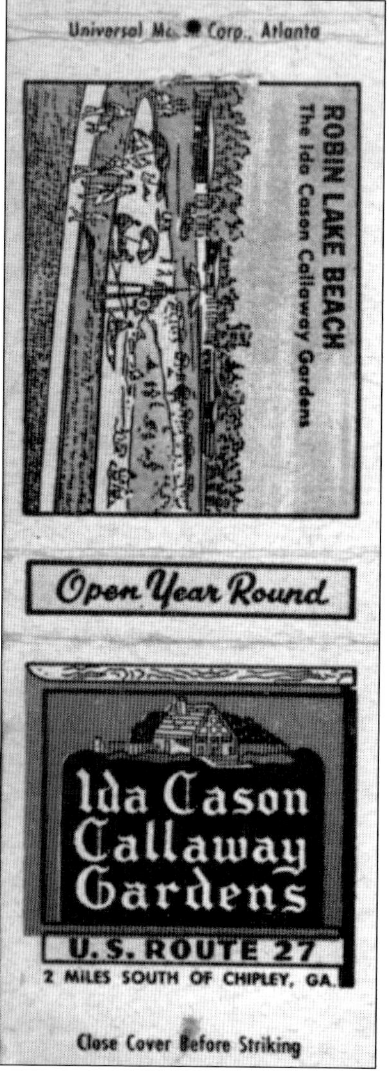

The gatehouse to Ida Cason Callaway Gardens was on US Highway 27. Built in an Old English style similar to the clubhouse, visitors could pay their entry fee, get information, and pick up maps for their tour of the gardens. Although Robin Lake Beach was open only during the summer, visitors could enjoy other parts of the gardens year-round, including beautiful azaleas in the spring. Fantasy in Lights, which debuted in 1992, draws a huge crowd from mid-November until the New Year to enjoy the Christmas lights and displays. The most recent addition is the Pumpkins at Callaway Festival from September through Halloween. (Above, Georgia State Department of Natural Resources.)

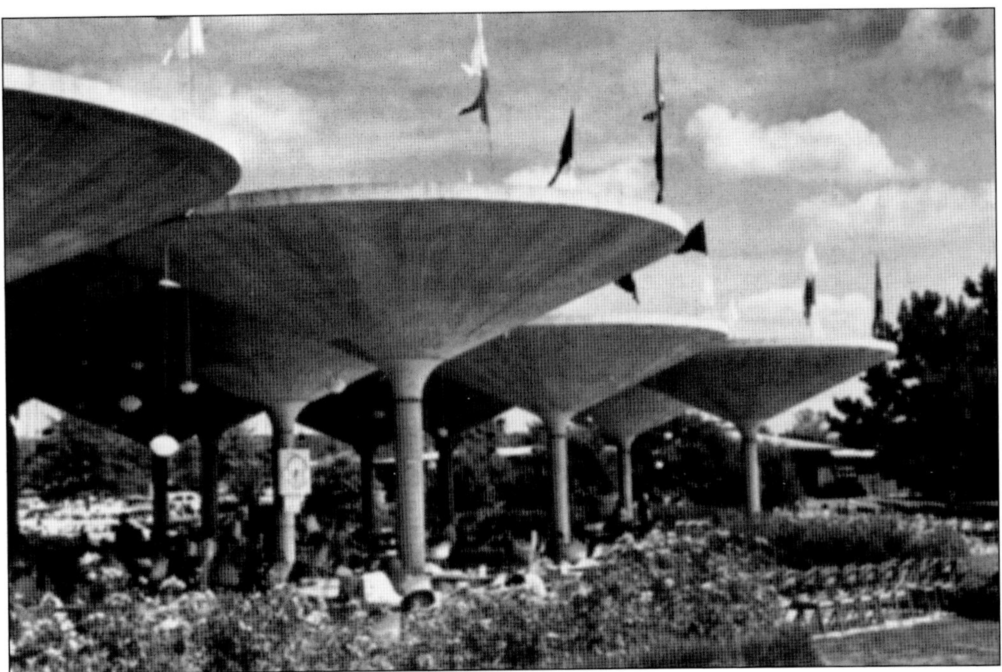

Construction on Robin Lake Beach began in 1953. The lake covers about 70 acres. A total of 32,000 tons (531 railway cars) of white sand went into creating this water sports center. The concrete structures over the picnic pavilion resembled "champagne glasses" of the 1950s. Sunbathers could gather on the beach itself or on the wide grassy strip next to the beach. Amenities included food and three bathhouses. The bathhouses were enlarged a few years later to serve a larger crowd. Annual visitation quickly approached a half-million just a few years after opening. The beach is open mid-May through Labor Day. Recent additions include a fireworks display on the beach on Saturday nights during the summer season. (Below, Amy Skinner.)

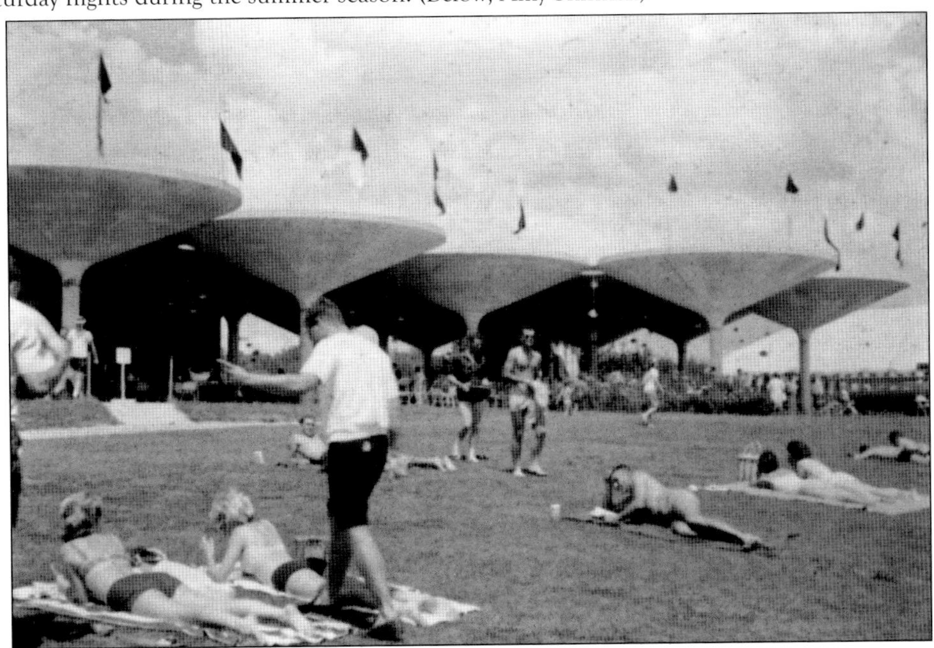

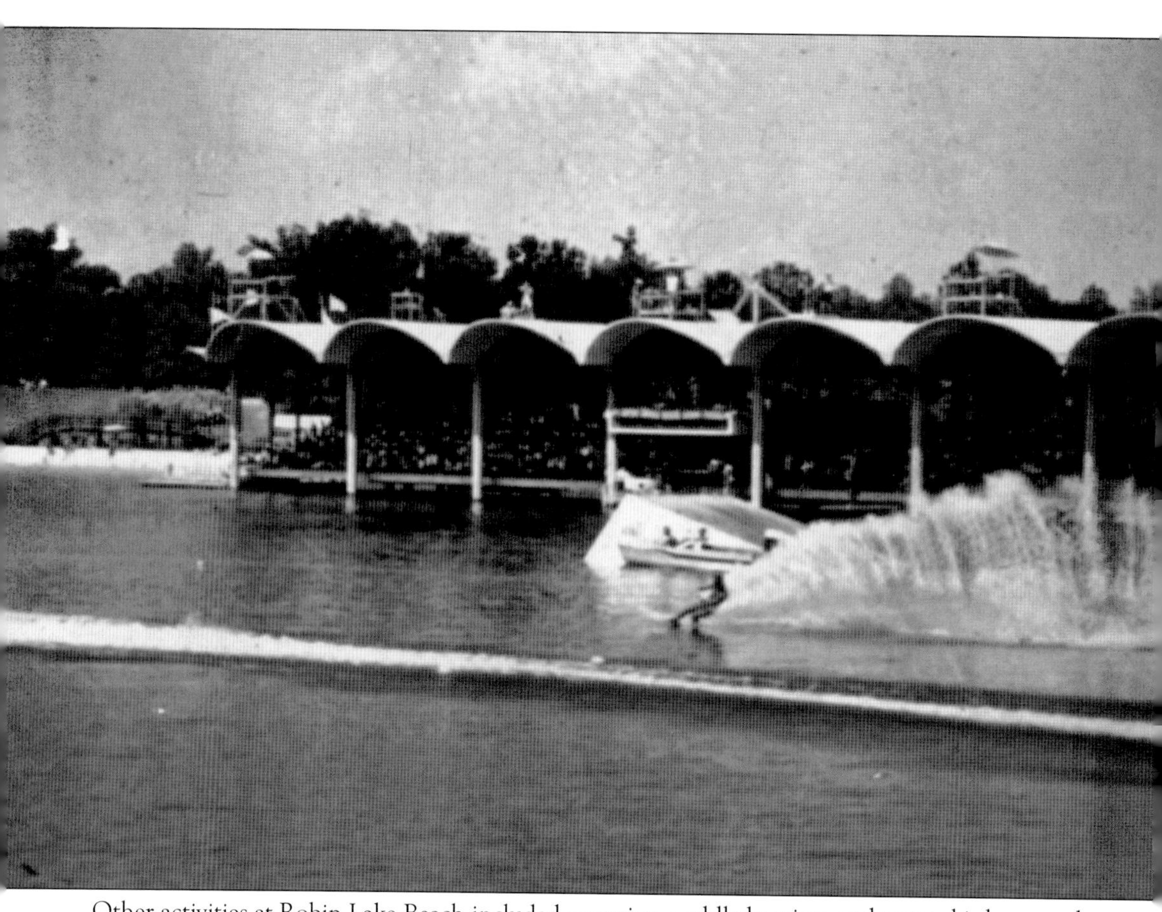

Other activities at Robin Lake Beach included canoeing, paddle boating, and water ski shows and lessons. A troupe of skiers from Cypress Gardens, Florida, gave ski shows during opening week, and two lucky winners' names were drawn from a hat for ski lessons. The Masters Water Ski and Wakeboard Tournament has been held here annually since 1959.

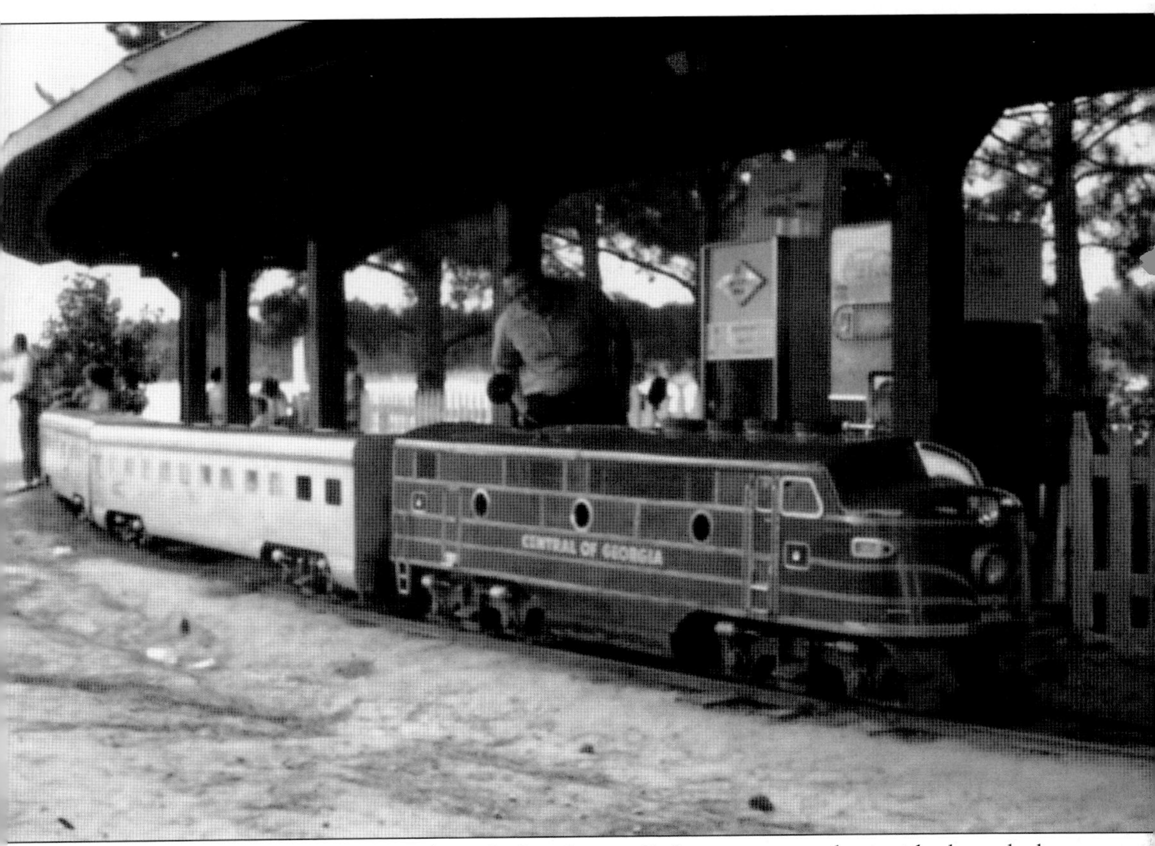

There was also a miniature train ride at the beach area. Riders were treated to a ride through the gardens around one of the lakes. Note the *Central of Georgia* name on the side of the train. The Central of Georgia was the railroad that ran through Chipley and Pine Mountain for many years. The train was removed around 2010. (Amy Skinner.)

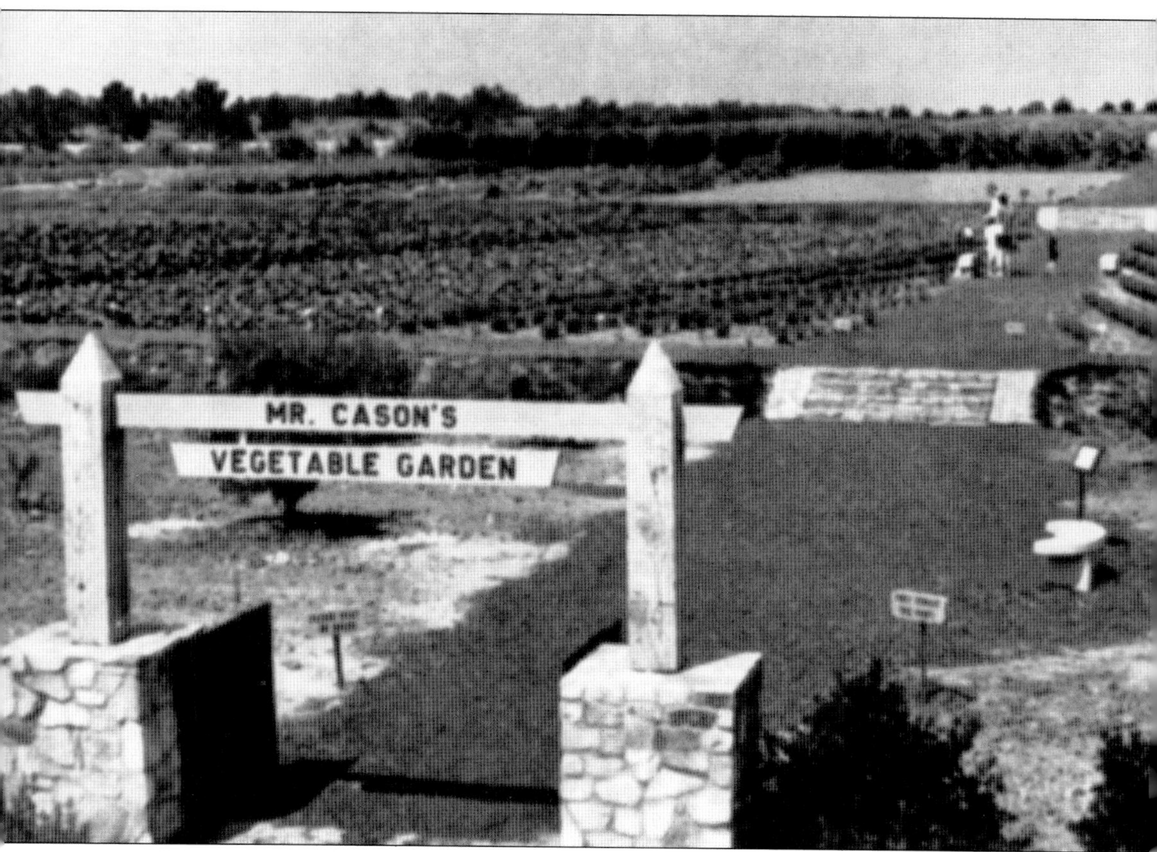

One of Cason Callaway's last projects before he died in 1961 was planning a 7.5-acre demonstration garden that became known as Mr. Cason's Vegetable Garden. It was often featured in "Victory Garden South" episodes on the Public Broadcasting System show *The Victory Garden* during the 1980s. The site now features a sunflower maze during the Pumpkins at Callaway Festival each year and a field of tulips in the spring.

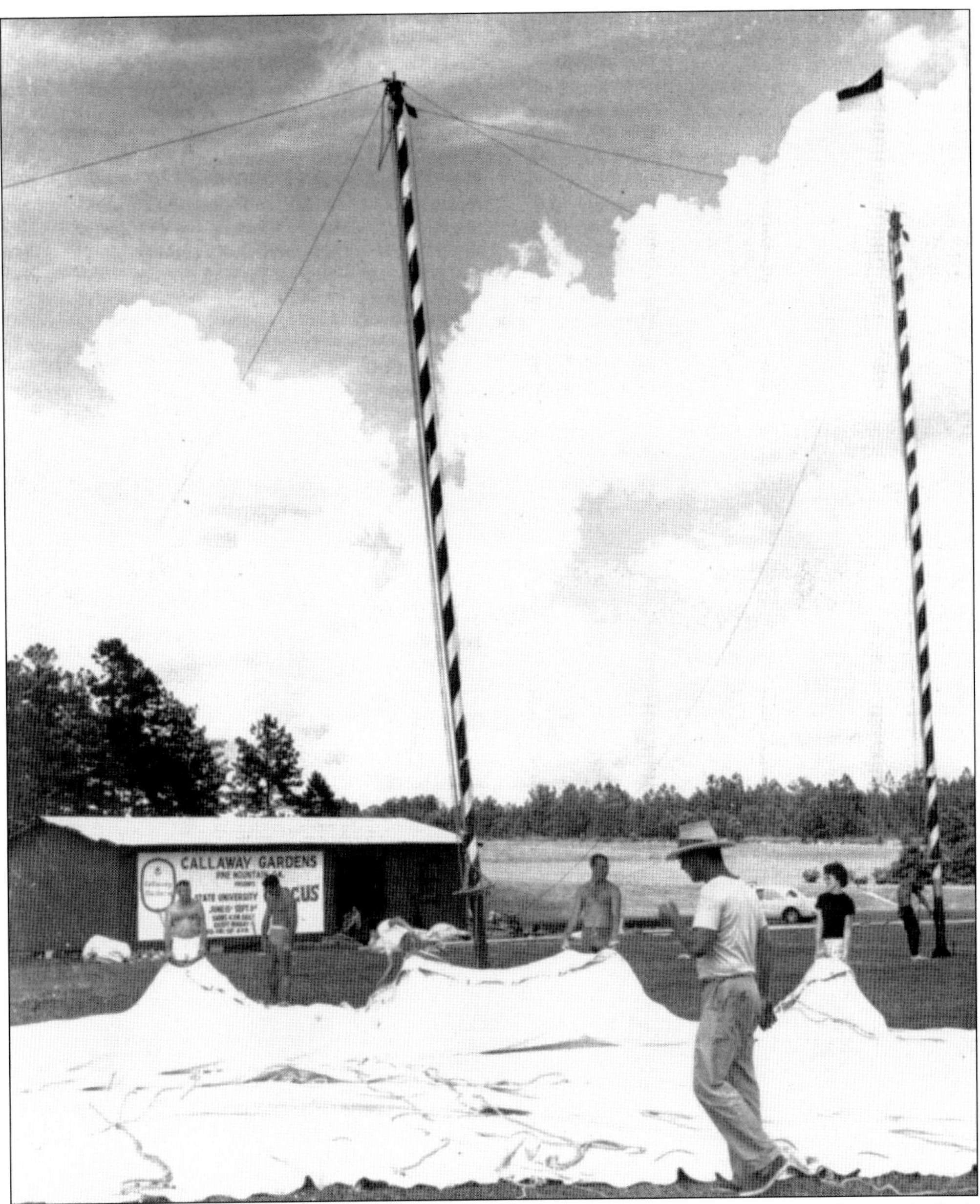

Beginning in 1961, the Florida State University Flying High Circus ran a recreational camp for kids as well as practicing and performing at Callaway Gardens during the summers. Attendees could try some of the same skills as the performers. Some of the activities included trapeze, aerial acts, and clowning. The circus was performed under a big top tent erected by Florida State University students. (Florida State University Flying High Circus.)

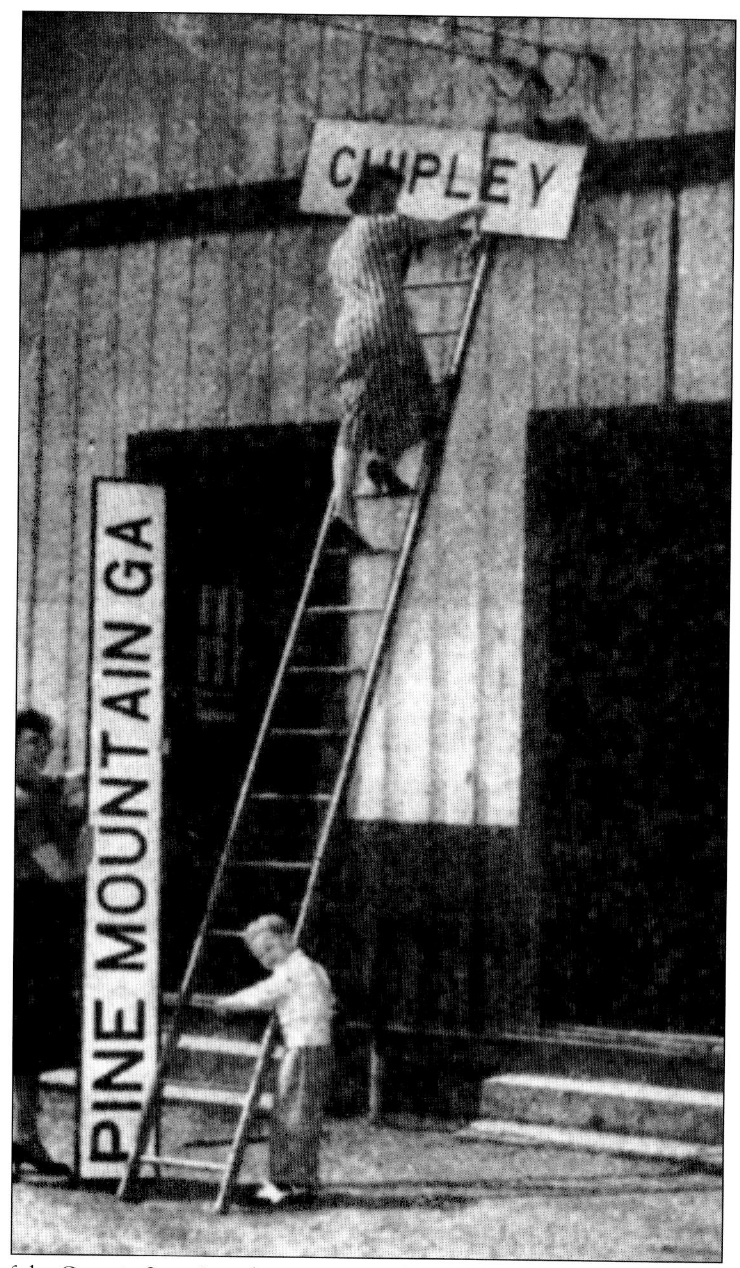

After an act of the Georgia State Legislature, required by law to change the name of a municipality, in 1958, Chipley became Pine Mountain. The change was strongly suggested, urged even, by Cason Callaway, who felt that the new name was more likely to attract tourists to the area than the name Chipley. The Chipley town council circulated petitions asking residents to show support for the proposed name change. Whether a majority supported the change was not publicized; however, there was strong opposition. Nevertheless, the state legislature approved the change, and "Chipley" was replaced with "Pine Mountain" throughout the town. In this photograph, Rachel Chambers and her son David are shown helping to change the signs with Catherine Chapman at the depot. However, Chipley has not disappeared entirely. Organizations, shops, restaurants, and family pets have worn the name Chipley. (David Chambers.)

Bibliography

Barfield, Louise Calhoun. *History of Harris County, Georgia 1827–1961.* Cherith Creek Designs, 1961.

Barnes, Margaret Anne. *Murder in Coweta County.* Reader's Digest Press, 1976.

Champion, Lillian. *History of Bethany Baptist Church, Pine Mountain, Georgia 1828–1978.* Bethany Baptist Church, 1978.

——. *Pine Mountain Reviews: Stories by the Plumber's Daughter.* The Chipley Historical Center of Pine Mountain Inc., 2008.

——. *William Dudley Chipley and Other Giants of Men.* Quill Publication, 1985.

Minchew, Kaye Lanning. *A President in Our Midst: Franklin Delano Roosevelt in Georgia.* The University of Georgia Press, 2017.

Moore, Dot. *No Remorse: The Rise and Fall of John Wallace.* NewSouth, 2011.

Schubert, Paul. *Cason Callaway of Blue Springs.* Blue Springs, 1964.

Woodruff, Marguerite. *They Yet Speak: A History of The First Baptist Church, Pine Mountain, Georgia 1887–1987.* Quill Publications, 1986.